HEROES in the NIGHT

Inside the Real Life Superhero Movement

TEA KRULOS

CHICAGO
REVIEW
PRESS

Published by Chicago Review Press, Incorporated

814 North Franklin Street

Chicago, Illinois 60610

ISBN 978-1-61374-775-9

Library of Congress Cataloging-in-Publication Data

Krulos, Tea.

  Heroes in the night : inside the real life superhero movement / Tea Krulos.

    pages cm

  Summary: "Tracing the author's journey into the strange subculture of Real Life Superheroes (RLSHs), this book examines citizens who have adopted comic book–style personas and have hit the streets to fight injustice in a variety of ways. Some RLSHs concentrate on humanitarian or activist missions—helping the homeless, gathering donations for food banks, or delivering toys to children—while others actively patrol their neighborhoods looking for crime to fight. By day, these modern Clark Kents work as dishwashers, pencil pushers, and executives in Fortune 500 companies, but by night—they become heroes for the people. Through historic research and extensive interviews, this work shares not only their shining, triumphant moments, but also some of their ill-advised, terrifying disasters"— Provided by publisher.

  Includes bibliographical references and index.

  ISBN 978-1-61374-775-9 (pbk.)

  1. Community activists—United States. 2. Crime prevention—United States—Citizen participation. 3. Superheroes—Social aspects—United States. 4. Social justice—United States. I. Title.

  HN90.C6K78 2013

  303.3'72—dc23

                          2013022099

Cover design: Sarah Olson

Cover photos: (clockwise from upper left) Phoenix Jones, photo by Lucien Knuteson, http://lucienknuteson.com; the Watchman, photo by Jerry Luterman, http://jerrylutermanphoto.com; Zetaman, photo by Pierre-Elie de Pibrac, www.pierreeliedepibrac.com; Terrifica, photo © Michele Abeles
Interior design: Jonathan Hahn

Printed in the United States of America

Dedicated to the Watchman—
Keep fighting the good fight.

CONTENTS

MEET YOUR FRIENDLY NEIGHBORHOOD REAL LIFE SUPERHEROES

"Real Life Superheroes," I had told my friends at the bar. "What's the worst that can happen, right?"

We all had a good laugh over that one.

The scene crossed my mind in a fleeting moment as I ran through the intersection of Alaskan Way and Columbia Street in Seattle. I had spent the night patrolling with a man who calls himself Phoenix Jones, the "Guardian of Seattle." Phoenix Jones and his team, the Rain City Superhero Movement, dress up in masks and body armor and patrol the streets, looking for crime to fight. He'd had some successes and some failures, but at this moment he was in big trouble.

At closing time, we had observed a group of men—Russians, as it turned out—fighting in the street near a bar. Phoenix Jones had brazenly run into the middle of the group of fighting men, yelled for them to break it up, then pepper-sprayed them. The men, and their girlfriends, became very angry, and soon we were running for our lives to escape them.

"Fall back! Cross the street!" Phoenix Jones yelled at me, videographer Ryan McNamee, and his teammate, Ghost. I looked at him across the street and determined that standing next to him wasn't safe—the Russians wanted to stomp him into the ground. One of their girlfriends had already beaten Jones repeatedly on his cowled head with a high-heeled shoe; the men made an effort to rush and tackle him before he blasted them with pepper spray again. Ryan and Ghost had been slammed into a wall and I had been punched in the face by an angry, confused Russian while I breathlessly tried to explain the scene to 9-1-1 dispatch.

I decided instead to stand on a little concrete island in the middle of some railroad tracks and an oncoming lane of traffic. If the Russians tried to attack me, I figured, I could kick them off the island into the street and run up the train tracks. But Phoenix Jones ran over to join me.

"Sorry about this, brother," he said, surprisingly calm. "Are you OK?"

I nodded, putting a hand on my right cheekbone. My eyes were blurry from running through a fog of pepper spray.

"I got punched, but I'm OK."

"I don't know where the police . . ."

Rrrrrrr! Rrr! Rrrrrrrrrrr! A loud revving cut Jones off.

We looked across the street. Some of the men were pointing at us and shouting angrily in Russian. One of them was in the driver's seat of a giant Escalade, and another one yelled and jumped in the passenger seat.

"Phoenix!" I said, "They're going to try to run us over!" The Escalade squealed out of the parking lot.

"Take cover!" Phoenix Jones screamed, running back across the street. "Protect yourselves! Take cover!" I ran to hide behind the concrete pillar of a nearby parking garage. I figured the pillar would shield me from the rampaging vehicle.

———

Welcome to the comic-book-turned-real-world lives of a growing group of people who call themselves Real Life Superheroes (or

RLSH).* It is a secretive subculture that I spent over three years getting to know. I found them to be alternately amusing, hysterical, inspirational, disappointing, and—in situations like this one—absolutely terrifying.

My introduction to the RLSH movement was in February 2009 after I read a short blurb in Chuck Shepherd's syndicated column, "News of the Weird," that said a growing number of men and women around the country were adopting their own superhero personas. Excited about the possibility of finding a local Milwaukee RLSH, and perhaps freelancing a short article on the subject, I began a search engine scan on "Milwaukee RLSH." I soon turned up someone who had named himself "the Watchman." He had a MySpace page, which was my first clue that RLSH varied drastically from their comic book counterparts. But I went with it, and sent him a message. He replied and we set up a late-night meeting at a city park near my house.

The night of March 1, 2009, was a freezing 9 degrees Fahrenheit. A frigid wind violently blew the pages of my notepad. I rubbed my mitten-clad hands together to keep the feeling in them and wondered if the story was worth the frostbite. The streets of the neighborhood were abandoned; only two people were crazy enough to be out in that weather, and one of them was me.

The Watchman might be called crazy for other reasons.

I forced my frozen hands to reach for my cell phone and stiffly dialed a number. The phone rang once, and a mysterious voice said, "This is the Watchman."

"Hi, Watchman, yeah, I'm in the park near the playground equipment," I said in a frozen cloud of breath. A swing creaked behind me in the wind. The Watchman told me he was pulling into the parking lot.

---

* "RLSH" (pronounced "R-L-S-H") is used much like the word "deer," used to describe both a singular superhero or a group of them—"an RLSH," "those RLSH," "all the RLSH."

He rolled up to the park, not in a high-tech Batmobile but in a pretty normal-looking four-door tan Pontiac. He left his car and walked through the empty park toward me, and for a few strange moments I felt totally unprepared to interview a costumed crime fighter.

Wow, I thought to myself, he's real and wearing a costume and walking toward me. Now what do I do?

He extended a motorcycle-gloved hand to me in greeting. The rest of his costume that night included a simple domino mask, a red hooded sweatshirt with the Watchman logo (a stylized letter *W* that resembles the tip of a clock hand) stenciled on it, army boots, and a black trench coat.

I had met my first Real Life Superhero.

The RLSH are described as a "movement," a "community," and a "subculture," depending on whom you talk to. They consist of mostly anonymous, costumed do-gooders trying to save the world in their own small ways. They have a wide range of missions—charity and humanitarian work, activism, and, most controversial, actual crime fighting. Like in the comic books. But not really.

Although their looks are inspired by the comic books, RLSH have in almost all cases adopted their own unique superhero persona, and this inventing process is often cited as the most personally empowering part of the experience.

RLSH should not be confused with other colorfully clad people. The term "cosplayers" refers to people who dress up in character, usually an already established comics or sci-fi character, to attend a comic con or similar event. RLSH sometimes use this term to insult someone they think is fake or just posing the part online—"that guy is just a cosplayer." Live-action role players, or LARPers, are in costume to act out a role-playing game. Costumed panhandlers hang around places like Grauman's Chinese Theatre in Hollywood or Las Vegas to solicit photos with tourists.

RLSH, as the Watchman informed me, are "trying to be the real deal."

The Watchman was also quick to point out to me that he did not have any superpowers. In fact, the RLSH who do believe they are supernatural are a very small minority, a few people who claim to have some kind of metaphysical abilities. These claimants—delightfully eccentric or completely crazy, depending on how you look at it—are mostly shunned by their embarrassed peers. RLSH say the movement is not about superpowers but rather embracing bravery and the willingness to make the world a better place, ideals that have made comic book superheroes so iconic.

My research eventually uncovered several early prototypes of the concept, a secret history dating to at least the 1970s. But the big, modern population explosion of superheroes didn't begin until the mid-2000s. It was then the RLSH seemed to become an almost overnight phenomenon, as though a radioactive cloud had rolled through the night, entering people's heads in a mass dream telling them they should hear the call of the superhero. This was mostly due to the viral nature of the Internet. The spread of the RLSH owes a lot to our social networking, meme-based culture.

As we walked around that night, the Watchman began to paint an honest-sounding account of what his life as an RLSH was like. Patrols were long, he said, and rarely adventurous or action packed; crime is a random thing, even when you're looking for it.

"Most nights are uneventful," he told me. "But from time to time something comes up." The Watchman told me of some small victories. One night he chased away a group of kids who were tagging a building with graffiti and trying to break into a shed. When he encountered a woman suffering from a heart condition, he called for help. He mentioned his annual Christmas toy charity drive, when he collects toys and delivers them in person to a local charity.

Another time he staked out an underage party. He saw some guys leading a drunken teenage girl to a dark corner of the backyard. The Watchman could tell the men wanted to take advantage of the intoxicated victim, so he sprang out of his car and caused a commotion. The girl's brother came out of the party and, despite some confusion—he thought the Watchman was the guilty party and pulled a knife on him—he got his sister into a car and drove her home.

"Real life isn't like a comic book," the Watchman admitted.

I asked the Watchman what message he hopes people take away from him and from the RLSH movement.

"What I hope and what I expect are two different things," the Watchman answered. "What I expect is pretty much basically what we hear from the public a lot. There are plenty of people out there who think it is a great thing, but I think a lot of people don't understand. They think that we are out there just looking for personal gratification, some kind of attention, that we're comic book geeks who, I don't know, were bored, lonely, or whatever, who just don't get it, and think we're a bunch of nuts."

The ice crunched as we passed under a street lamp on the park path. The light cast strange shadows on the Watchman's masked face.

"What I hope people do think is that we're actually out there trying to do something good, and we're trying to make a difference. Yes, we're trying to get attention. But we're not trying to get personal attention. If I were out for personal attention, I wouldn't be wearing a mask. I wouldn't hide my identity. We're looking for attention for our various causes. That is what I would like the public to think about: hey, maybe these people are doing some good, taking notice, and hopefully getting a little bit of inspiration, not exactly to dress funny and go out the way we're doing it, but to do something."

The Watchman stopped walking for a moment. He turned to me and gestured broadly. "You know, if everyone made little changes in what they did, gave a little more to charity, watched out for their neighbors, we wouldn't have the problems that we have. That's really what we are trying to accomplish."

I asked the Watchman if he might help me contact other RLSH to talk to.

"While there are RLSH who seem to jump at any chance to be involved with the media, there are also many who stay away from it," he explained. "I can let some of them know about you and that may help. To get the whole picture, you'll have to talk to plenty of us and keep an open mind. There are some who pretend and some who are the real deal."

He turned back to the path leading to his car. We shook hands again and parted ways.

I headed home to warm up and contemplate everything I had heard. I thought about this growing secret society based on the pages of comic books, an anonymous army of superheroes patrolling the streets of their neighborhoods at night. Walking home, I realized my interview had created more questions than it answered.

Who were these people, and where did they come from?

Could they actually be successful in stopping crime, or were they facing a gruesome death?

What did their poor parents think of this?

Who was designing their wardrobes?

Did they team up like the Avengers or the Justice League?

I was certain about one thing—I was hooked on the Real Life Superhero story. What I couldn't predict was how weird my life was about to get.

AMERICAN SUPERHEROES

The Watchman. PIERRE-ELIE DE PIBRAC

As I walked around the park with the Watchman that cold evening, he told me that he had first adopted his costumed alter ego in the mid-1990s. At the time, he wasn't aware of anyone else who had explored the Real Life Superhero concept. He would mask up and sweep the streets in his car—known as a "rolling patrol"—all alone. And in 1997, feeling generally burned out on the superhero idea, he hung up his cape and called it a day.

What encouraged him to reenter the arena of real life heroics was the incredible discovery that he wasn't alone in his vision. In fact, he found, a whole superhero movement was quickly developing. He returned to costumed patrols in 2008 after deciding that "Wisconsin needed the Watchman again."

By 2008, the RLSH had grown to at least a couple hundred people. It's a hard group to get a head count on, due to their mysterious nature. Often an RLSH will set up an online profile, interact for a few weeks, then, out of boredom or disappointment or whatever other reasons, disappear, his or her online profile falling dormant. Others "retire" and then return, sometimes switching their superhero personas.

All of this confusion leads to a somewhat shaky current estimate of between two hundred and five hundred active RLSH claiming to hit the streets. The majority of these heroes are Americans, located in most major cities coast to coast—but also some not so major ones like Spearfish, North Dakota, and Mountain View, California. There are a small number of foreign RLSH, too, in locations ranging from London to São Paulo. The biggest RLSH populations are found in New York, San Francisco, Seattle, Minneapolis, San Diego, and Salt Lake City. Some RLSH are the sole defenders of their city or even their whole state.

The first reaction many have to RLSH is to assume they are all dorky, squeaky-voiced, white male virgins in ill-fitting spandex, living in their parents' basements. Some people think of the title character of the movie and comic book *Kick-Ass*, an over-the-top, violent interpretation of the RLSH concept. This description does match up in part with some, but in actuality, RLSH span a very diverse demographic. Most of them look like average, everyday people—the kind who might sit next to you on the bus or stand in line in front of you at the grocery store. They include people from their early teens to early sixties and come from all ethnic backgrounds. There are a rapidly growing number of women, so many that they have developed their own web magazine, *STAND* (Superheroine Tips and Networking Department).

One of *STAND*'s contributors is a professional bodybuilder who smashes the nerdy white dude stereotype with her ripped biceps. Miss Fit is a Puerto Rican woman who lives in Los Angeles by way of Brooklyn. Her mission as an RLSH is to promote health and fitness, and her alter ego has placed in several bodybuilding contests like the Miss Universe and Miss Olympia competitions.

The day jobs RLSH hold run the full gamut of American society. I've met caterers, graphic designers, pencil pushers, mechanics, radio DJs, and security guards. Some were college grads, others high school dropouts. I met RLSH who had former military training and others who had been in jail.

The economic gap varies vastly. The simple-living Catman walks around McMinnville, Tennessee, offering to do good deeds dressed in a samurai-style outfit with cat ears perched on his hood. He worked for a long time as a dishwasher at Waffle House and lived at various times in a tent and in someone's basement. On the other end of the scale, Citizen Prime, who lives in the suburbs of Salt Lake City, has a prominent position with a Fortune 500 company. He built an elaborate supersuit of armor that cost somewhere between five and seven grand.

The religious beliefs of RLSH are also an eclectic mix. I've met quite a few Christian superheroes of all denominations, Protestant and Roman Catholic. There are pagan superheroes, and Jewish superheroes who are careful to observe Shabbat. There are atheists and agnostics and ones who have made up their own beliefs.

The RLSH concept has been interpreted by people of all political stripes, from radical liberals to extreme conservatives. I have had RLSH tell me they are anarchists; others are Tea Party supporters. Many are indifferent to politics and cite a frustration with the two major political parties as a motivation to participate in this new movement in the first place.

Nadra Enzi, who also calls himself Captain Black, of New Orleans, argues that the RLSH are a political party unto themselves. They've tapped into a sentiment shared by conservative and liberal activists alike: the belief that the system is ineffective, that there is too much gridlock and red tape and not enough action.

"America has tea parties and coffee parties offering nonpartisan involvement. RLSH do the same, minus political arguing!" he declared in an impassioned blog entry. "We just suit up and serve the community—simple as that. I offer us as an option for anyone sick and tired of political grandstanding while problems go unchallenged. Those preferring really creative outreach to hot air ought to check this Movement out."

Arguments occur between RLSH online often, about patrolling techniques and media policies and any number of other things. In fact, it is not dangerous criminals but "Internet drama" that is ranked as the number one problem for the RLSH movement to gain serious momentum. Strangely, these arguments rarely gravitate toward their politics, religion, or other factors. In fact, these people collaborate on a lot of things in spite of their differences.

One of these odd couples is Treesong of Carbondale, Illinois, and Crossfire the Crusader of Hot Springs, Arkansas. Crossfire is forty-four, has been married for twenty years, and has two daughters and a granddaughter. He is a rather large, rotund man. He is a Southern Baptist who incorporates religious symbols into his costume. He describes his political beliefs as "very conservative." He works as a clerk at a hotel and in his spare time as a Christian children's entertainer, performing as a clown and puppeteer. His hobbies include model building, writing sci-fi stories, and karaoke.

I would describe Treesong, thirty-three, as a hippie superhero. He is a single, bearded, rail-thin vegetarian, a former vegan. Even before he became an RLSH, he legally changed his name to Treesong. He is a Wiccan high priest. He describes his political views as "social anarchism" but also identifies with the Green Party. He works as a cashier at an organic co-op grocery store and has authored three books: collections of poetry and essays on self-improvement. Treesong's interests include spending time in the outdoors, role-playing games, and karaoke.

So the two seem to have one thing in common. But besides maybe an encounter at karaoke night,* they should want to have absolutely *nothing* to do with each other, right?

"He shows respect for my beliefs and I do the same for his," Crossfire told me in an e-mail, "and that's how it should be."

These two not only know each other but have collaborated as moderators on an RLSH forum, and Treesong was a guest on Crossfire's Internet radio show, *Superhero Academy*. Treesong shared tips on the show for simple things people could do to save the environment. Crossfire and Treesong got to meet each other in 2010 to hang out in costume at the annual "Superman Celebration" in the small town of Metropolis, Illinois.

"As long as we stick to talking about concrete ways to help others (and the environment)," Treesong wrote in an e-mail, "we seem to be able to work together just fine regardless of our differences."

As time went on, I slowly learned more details about the Watchman's life. The more I found out, the less crazy he seemed, despite his odd hobby. I found out he had been married for more than ten years. He met his wife while he was still enlisted in the army. The couple now have three young children. They both have jobs, and on top of that the Watchman was going to night school for a while to pursue an interest in graphic design and filmmaking.

The Watchman and his family live in a city outside of Milwaukee (he's asked me not to name it) in a nice, modest home on a quiet suburban street. There's a basketball hoop above the garage door, a grill, and a yard with playground equipment. Inside, the kids have their artwork hanging up on the fridge and the living room has a wraparound couch and a pile of toys—superhero action figures, of course—on the floor.

They are the average American suburban family—except for one thing. Instead of going to sleep or watching the game after work, the Watchman goes down to the "man cave" in his basement and

---

* Crossfire's favorite karaoke song is "Sweet Home Chicago," Blues Brothers style. Treesong's jam is "Light My Fire" by the Doors. Not a bad combo.

carefully puts on his red rubber cowl, red leather gloves, spandex shirt, utility belt, and trench coat. His dog, known as the Watchdog, sometimes joins him. And while his wife and kids are sound asleep, the Watchman cruises the streets, keeping a watchful eye out for the safety of his neighbors.

Comic Book Fans

Like most RLSH, the Watchman is a fan of his comic book counterparts. He told me that one of his dreams is to someday open his own comic book shop. He told me his personal favorite is DC's powerhouse, Superman.

Superman, in fact, is pretty important to this story. That's because the SH part of RLSH really traces back to the Man of Steel and the birth of that great American art form: the superhero comic book.

Action Comics #1 was published in June 1938, and the cover of the comic book depicted something not quite ever seen before. Superman is lifting a car over his head with ease and smashing it into a rock, his red cape floating behind him. A trio of terrified no-goodniks is trying to make a getaway.

There are other mysterious characters that predate Superman—cowboys and detectives like Zorro, the Lone Ranger, and Green Hornet—but Superman was different. He was an alien, an orphan of a doomed planet, born with incredible superpowers. He was also a huge success and launched what became known as the Golden Age of comics.

Competing companies raced to get as many superhero titles on the market as they could, to ride the wave of Superman's selling power. Soon the shelves were overflowing with comics starring Batman, Wonder Woman, Captain America, the Spirit, Captain Marvel, and more.

These characters soon became our own American mythology, updated versions of the Greek and Roman gods. These warriors were our hope, our champions. They were rays of light in the darkness. The superheroes became the gods of our pop culture religion.

Comic Book Revisionism

Yet if superheroes are godlike, how did they move from the pulp page heavens to wandering around downtown Cincinnati in real life? That might have something to do with what comics creator Bob Burden calls "comic book revisionism."

When I first heard of the RLSH, one of Burden's creations, the Mystery Men, immediately came to mind. Burden's surrealist superhero, Flaming Carrot, first appeared in 1979 and was an oddball interpretation of the American superhero—he wears scuba flippers and sports a gigantic carrot head with a flame shooting out of the top. His utility belt is equipped with a yo-yo and sneezing powder, and one of his few powers is entering a state of "Zen stupidity." The title became a cult hit in the direct comics market in the 1980s.

Burden introduced the Mystery Men, a team of superheroes with subpar, questionable powers in a 1987 story line. The characters were also a hit, spawning a 1999 film adaptation. Burden says they were another step in devolving the superhero mythos.

"The original superheroes were sort of all powerful and mythical," Burden explained in an interview. "The Marvel superheroes were more middle class, more antiheroes. They were revisionist in that sense. It was a revolution. And when they came along, there was a tremendously big middle class and they appealed to middle class kids."

Burden cited an example. "I remember reading a Spider-Man comic where he couldn't find his costume. Aunt May took it and threw it out, so he had to get a costume quick. He went into a department store and got a Halloween costume, and all during the adventure it was coming loose on him and he had to keep using spiderwebs to pull it back up.

"That's not the type of thing that would happen to Superman, who was kind of an all-powerful character, or Green Lantern. Unthinkable.

"With the Mystery Men, I kind of usurped the Marvel middle class by coming up with a working class, blue collar, rust belt superhero. The Flaming Carrot shops at K Mart, hangs out at a bowling alley, and owns a broken-down Laundromat. He catches the catfish dinner special on Friday nights and hangs out in strip clubs. This was another level down from the middle class superhero."

At the same time Burden was working on his surreal action farce, comic book revisionism was also being plotted as an apocalyptic drama by writer Alan Moore.

The Scriptures of Alan Moore

RLSH list a wide variety of literature that has inspired them, but one book is cited as key to the movement in general: Alan Moore's *Watchmen*, often regarded as one of the best-written comics of all time.

The original series was created in 1986 and 1987 as a twelve-issue series for DC Comics with illustrator Dave Gibbons. The story line deals with intense, real life issues facing its group of dysfunctional superheroes, while a nuclear clock ticks in the background.

The importance of the book was conveyed to me early on by the Watchman, when I asked if his name was in reference to the book.

"As for my name . . . it is not directly inspired by Alan Moore's *Watchmen*, nor am I a Jehovah's Witness who reads *The Watchtower*. Those are two things that people seem to wonder about. I am a fan of the book though, as are most Real Life Superheroes. Many have called it 'the RLSH Bible,'" the Watchman said.

The influence of *Watchmen* is notable among the RLSH. One of the iconic symbols from the book is a smiley-face button with a blood splatter on it, found in the first couple pages by one of the story's protagonists, Rorschach, a psychotic vigilante. Rorschach finds the button in the gutter near the scene of the murder of one of his fellow superheroes, the Comedian.

Several RLSH have included a replica of the crime-scene button pinned to their costumes. Others wear a costume similar to Rorschach's—a trench coat, fedora, and mask. Rorschach-isms are also popular on social networking sites and as the signature line of forum profiles, lines such as, "We do not do this thing because it is permitted. We do it because we have to. We do it because we are compelled."

I've always been puzzled and a little freaked out by Rorschach's popularity with the RLSH. Rorschach is portrayed as a psychotic, obsessive vigilante who beats people up and breaks fingers to get criminals to spill information. In one flashback, he captures a child molester and murderer and gives him a choice: he can burn to death in the abandoned house he has been using or saw through his hand-cuffed arm to escape.

The cast of *Watchmen* resonate with RLSH as complicated, rebellious characters. As in other of Moore's works, like *V for Vendetta*, the heroes and antiheroes of *Watchmen* struggle with the idea that the only way to build a better future is to destroy the present. They lead dangerous, clandestine lives and operate outside the corrupt bureaucracy of the government, and it's likely that such romantic, revolutionary ideas appeal to the RLSH.

Batman: The Ultimate RLSH

I conducted an informal poll on an RLSH forum, asking them to share their favorite comic books. Many of their answers reflected their own style. RLSH who sport domino masks and ties are basing their looks on classic pulp heroes like the Spirit or Green Hornet. Some of the creepier, occult-looking costumes are inspired by characters like Spawn or Ghost Rider.

The RLSH mentioned a lot of favorite heroes—Spider-Man, Green Arrow, Daredevil, superheroes famous and obscure, a list that would make Comic Book Guy from *The Simpsons* swoon. But there was one name that popped up over and over: Batman.

The character has a lot of appeal—he's a mysterious billionaire ninja, the world's richest, smartest man, the best-trained fighter with the coolest crime-fighting gear. Unlike most of his Justice League colleagues, he has no superpowers. He is a mere mortal, a "real life" person defending the night against the forces of evil.

But he does have a huge advantage over the RLSH—he is a work of fiction.*

Batman has unlimited resources and technology and can withstand physical trials beyond reality—he is beaten and stabbed, has his back broken, and bleeds buckets of red ink, but still carries on with his one-man war against crime.

The concept of Batman may lie somewhere within the realm of reality, but the reality is hardly a glamorous or safe one.

Real Life Influences

Comic book scripts aren't the only influencing factors for the RLSH. Many RLSH list personal reasons for what they do—a difficult family life or a need to improve the world for their own children. Some have witnessed or been victim to a crime, or have a loved one who was. For others it is an opposite reaction: their past is shady, and becoming an RLSH is a way for them to atone with the universe—a last step of a twelve-step program, with themselves benefiting as much as anyone they happen to help out.

There are certain real life events that have helped mold the movement, too. The overpowering feeling of tragedy and helplessness after the 9/11 attacks was a calling to some RLSH. They wanted to do something to make the world a better place but were unsure what to do until they heard about the RLSH, and the idea spoke to them.

Another story often cited as a call to action is the murder of Catherine "Kitty" Genovese. On March 13, 1964, Genovese arrived

---

*Economics students at Lehigh University studied Batman and calculated what the real life price tag would be to operate as the Dark Knight: $2.8 million.

at her New York apartment building after closing the bar where she worked. Outside her building she encountered Winston Moseley, who stalked, robbed, raped, stabbed, and beat Genovese for over an hour while her neighbors, tallied by a *New York Times* report at thirty-eight, sat idly by, afraid to act. Some later said they "didn't want to get involved," or were afraid. Eventually police were called, but it was too late. Genovese was dead. Moseley told police the motive of his attack was simply "to kill a woman."

There was a lot of public outcry after the story started rolling off the press. "Dear God, what have we become?" was one reaction recorded at the time. It was hard to believe that thirty-eight people had numbly sat on their hands while a woman was being brutally murdered in the street below.

The incident led to the coining of the terms "Genovese Syndrome" or "bystander effect." The incident made its way as a reference into various bits of pop culture including *Watchmen*, which may be why many RLSH have taken to treating the anniversary of her death as a sort of memorial holiday.

"This is why we exist" is a common phrase among RLSH sharing the Genovese story.

MARCH 13—KITTY GENOVESE DAY

Catherine "Kitty" Genovese. DAVID BEYER JR.

Many RLSH patrol the streets in memory of Kitty Genovese on the night of March 13. Some hand out flyers detailing the case and warning of the dangers of apathy.

"Take a good look at her and never forget her and what happened to her," concludes the flyer made by Thanatos.

"It speaks to me because it is a well-known example—even if exaggerated—of something fundamentally wrong with people not caring to get involved," Silver Sentinel told me. Silver Sentinel patrols his hometown in upstate New York with his wife, Golden Valkyrie, every March 13.

Not everyone is sold on the idea of the date becoming an RLSH holiday. Portland's Zetaman believes many RLSH care about it simply because the story worked its way into the plot of *Watchmen*. "This is a very sad case of apathy, but it happened a long time ago. I can think of numerous tragic events that the RLSH community can draw inspiration from and possibly should," Zetaman says. "I have felt that it was bizarre of so many RLSH to want to 'patrol' on her death day and not be inspired by other injustices in our nation to do a national patrol as well."

Another issue with the Kitty Genovese story is that it has been disputed as more myth than fact. An analysis of the building layout revealed very few "witnesses" could have seen the attack. Initial screams were probably mistaken for bar noise, so the image of thirty-eight people gazing down coldly at the murder is an exaggeration.

Despite the myth, or maybe because of it, the story is important to many RLSH, who use it as a textbook example of citizen apathy.

Walking Through the Door

Today, superheroes are as popular as they were in the Golden Age. The media has changed, but the characters have changed with it. The past decade has seen Hollywood repeatedly smashing the summer box office like the Incredible Hulk on a rampage, with franchises starring Batman, Spider-Man, Iron Man, Superman, the Avengers, and the X-Men.

Graphic novels have made the leap from comic book specialty stores to the shelves of mainstream booksellers. There have been TV shows like *Heroes* and *Smallville*, Saturday morning cartoons, and video games. Comic cons have grown from hotel rooms full of card tables with nerdy guys trading dusty back issues to huge multimedia extravaganzas with megawatts of star power.

The evolution of our culture has something to do with Real Life Superheroes, too. We've become increasingly vicarious, catering to our fantasy lives. We're assuming the lives of rock stars, soldiers, and athletes in video games, and immersing ourselves completely in characters created in *World of Warcraft*, *Second Life*, and other online (and real life) role-playing games. We watch artificial realities on TV and read celebrity blogs on MySpace and Twitter.

It's easy to see the yearning of your everyday Clark Kent for something, well, more super.

When I spoke to Bob Burden, though, he told me to be careful not to be too derivative theorizing about the RLSH origins. He noted that the main motivating factor might be the group's own initiative, their desire to do something new and bold, that has caused their existence.

"Something like Mystery Men or *Watchmen* can be a doorway," he noted, "but they have to choose to go through it."

BOY SCOUTS AND BATMEN

DC's Guardian. PIERRE-ELIE DE PIBRAC

Part 1: Boy Scouts

July 4, 2009, 9:15 AM. That's when you would have found me peeking around a stone wall near the Tomb of the Unknowns in Arlington Cemetery.

It was a beautiful summer morning. My friend Groschopf (most commonly known by just his last name) and I followed signs pointing to the tomb. We were there before the first wave of tourists, and it was silent, completely still. The thousands of grave markers of our fallen soldiers spread as far as the eye could see. It was a moving sight.

All the more reason why I myself was feeling sort of like a lowly superhero paparazzo. After all, I was sneaking into a superhero wreath-laying ceremony on hallowed ground.

The ceremony was held with a "costumed activist" named DC's Guardian and three of his Skiffytown League of Heroes teammates, and more of the team watched from the side. None was dressed in costume, as there is a dress code for the wreath-laying ceremony.

They were announced as Skiffytown, and the quartet was escorted down the stairs. They were presented with a wreath, which was placed on the tomb. A sentinel then played "Taps" and they were led back up the stairs.

There was a reason for us sneaking in. Although the group had at first told me about the ceremony and their appearance in our nation's Fourth of July parade, they soon had a change of heart about talking to me, after I had purchased my plane tickets to Washington, DC. They didn't want to tell me when the ceremony took place. In fact, after a certain point Skiffytown was pretty much not up for talking with me about anything, at least not for a while.

Why? Let's make a trip back in time, true believers!

November 1961

This is the year young Atlas (soon to rebranded Marvel) Comics editor, writer, and art director Stan "the Man" Lee helped launch a new revival after comics from the Golden Age had waned in popularity. This new era is referred to as the Silver Age of comics. Lee did this with an innovative new line of comics, well received by the comics-reading public. Lee's first hit was a team called the Fantastic Four, which he developed with legendary artist Jack Kirby. Lee's publisher wanted a comic that could compete with National (later to become DC) Comics' successful superhero team title, *Justice League of America*, which had been created a year earlier.

Lee thought it was a good chance to try an idea he had. As he explained in his autobiography, "I tried to make [the Fantastic Four] like real people, with all their warts revealed." The Silver Age's success was built on this comic book revisionism of superheroes who acted more like normal people than superhero gods.

The *Fantastic Four* title was a smash hit, and Marvel began to develop a dedicated following of readers, which Lee dubbed "true believers." Lee and the Marvel bullpen set to work inventing more groups of heroes, including the Avengers and the X-Men.

It may be a testimony to Lee's creative powers that he helped form a super group, the Skiffytown League of Heroes, without even knowing it. To better explain, you have to move forward forty-five years.

Who Wants to Be a Superhero?

On July 27, 2006, one of Lee's more recent projects premiered, a superhero-themed reality show titled *Who Wants to Be a Superhero?* Featured on the Sci-Fi Channel, the show followed a basic reality show premise. Ten or eleven invented superhero personas were chosen from a field of hundreds of auditioners. This group then lived together in a camera-rigged house, and personalities clashed.

Although it was billed as a "reality" show, there was a lot of over-the-top comic book–style scripting, which led to moments like the contestants turning in for bed at the end of the day fully dressed in their bulky costumes.

Stan Lee himself popped up here and there throughout the shows via satellite, sending the group on competitive challenges designed to see who had the "right stuff" to be a superhero. Those who fell short were sent packing each episode in an elimination round that took place on the roof of a warehouse with a lot of dramatic music and commercial breaks.

The show produced two winners—Feedback, who was crowned champion of season one, and the Defuser, who was the winner of the show's second season. Two winners, but what about all of the also-rans and others who auditioned? Not to mention a league's worth prepping their characters for season three. But rumors of a third season flattened out into limbo, and the streets were then filled with hundreds of disappointed homemade superheroes.

Many of them were not ready to pack up their tights and capes and call it a day. Their characters began to communicate and befriend each other via the forums on the Sci-Fi Channel website. They began to write fan fiction about their characters and soon banded together in the fictional city of Skiffytown. The superhero castaways pulled themselves up by their bootstraps.

Fast forward to me standing on the corner of East Constitution Avenue and Ninth Street with Groschopf. July 4, 2009. Twelve noon. Washington, DC. We were waiting for our nation's official Independence Day parade to start. The weather was hot and the National Mall was crowded with tourists enjoying the day, wearing sunglasses, visors, fanny packs. Many people were waving flags, and the lampposts were decorated in red, white, and blue.

The parade started with the blare of police sirens. Then, after the battalion of Daughters of the American Revolution, there they were, the Skiffytown League of Heroes. They were led by DC's Guardian—or just DC—who had quickly changed into costume between Arlington and the parade route. DC looks like an alternate-universe version of Captain America crossed with Spider-Man, with the Flash's ear wings. He waved broadly to the crowds. His wife and kids, also dressed as heroes, had joined him for the parade, along with Skiffytown members from all over the country.

Near him was Dragonheart of Miami, sporting a spandex suit and a bleached streak in his hair and some red rectangular shades. Working the other side of the spectators was Blue Lotus of Detroit. She wore a silky blue shirt straight out of a kung fu flick. Knight Vigil of Tampa had metallic shoulder and chest pads, a utility belt over black spandex, and a metallic mask.

This was the Skiffytown crew, but not in full force. There were about twenty members in the parade, but the group has at least eighty members on its online forum.

Following the heroes on foot was a jeep pulling a trailer with Skiffytown banners along the sides. Inside the trailer, waving in friendly fashion, were the mountainous Noir and Kryhavoc, also of heroic proportions. And joining them in the "Good Ship Skiffy," as she called it, was Agent Mixsae (later just Mixsae), second in command of the group at the time. She was dressed in a patriotic ensemble with a tricornered hat. The group in the trailer waved and threw candy to the crowd. Behind them, a giant balloon of cartoon aardvark Arthur hung suspended in the air, looming lazily on the horizon.

Groschopf and I tried to work through the crowd to stay with the group as they paraded along. Eventually we reached the end of the route—Seventeenth Street, where they were announced by a man with a microphone, speaking in the rich tones of a movie narrator.

"Skiffytown League of Heroes is a nonprofit group of people from around the country banding together to help charities large and small. They travel across the United States visiting children's hospitals and helping local charities. Wherever duty calls, they are more than willing to step up and lend a helping hand when they can," the announcer declared with gusto.

Groschopf and I watched from a distance. We didn't approach them. We had been told Skiffytown was not down with talking to me.

"Guilt by Association"

In mid-May 2009, I began planning some travel to the East Coast. I saw a MySpace bulletin saying that Skiffytown would be in the Fourth of July parade. I liked the idea on paper—superheroes marching in our nation's capital, celebrating the birth of the United

States of America. I emailed DC, and he seemed receptive to the idea of my being out there.

"I look forward to hooking up with ya," he said in an e-mail, and in a follow-up, "Can't wait to see ya. We have not only the parade, but we've also been invited to lay a wreath at the Tomb of the Unknown." Dragonheart, a top-ranking Skiffytown member, was also receptive to the idea, talking with me about the group's plans for the day.

"This is great," I thought. "This will obviously be the easiest part of my journey into the world of superhero." I believed they would be the most open to talking to me, since they had auditioned for a reality show and were walking down the street clad in superhero costumes in front of thousands of people.

I assumed we'd hit it off so well that there would be a Fourth of July superhero barbecue. I could just imagine it: DC's Guardian, in costume and an apron, grilling up some all-American cheeseburgers while I tossed the old Frisbee around with Kryhavoc and Justice Boy. Lemonade and lawn darts—the perfect American afternoon.

Things hit a major snag, though, when I introduced myself to Agent Mixsae. She didn't like the idea. To use a term from her home state of Tennessee, the idea put a bee in her bonnet. She brought the idea up for debate in a private forum with the Skiffytown members. I was told they concluded that being a part of this book would be something they didn't want.

The reason? (Gavel cracking!) "Guilt by association."

I was informed that the group didn't want to share the space between these book covers with those guys referred to as the "V" word. Yes, that's right, the dreaded "member of a volunteer committee organized to suppress and punish crime summarily (as when the processes of law are viewed as inadequate); also: a self-appointed doer of justice." The vigilante. Mixsae, who was the group's "chief of staff" at the time, sent me an e-mail explaining their position.

"The one biggest voice I did need to listen to was a member of our group who is a law enforcement officer," Agent Mixsae wrote. "The term RLSH has come on their radar, mostly thanks to the vigilantes. The activity is frowned upon by law enforcement as well as some government outlets who are aware of the activity. Several voices then spoke up and commented that they would not like to see the charity organization that works so closely with sick children and with kids in general associated with 'vigilantes.'

"Therefore we would ask that the organization as a whole not be discussed in your book. Your book is about RLSH, that's something our organization is not and parallels could result in 'guilt by association.' We would like to avoid that if at all possible."

I found this response to be somewhat puzzling. First, because DC's Guardian, Skiffytown's president, was heavily involved in the RLSH world—he had hosted RLSH panels at a Florida comic con, was signed up on their forums, and participated in several RLSH media projects. Second, as I stated in a follow-up e-mail—wouldn't having them represented *help* them clarify that they are not vigilantes?

The Skiffytown League of Superheroes is not a group of vigilantes.

See? There you go, I did it.

Skiffytown and others like them prefer the term "costumed activists" to "RLSH." Costumed activists do not fight crime—their superhero personas are used solely for charity, humanitarian, and sometimes activist causes. They visit children's hospitals and classrooms, hand out supplies to the homeless, do charity walks and fundraisers. And again, they are not vigilantes.

Reconnecting with the Skiffies

Fortunately, I got to know DC's Guardian better despite the initial misadventure. I found out the reason for the specific design of DC's costume: not a single inch of flesh is showing; even the eyes are covered with reflective lenses. DC says this is because he wants his ethnicity to remain a mystery so children can imagine a man of any race under the star-spangled spandex.

DC, who actually splits his time between Washington, DC, and Southern California, used to be in the military. His favorite comic book influence, obviously, is Captain America. One of his activities outside of charity work has been to hand out pocket-size editions of the Constitution and Bill of Rights.

I heard a very emotional description of a visit by the group to a children's hospital where they were able to bring some joy to terminally ill patients. I heard about other charity work and simple civil acts, such as Skiffytowners volunteering to work the "lost children" booth at a comic con.

I also was finally able to ask him why the group was so vehemently opposed to the RLSH label. He explained that he didn't really care about the term, but had to follow his group's consensus.

"RLSH is a term, that's about all I think of it as, as a label to lump in several different types," DC told me. "Does it matter to me what you call me? No. I will still do what I think is needed, within the law. Now, Skiffy as a whole prefers the term 'charity group.'"

So that's the charity end of the spectrum, the costumed activists. Now brace yourself to take a look at the flip side of the RLSH coin.

Part 2: Batmen

It was a hot night in Richmond, Virginia. The Death's Head Moth was staking out a drug dealer, watching him working an operation out of a parking lot. He was watching him and watching his drug deals, trying to get a sense of his rhythm and setup.

"A lot of times they work with a partner," Death's Head Moth explained to me later over the phone in a baritone voice with a slight southern accent. "It's common to have one guy selling and another guy holding who goes to get the product, which gives them kind of a buffer zone. There's a variety of different ways they do it. I staked him out and determined he was working alone."

Death's Head Moth then began to sneak up behind the drug dealer. His appearance is certainly designed for the element of sur-

Death's Head Moth.
COURTESY OF THE NEW YORK INITIATIVE

prise. His outfit and gear include a black spandex bodysuit and elbow-length gloves called hatch dominators, used by law enforcement for riot control. His feet are also protected with tall, tough steel-toed boots.

DHM also wears a "utility belt" that holds his two rapid-rotation batons. The batons have two handles, which makes them versatile defensive and offensive weapons. Other gear in the belt includes a collapsible grappling hook and rope, flashlight, and camera. He wears a padded shirt underneath a protective vest that can deflect blades, and a "protective metal nut cup."

For imagery he has a skull and crossbones on the chest of his uniform, and a creepy, kind of spiky, dull metal mask. In a phone interview, I asked DHM about his spooky imagery.

"I find the frightening appearance to be to my advantage. There is something unsettling about not being able to see someone's eyes and face. They can't see my facial expressions and can't really see what muscles I'm moving if I'm preparing to move."

As he crept up on the drug dealer, the element of surprise was ruined by the crunching of glass from a broken car window beneath his boots. The drug dealer heard him. "He immediately turned around and punched me in the face. And then he began to yell and kick at me."

Death's Head Moth was prepared for this moment, he said. He sprayed the drug dealer with MK-4, a high-octane pepper spray. After being sprayed, the drug dealer coughed up a plastic baggie and spit it on the ground. Death's Head Moth grabbed it and took off. The baggie contained crack rocks, which he dumped down a sewer drain. He felt his mask, which was wet, and he could feel something loose in his mask. The punch had broken part of his front tooth.

The journey to becoming Death's Head Moth had begun about four years before. He had seen a report on an Indianapolis RLSH named Mr. Silent and it got his imagination rolling. "That thought of that guy out there gestated in my brain and I turned the thought over in my mind. I was thinking maybe this is something I could try—maybe I could do it," Death's Head Moth told me. "I started putting things together."

Death's Head Moth began to work out seven days a week and swore off fast food and soda. He practiced a variety of martial arts and "started working on pseudonyms and collecting gear."

His imagery was inspired after his eyes fell on the movie poster for *The Silence of the Lambs* that famously features Anthony Hopkins's face partially covered by an actual death's head moth. He began sketching costume designs and was doing legwork on the streets. Soon he was patrolling. Some of the victories he claims are stopping a mugging, a rape, and a guy beating up his girlfriend, all of which were reported to police.

But why risk it? Why spend your Saturday nights scoping out drug dealers and potentially getting punched in the face, or worse?

"Because it needs to be done. I see these things going on everywhere, and I want to do something about it. I'm an objectivist," DHM says. "Some of it is my upbringing. My parents taught me what was right and what was wrong. And that you can't wait for someone else to do something."

The Crime Fighters

This is the grittier side of the RLSH concept, the "crime fighters." This breed of RLSH has no interest in marching in a Fourth of July parade. If they were to visit a children's hospital, they would probably scare the kids half to death with their frightening costumes. They don't really care if you throw around the term "vigilante" to describe them—and, in fact, some would prefer you did.

Whether we like it or not, vigilantes are as American as apple pie, with a long history from the frontier justice of the Wild West to fighting thugs on the subways of New York. They have long been a source of our entertainment. Our eclectic vigilante heroes include characters portrayed by Clint Eastwood and Charles Bronson. They appear in TV shows and comic books—where almost every superhero operates as a vigilante.

THE BALD KNOBBERS: A CAUTIONARY TALE OF MASKED VIGILANTES

A lawyer modeling a Bald Knobber mask from the late 1880s. THE STATE HISTORICAL SOCIETY OF MISSOURI

Our purpose is to punish the evil doer among us. The courts have failed us. We administer punishment to those the arm of the law cannot or will not reach. In doing this, we do not break the law, because we have no evil intent.

—The Oath of the Bald Knobbers

A short-lived but interesting entry in vigilante history is a group called the Bald Knobbers. The Knobbers, named after their mountaintop meeting grounds, operated in Missouri from 1885 to 1889. They were founded by saloon owner Nathaniel N. Kinney, a giant muscular man with a "dynamic, persuasive personality and a gift for oratory." At first glance their posse, who wore matching masks and rode at night to dispense their version of justice, bears a resemblance to the longest-running vigilante hate group, the Ku Klux Klan.

The Bald Knobbers, however, were not racially motivated. They were determined to deliver prairie justice to invading bandits, whipping and sometimes hanging horse and livestock thieves. These thieves would experience a terrifying confrontation—a mob of men on horseback with devilish-looking masks, red and white stitching around the eye and mouth holes, and tassels of red yarn hanging off the cork horns mounted on top of their heads. The men wore their suit coats backward to help prevent identification.

But the Knobbers began to lose any support they had when their power went to their heads. They began punishing anyone who didn't follow their idea of morality. Unwed couples were common in the area, because they were poor and wanted to avoid marriage license fees, and the Knobbers began beating them for living in sin. One offense that could summon a late-night visit from the Knobbers was simply "being ornery."

Things ended badly for the group. A Knobbers chapter in Christian County had several young members who decided to kill a critic, William Edens, over remarks he made about the group. A shoot-out at Eden's cabin left two of his family dead and other family members and Knobbers seriously injured.

The Knobbers were rounded up and jailed and three of them were sentenced to death. Nathaniel Kinney was also assassinated in retaliation. The condemned Knobbers were hung on a poorly constructed gallows in 1889 in a scene described as "gruesome"—the Knobbers' feet dragged on the ground as they writhed in pain. The gallows were quickly fixed and the Knobbers were hung again. The remaining Bald Knobbers disbanded.

Modern vigilante groups exist today with a wide range of goals. The Sea Shepherd Conservation Society travels the oceans trying to prevent whaling boats from capturing their quarry. The Minuteman Project patrols the US-Mexico border trying to capture illegal immigrants. Perverted Justice sets up sting operations to catch pedophiles.

Many crime fighters are careful with the vigilante title. They say they are operating within the law, even if they might be pushing the limits a bit.

Ironically, the very people who have made the costumed activists shy away from the RLSH title also do not want the label. "I will not associate myself with 'RLSH,'" a crime fighter from Philadelphia named Ecliptico told me in simple terms. He did not respond to a follow-up inquiry.

Another reluctant interview subject was Nightwatch, who lived near Denver, Colorado, with whom I exchanged e-mails briefly in 2009. He had recorded videos of himself brandishing his collection of nightsticks and threatening criminals in a gravelly voice. Nightwatch preferred the term "mask" and dressed in full bulletproof body armor and a riot cop helmet.

He stopped posting online updates in 2010, but his MySpace page still floats in limbo, warning criminals who may be perusing it: "Know that if you commit a crime in my area and the outstanding [Colorado] PD does not pick you up for it—I will find you, and you will wish they had."

"I am only in contact with a brief few RLSH," Nightwatch explained to me in an e-mail. "Most I do not like, simply because to me, they seem exceedingly fake. I will not hold what they do against them—live and let live—but that does not mean I have to actively associate with them. I find most (75%) to be embarrassing at best, and disgraceful/mentally unstable at worst. Most do not deal in reality. I try to. Keeps me level and un-bullet-holed."

The crime fighters also despise the term "costume" to describe their attire. They say this implies Halloween or a costume party. Some prefer the term "uniform," although I never understood this as the unique nature of the attire defies the definition of the word. "Gear" is frequently used, although that usually refers specifically to armor and equipment. "Gimmick," a term borrowed from the wrestling world, refers to costume and overall persona. Some RLSH are sensitive to this lingo; others couldn't care less.*

I was not sure what to make of this group of people. I couldn't tell if they were exaggerating, if they were just tough guys on the Internet or, as the Watchman had put it, "the real deal." The story by Death's Head Moth about his late-night punch and pepper spray exchange with a drug dealer—was it an actual scenario or a tall tale? The story left only himself and the dealer as witnesses.

When this crime-fighting movement began, there were very few teams; the network consisted of random people working solo or in pairs in random cities. They shared tips and war stories on a forum called the Heroes Network that was established in 2007 by a young RLSH from New Jersey named Tothian. There is a very divisive, mixed reaction to Tothian—just mentioning his name can lead to an angry rant describing him as insane and manipulative. Others give him credit as an early force, organizing RLSH into a connected network.

---

* "I can't believe the amount of fighting that takes place over this subject," the Watchman told me, tired of Internet drama on the terminology. "If you wish to refer to my attire as a fruitcake wrapper, so be it."

Another infamous crime fighter from this early group was Nostrum, who became an RLSH urban legend. Nostrum patrolled post-Katrina New Orleans, wearing a sleeveless black shirt with an *N* logo on the front and a black hood like a medieval executioner would wear. One of the eyes of the hood was patched out. According to an online entry, he lost his vision in one eye in an altercation on the street.

"A good few weeks ago, had a struggle a few blocks from Bourbon Street with some punk. Resulted in a harsh fight and him jabbing a knife through my left goggle and into my left eye. A more recent doctor's appointment has confirmed I will not be getting sight back in that eye. None too pleased about this."

He was also rumored to patrol with a firearm, although reports ranged from a pistol to a sawed-off shotgun.

Nostrum left the online grid in 2009 and his current whereabouts are unknown. I was not able to get a message to him or find anyone still in contact with him.

"Every conversation I've ever had with the man has been him talking about how crazy he is, or how powerful," Zero, of the New York Initiative, recalls. "He told us all a story about him witnessing a man slapping his wife, in which case Nostrum claimed to beat the man half to death, and then lifted his head up and bit part of his ear off."

Crime-fighting groups slowly began to form and with them came more reliable media reports, video footage, and police reports that confirmed these people were actually butting heads with criminals or alleged criminals on the street.

One of the earliest of these crime-fighting groups was the Black Monday Society, based in Salt Lake City. Their membership fluctuates from eight to twelve strong. The group's founder, Insignis, is a tattoo artist, and the team uses his tattoo shop as a headquarters, where they work on costume and mask designs. The BMS is known for their monstrous-looking masks and gear, often based on demon or skeleton images of dark occult avengers, creepy antiheroes. The group does foot patrols of Salt Lake City. Leadership passed from Insignis to a newer recruit, Red Voltage. Serious members of the team show their allegiance by getting Black Monday Society tattoos at Insignis's shop.

Conflicting Methods

Not surprisingly, costumed activists and crime fighters don't see eye to eye on their missions and can be highly critical of each other's methods and goals. On the Internet radio show *Creature Feature*, for example, Ecliptico railed at fellow guest DC's Guardian, telling him that charity workers soften the impact that crime fighters could have.

"You guys are making us a target by going out there and flaunting your ass in spandex; you're making vigilantes a target. You are making our jobs harder because we put our asses on the line, like literally," Ecliptico said. "And when [the public] see people in costumes doing shit that normal people do on a daily basis, it makes it fuzzy. It fuzzes the line because they are not as afraid as they should be. We don't have the upper hand anymore."

Costumed activists and many RLSH counter by saying that crime fighting needs to be handled by proper law enforcement.

"I do not believe in vigilantism," Zetaman, an RLSH from Portland, Oregon, told me. "I believe we have to act like responsible citizens, which includes reporting to police, and following up by being prepared to give statements, testify, and present evidence."

He also believes a lot of stories told by crime fighters are fabrications and that their expectations are delusional. "I think these stories are far-fetched and I do not believe it happens, and they are presenting a false sense of security by running around with bulletproof vests and swords. People are going to notice someone running around dressed as a ninja and they are going to be scared and call the police. They're going to think there's a guy dressed up like a ninja in a trench coat that's running around flashing people."

Zetaman also thinks that vigilante justice doesn't help in the long run. "You're not really changing anything running around beating up crackheads and then disappearing. What does that change? The only thing the person is going to do is get a crew together to walk around with so they can beat you up next time they see you."

Crime fighters and costumed activists are the two extreme wings of the RLSH community, but most RLSH fall somewhere in the middle. They participate in charity events and humanitarian missions, and they also have a crime-fighting angle. Usually this is more passive than Nightwatch or Nostrum's approach, something more like a costumed neighborhood watch, looking to report, deter, and intervene only in case of emergency.

What is amazing about these people is that their "subculture" has a lengthier secret history than you would expect.

EARLY PROTOTYPES

The Human Fly poses with rocket builder Ky
"the Rocketman" Michaelson and entourage,
1976. COURTESY KY "THE ROCKETMAN" MICHAELSON

So, who was the first Real Life Superhero? Legends of mystery men have long
captured the imagination. The first story of Robin Hood, a ballad
titled *Robin Hood and the Monk*, was written in 1450. There have
been many theories on who the real Robin Hood was, although one
theory says "Robin Hood" was a stock alias used by thieves. Almost
six centuries later, the character's story still entertains us.

Zorro, created by pulp writer Johnston McCulley in 1919, was possibly based on stories of Portuguese bandits, or on the tale of William Lamport, an Irish soldier and pirate who lived in Mexico and was burned at the stake by the Spanish Inquisition in 1659.

My research into the secret history of the modern RLSH kept going further and further back, as I found costumed prototypes reaching back as far as the 1970s. It's possible this history could go back further—someday someone might be going through their grandparents' attic and find a dusty, neatly folded homemade superhero costume inspired by the Golden Age Batman or Captain America. The furthest back I followed the time line was to 1969, where I found a mysterious man known as the Fox, who began a mission that was often compared to Robin Hood and Zorro, the mysterious folk heroes who preceded him.

A science teacher from Aurora, Illinois, the man who would become the Fox was irritated by the black smoke and toxic sludge a new soap company was spewing into the sky and river. One day he found a mother duck and her ducklings dead and floating in soapy by-product and declared war on the company.

What few antipollution laws existed then were very primitive. The Fox explained, "Essentially what we had was a group of ineffectual local, state, and federal entities who really couldn't enforce the environmental laws; even if those people who were responsible for enforcing what laws we had wanted to. Locally, we had a severe pollution problem and local authority was looking out the window."

The Fox formulated a plan to jam the company's sewer pipes with boards and garbage so the waste would back up into the factory. Although he was determined to send a message, the Fox struggled with the morals of his mission. He described his inner conflict before his first raid on the soap company's sewer drain, tormented by the slight possibility that the backed-up industrial waste could cause a fire or explosion.

The Fox wrote, "What if my actions caused somebody to get hurt, or even killed? I sank to my hands and knees at this last thought and threw up. I could never live with myself if that happened." Throwing up from nervousness became a common pre-mission ritual.

After accomplishing his mission, he left a note on the scene, admonishing the soap company. It was signed "The Fox," with the face of a fox drawn peeking out of the letter *O*. It was a dually clever name: not only did it allude to the Fox River, but also "fox" in Spanish is "Zorro."

The Fox reflected on his direct action approach in his 1999 autobiography, *Raising Kane: The Fox Chronicles*.

> Over the last twenty-nine years, I've capped smokestacks, plugged sewers, and hung signs. [I've] distributed broadsides, defaced products, and dumped sewage and rotten fish in corporate offices. I have also deposited, hung, sailed, and poured (yes, poured), more dead skunks in more unusual places than anyone I know of. I'm probably the only person in North America who considers a road-killed skunk to be a natural resource.
>
> Some of my little wars were one-raid affairs, and some lasted off and on for several years. I won some, lost some, and some were rained out.

The Fox was a pioneer of monkey-wrenching tactics that have become commonplace among activists ever since, from mainstream groups like Greenpeace to the more extreme Earth Liberation Front.

The Fox consistently proved himself to be a gentleman. In one mission he dumped chemical sludge and dead wildlife in the reception room of a company, along with a written message. He was concerned he had frightened the secretary, so he sent her a bouquet of flowers with a note apologizing for scaring her.

The Fox continued his fight against the soap company and other industrial polluters, leaving dead skunks at aluminum refineries and chaining and locking shut an asphalt company.

Other activities included an orchestrated mailing of 10,000 Day-Glo stickers for a network of people to stick on products from offending companies. He held a mock funeral for the Fox River in April 1971, attended by hundreds of people. Along the way, the Fox befriended many allies—concerned citizens, politicians, journalists, even sympathetic police who tipped him off about searches for him. Despite these warnings, the Fox had to run from the law at least three times, running once through the freezing Fox River in February, and once through the streets of Chicago after hanging a giant political cartoon on the Picasso sculpture in Daley Plaza.

"I have been praised, vilified, emulated, harassed, admired, hated, and loved. About the only thing I haven't been, is ignored," wrote the Fox.

After his death in 2001 at age seventy, it was revealed that the Fox was an environmental science teacher named James F. Phillips. He was cremated and his ashes spread over the Fox River, the river he had spent thirty-plus years defending. A small memorial bearing his signature carved into a rock and a plaque sharing his story rest peacefully on the Fox River bank in Oswego, Illinois.

RLSH Hall of Fame: 1970s–Early 2000s

In the 1970s and decades that followed, various news reports substantiate that superheroes popped up in random corners of the earth—London, Mexico City, and Jackson, Michigan, among other locations. Many of these crusaders were looking to draw attention to specific causes like workers' rights or unfair parking laws. Online social networking later played a key role in the RLSH movement, but here is a look at ten superheroes who were on a mission before they were online.

Captain Sticky (Deceased)

San Diego
Active: Early 1970s–2003
Mission: Watchdog and consumer rights advocate

The Fox wanted to remain an anonymous shadow, but Richard Pesta—also known as Captain Sticky—wanted all eyes on him. He was the first to experiment with "raising awareness" through a flashy superhero disguise.

The 350-pound superhero, named after his love of peanut butter and jelly sandwiches, wore a bright blue jumpsuit and a gold cape and cruised around in the "Stickymobile"—a Lincoln decorated with flashing lights and flags. He apparently also invented a gun that shot peanut butter. He attracted a lot of media attention. As a writer from the British *New Musical Express* noted, "It would take a strong person indeed to remain oblivious to a bearded, crash-helmeted Rasputin running wild in nightmare pajamas, gold lamé boots, and a peanut butter bazooka."

Captain Sticky was a consumer rights activist campaigning against everything from rental car rip-offs to sugar-coated cereal. He would stage protests, yelling through a bullhorn and often followed by an entourage of media attracted to the strange spectacle. One such campaign is credited with launching an investigation into nursing home abuse, resulting in new regulations for safer conditions.

Pesta ran into some sexploitation problems in the 1990s, getting busted for running a sex tour service in Thailand. He changed careers and became an entrepreneur specializing in environmentally friendly soil products. He died in 2003 at age fifty-seven from complications of heart bypass surgery in Bangkok.

Human Fly (Unknown)

Montreal

Active: Mid-to-late 1970s

Mission: Costumed, charitable stuntman who became comic book hero

The Human Fly, whose real name may or may not have been Rick Rojatt, is a mysterious entry in this history. A masked stuntman, the Fly did stunts like walking on a DC-8 airplane wing while it was flying at 250 mph. He even broke one of Evel Knievel's records by jumping a rocket-powered motorcycle over twenty-seven buses in 1977. The stunt cost him, though: he crashed upon landing and broke his ankle, as well as sustaining other injuries.

"Frankly, I'm not worried about death," the Human Fly told *People* magazine in 1976. "I don't have a death wish, I have a life wish." What nominates him for RLSH status is that he reportedly donated his earnings to charity, although specifics on this aren't mentioned.

Marvel Comics created a short-lived series that was a highly fictional imagining of the Human Fly battling bad guys with his stunt performances. The series ran for nineteen issues in 1977–78 and its star was billed as "The wildest superhero ever—because he's real!" After the comics series ended, the Human Fly performed one more stunt—he disappeared without a trace.

Super Barrio (Retired)

Mexico City
Active: Mid-1980s to early 2000s
Mission: Fair housing and workers' rights

Wearing a bright red and yellow costume with a cape, similar to ones worn by Mexican wrestlers known as *luchadores*, Super Barrio (translated: Super Neighborhood), the masked hero activist of Mexico City, kept his identity secret for a long time. Eventually he revealed himself to be an activist, now in his early sixties, named Marco Rascón Córdova, a restaurant owner, political journalist, and founding member of the Party of Democratic Revolution, a socialist party.

Super Barrio became a folk hero to the working class and poor and was celebrated in books and folk songs. His followers erected a statue of him sometime around 1997. At the statue unveiling, the crowd chanted "You see him. You feel him. Super Barrio is here!"

Super Barrio declared himself a candidate in the 1996 US presidential elections, holding mock campaign stops on both sides of the border, promising to abolish the US Border Patrol and Drug

Enforcement Agency to allow free migration to the United States. He also inspired others to become "social *luchadores*" of Mexico City, grappling with issues like animal rights.

MORE *LUCHADOR* ACTIVIST HEROES

Director Arturo Perez Torres reveals in his documentary *Super Amigos* (2007) that Super Barrio wasn't Mexico City's only "social wrestler." Three others inspired by Super Barrio tackled a multitude of problems through the 1980s and into the mid-2000s.

Super Animal (along with a sidekick—Super Animalito) fought for animal rights, particularly against bullfighting. In *Super Amigos*, Super Animal gets arrested trying to enter a bullfighting ring to challenge the matadors to fight him to the death instead of the bulls. In another scene, he dumps bull intestines and bones on the front stairs of City Hall during

Super Animal, 1993. YOLANDA ANDRADE

a city council session. He even has a Super Animal–mobile, a black VW bug with the outline of a bull painted on the hood.

The man known as Super Gay sports a rainbow-striped *luchador* mask. His origin story is that his boyfriend was beaten to death; after that, his mission was to stand up to gay bashers. He makes appearances at gay pride events and works as a counselor to those who have suffered from homophobia.

Ecologista Universal makes a great two-hundred-mile pilgrimage by foot in the film and battles environmental destruction, protesting deforestation of pines for Christmas trees and wasteful packaging.

The documentary also features Fray Tormenta, who lived on the street as a child, but joined the seminary and became a priest. He also became a *luchador* wrestler in 1983. He wrestled in over four thousand *lucha* matches and used the money he earned to fund two orphanages that he still operates. He gives sermons in his gold *luchador* mask—a man of the cloth and the spandex.

Terrifica (Retired)

Manhattan
Active: Early 2000s
Mission: Protecting inebriated women

Terrifica is one of the first documented female RLSH. She moved from Pennsylvania to the Big Apple in her early twenties. It was there that she had some bad encounters with men and was inspired to dress in purple and pink tights, a blonde wig, gold mask, and Valkyrie bra. She would patrol bars in Manhattan, looking for "male predators" and offering to call cabs for inebriated women.

"When a woman falls prey to a man who is willing to seduce her for one night or a lifetime, she is destroyed," Terrifica explained to me in an e-mail. "She is the victim of the mythologies of love and social order that men perpetuate in order to keep women in the role of servant, whore, wife, or mother."

Captain Ozone (Still semi-active)

Bellingham, Washington, and Belfast, Ireland
Active: 1989–present
Mission: Promoting renewable energy

Captain Ozone's first appearance was in 1989. He claimed he was sent back from the year 2039 to warn about the "petroleum apocalypse of World War III," saying that the only way to avoid it was to invest in renewable energy. "We have no choice—green power or World War III," Captain told me.

Ozone, who lived in Bellingham, Washington, before moving to Northern Ireland, soon teamed up with Environmental Media Northwest to make classroom visits and appearances in environmentally themed public service announcements. For a more mature crowd, he made an appearance at Seattle Hemp Fest, demonstrating a hemp oil–powered chainsaw.

More recent efforts include hosting a 2010 "Green Power Rally," but for the most part he lives a quiet life, he told me. "I've turned down most reporters in the UK who have wanted to interview me. I despise reporters and, like most superheroes, enjoy a clandestine lifestyle."

Angle Grinder Man (Unknown)

London
Active: Early 2000s
Mission: Sawing "boots" off illegally parked cars

The "boot," also called a "wheel clamp," is a metal device clamped to the wheel of your car when you are parked illegally. You then have to pay a fee to get it removed. Most people agree it is a frustrating experience. But this frustration made one man snap. He created a spandex outfit and began sawing the boots off cars with a gas-powered angle grinder.

Angle Grinder Man set up a hotline for motorists to call. He would drive out to their assistance, sawing through the boot in a forty-five-second shower of sparks in the streets of London and his hometown, Kent.

"There are not enough parking spaces for people, and no public transport to speak of," Angle Grinder Man declared in a 2003 television interview. "It's a complete joke, and yet instead of us suing the government for shambolic mismanagement, we allow them to take back money from us, the very people they have let down."

After a couple reports in 2003 and '04, and evidence of a MySpace page in 2005, Angle Grinder Man seems to have gone off the grid.* The potential threat of jail time for criminal damage and theft is a likely factor in his disappearance.

Birmingham Batman (Deceased)

Birmingham, Alabama
Active: 1970s–1985
Mission: Roadside assistance

In the 1970s and '80s, stranded motorists in Birmingham, Alabama, were relieved to see an oddly dressed man cruising the highways in a customized 1971 Ford Thunderbird. He called himself the Birmingham Batman, although his style was similar to Evel Knievel, wearing a white jumpsuit, helmet, and cape.

Willie James Perry was a window distribution company manager; in his spare time he suited up and worked on his car, which he called the "Bat Rescue Ship." It was decorated with fins and flashing lights and equipped with CB and police band radios. "I remember

---

* Angle Grinder Man did inspire a copycat to take up his cause. Wheel Clamp Man, clad in green spandex, helmet, and a fake mustache, began sawing clamps off cars in Perth, Australia, in 2012.

a rocket launcher too, but that's probably an embellishment of my childhood memory," Birmingham writer Lou Anders recalls in a blog entry describing the Birmingham Batman.

The superhero is still fondly remembered in Birmingham for helping motorists with car troubles, giving free rides to people who had had too much to drink, and taking seniors to doctor's appointments and kids to birthday parties.

Tragically, the car that was so important to his life and had transported so many others was also the cause of his death. He reportedly was tinkering on the car in 1985 when the garage door slid shut and he died of carbon monoxide poisoning. The City of Birmingham purchased his car and displayed it for years at the Southern Museum of Flight and later at Alabama State Fair Park.

Captain Jackson (Still active)

Jackson, Michigan

Active: 1999–present

Mission: Deter street crime

Captain Jackson started as a simple prank in 1999, he told me in a phone interview, but soon he took the idea seriously.

"I thought, hey, maybe this is a way I can make a difference in society," he told me. He took a trip to a craft store and made a purple cowl and cape to go along with gray leotards and a crudely made "CJ" logo on his chest. He soon also enlisted his girlfriend to become the Queen of Hearts and his daughter to become Crime Fighter Girl. The trio called themselves the Crime Fighting Corps, probably the first RLSH team. Captain Jackson patrolled downtown Jackson looking to prevent and deter crime, patrolling and doing door checks. The trio also made public appearances at events like car shows and chili cook-offs.

Small town scandal hit the superhero, though, when he was busted and the local newspaper had a field day. "I got popped for drunk driving," Captain Jackson explained to me. "I had too many beers and was pulled over for speeding. The *Jackson Citizen Patriot* picked up on the story, and the AP put it in five thousand fucking papers," he lamented.

He had been drinking before he called me and seemed very bitter about his treatment and about the new wave of RLSH. "I have nothing to do with those fucking costumed idiots," he told me. After a hiatus following his drunk-driving bust, he eventually made a comeback and still makes a public appearance as Captain Jackson from time to time.

He told me his strategy for keeping his downtown district crime-free: "In my district I tell the panhandlers and prostitutes to leave. Go do it across the street, but not in my district. You got to make a zone."

The Eye (Still active)
Mountain View, California
Active: 1990s–Present
Mission: Leads community block watch and builds gadgets

Captain Jackson was able to find an early colleague in the Eye, who dressed in the classic detective noir style of trench coat and fedora. He patrols and helps with a community block watch in his peaceful Silicon Valley town.

His crime-fighting gadgets include the "Dragon's Eye," a ring with a bright light used to temporarily blind a potential attacker, and a "sonic screamer tube" that sounds a loud 107-decibel alarm. He says he has developed his own style of kung fu that he calls "Jade Mantis." He sometimes gives newer RLSH advice on their gadget arsenal.

Superhero (Still active)
Clearwater, Florida
Active: 1998–Present
Mission: Various

Superhero is still an active member of the RLSH community, helping to found the first nonprofit RLSH team, Team Justice, in 2010. The team does charity events, patrols, hands out supplies, and offers roadside assistance. It all started for Superhero when he entered a brief foray into wrestling. He sat down with wrestler Dave Tristani to discuss a superhero wrestling persona.

"Dave said, 'Why not just call yourself Superhero?' I was born," Superhero told me about his simple name. His wrestling career was cut short after he landed badly and tore a ligament, but the character lived on as he discovered the RLSH movement. In addition to his seniority and booming radio announcer voice, Superhero is well known for patrolling in his flashy red Corvette.

The Secret Text of the RLSH

That is a rundown of early RLSH who can be substantiated with media reports, but it is by no means an exhaustive list. I encountered other RLSH who claimed to have early beginnings.

Max Mercury says that his first patrol was in 1976, when he was going to college in Sherman, Texas. He walked the streets, "looking into dark corners."

"Boy, was I green," Mercury told me in an e-mail. "I had a primitive outfit: olive drab overalls and a lower-face bandanna. Nearly got caught one night coming out of a building that I had found unlocked." He says he still patrols in plainclothes today.

A man calling himself Knight-Hood also still patrols in St. Petersburg, Florida, and claims he has been doing it since 1989, inspired by Tim Burton's *Batman* movie. "I saw it twelve times that year," he says.

One document that sheds light on the possibility of more early crime fighters is a rare book published in 1980, usually referred to by RLSH as "The Night Rider Book."

The fifty-four-page book, titled *How to Be a Super-Hero*, has a homemade, self-published quality and was produced by GEM

Enterprises of Morgantown, West Virginia. It is credited solely to an author calling himself "the Night Rider." Only Night Rider and his possible collaborators can answer further questions on the print run and distribution of the book.

The book was discovered after Night Rider read a report on an RLSH named Knight Owl, whom I was to meet several times in person. Night Rider got his phone number and called him, but Knight Owl had phone issues and the number was lost. In his brief conversation, Night Rider told Knight Owl about his 1980 manual. Curious, Knight Owl told the story to a Toronto-based RLSH detective, Wolf, who runs Wolf's Detective Agency. Wolf tracked a copy of the book down at Michigan State University's library, where it is available only for in-library use in the special collections department. Knight Owl and Wolf went to Zimmer, who at the time was president of the Heroes Network forum. He checked the roster and found a Michigan RLSH—Blue Lightning—who went to the MSU library and photocopied the entire book.

In the book, Night Rider provided chapters on physical and mental training (mostly "visualize yourself as the person you want to be"–type techniques), a chapter on selecting an effective "uniform," and a chapter mostly about different ninja weapons.

One of the most interesting segments is the last chapter, titled "More True Stories of Real-Life Superheroes." Night Rider used this term a few times in the course of the book more than thirty years ago! According to Night Rider, he was not alone out there; he included short accounts of the Phantom Avenger and Ms. Mystery.

Phantom Avenger, he wrote, helped his wife give one of their friends shelter from her abusive husband, then went over to their house to beat him up. He continued on a quest to beat up abusive husbands.

Ms. Mystery, Night Rider reported, was part of a pool of secretaries being propositioned and felt up by their bosses' horny hands. Ms. Mystery created a disguise, then lured the boss to her workplace at night with a suggestive phone call. When he arrived, she handcuffed him to a desk and flailed him with a pair of nunchuks.

Although these stories are interesting, no evidence exists to suggest that these two, along with Night Rider's own activities, actually existed outside of Night Rider's imagination. He did mention two people who have been documented, though: the Fox and Curtis Sliwa.

Sliwa's first organization was the Magnificent 13. Their name was inspired by a classic 1960 western, *The Magnificent Seven*. This movie was in turn an adaption of the 1954 Japanese film *Seven Samurai*. Both tell the story of a village of farmers being bullied by greedy bandits. The villagers enlist the help of cowboys (or samurai) who not only run off the bandits but also teach the villagers to defend themselves.

Sliwa gathered a group to patrol streets and subways. The group's membership rapidly expanded, and Sliwa renamed the growing group the Guardian Angels, who soon became easily identified by their red berets and jackets.

As for Night Rider, we can only guess. There was no network or "recruitment center" for these early prototypes. Occasionally their paths crossed. Night Rider had heard of the Fox. The Eye and Captain Jackson became friends in the early days of the Internet. Other than that, these early costumed crusaders thought they were alone in the world.

After some Internet chatter on superhero-related forums, that all changed. The RLSH phenomenon began to blast off in 2004–05, rapidly spreading mouse click to mouse click. Superheroes were hitting the streets in growing numbers.

The Craziest RLSH Story Ever Told

A frightening, intense, and relatively unknown RLSH story is the tale of Richard McCaslin, also known as the Phantom Patriot. There are a lot of interesting aspects to McCaslin, but for the purposes of this book, his major claim to infamy was a raid on the Bohemian Grove.

McCaslin served in the US Marines and even as Batman for a Six Flags stunt show in the late 1990s. He started dreaming up superhero personas as early as 1981, when he invented the persona of the Stranger on paper. It was around this time that he had also read Night Rider's *How to Be a Super-Hero*, which he had ordered from an ad in the back of a Marvel comic book.

He adopted a new persona, the Lynx, in 1985, and patrolled the streets of Zanesville, Ohio, with a teenage sidekick named Iron Claw. He developed other personas over the years, mostly for TV, stage, or movie ideas.

In 2001 he developed the Phantom Patriot, who had the goal of protesting the "New World Order." Phantom Patriot's gear featured a navy blue jumpsuit, boots, and a skull mask with an American flag wrapped bandanna style on the head. An elephant decorating one arm and a donkey on the other were both canceled with a red circle and slash.

McCaslin was living in Austin, Texas, when one night he saw a documentary produced by conspiracy theorist Alex Jones on public access television. The documentary, *Dark Secrets: Inside Bohemian Grove*, claims there are satanic rituals held at a place north of San Francisco.

The Grove, owned by the Bohemian Club, is a twenty-seven-hundred-acre resort deep in the redwood forest. It is members only, men only, with no media access allowed. Members include the most powerful and wealthy men in the country—every Republican president since 1923 has been a member, as have several Democrats, as well as lots of high-level politicians, CEOs, businessmen, actors, and entertainers. The Grove is open year-round, but the big party happens in July, when they have a giant two-week celebration. The main activities seem to be networking, getting drunk, and partying in the woods.

Conspiracy theorists have targeted the opening ritual for this elite gathering of powerful men—a bizarre ceremony called the Cremation of Care. In this production, several members of the club (Phantom Patriot calls them "Bohos") dress as druids and burn an effigy at the foot of a forty-foot owl statue, the "Great Owl of Bohemia." There is eerie music and pyrotechnics, and the owl statue even speaks to them in some cryptic poetry. To make things even weirder, the owl's voice is a recording made by beloved news anchor Walter Cronkite—I can't make this stuff up! Many people suggest that this is nothing more than theatrics—a frat boy ritual for rich old men. The Phantom Patriot didn't think so, though, as he informed me through a series of handwritten letters. He was (and still is) convinced that live human sacrifice took place, and he planned a raid to save the victims and expose the Grove.

On January 20, 2002, he slipped into the Grove with the following: a rifle, a pistol, a knife, a sword, a bulletproof vest, and a homemade smoke bomb launcher. He also had a crossbow and a baton in his truck. What he didn't have were adequate batteries for his flashlight, so after he entered the Grove he found himself lost in the dark. He broke into a cabin and spent the night.

At daybreak he found the Owl of Bohemia, which he had planned to destroy, but discovered it was made of concrete instead of wood as he had anticipated. He decided to burn down a nearby mess hall instead. He lit it on fire, but the sprinkler system extinguished the blaze and sounded an alarm. After a short but tense standoff with the sheriff's department, he surrendered.

McCaslin was sentenced and imprisoned from 2002 to 2008, then released on parole until May 2011. His parole conditions stated he must stay thirty-five miles away from the Bohemian Grove, and informed him, "You will not possess or have access to costumes-clothing."

After parole, McCaslin did a tour peacefully protesting in cities in the lower forty-eight states. On January 21, 2012, he re-created his Phantom Patriot costume and marched to the Bohemian Club headquarters in downtown San Francisco to stage a protest commemorating his Bohemian Grove raid ten tears prior.

McCaslin currently lives in Las Vegas, where he continues to stage protests and draw comic books based on his life. His story has had a mixed reaction from RLSH who know about him. A few have been supportive; others have distanced themselves from him.

GREAT LAKES ALLIANCE

Razorhawk (left) and Geist in Minneapolis. HEATHER HAYNES

Among the earliest RLSH teams formed was the Great Lakes Alliance (GLA),* a regional team founded by three RLSH: the Watchman, Razorhawk, who lives in a suburb of Minneapolis, and Geist, of Rochester, Minnesota. The team is also one with longevity. A few other RLSH teams have already come and gone, disbanding before they really got started.

---

* There is a comic book precedent for a GLA—Marvel's Great Lakes Avengers. The team, based in my hometown of Milwaukee, first appeared in 1989. They were presented as a humorous, third-rate team of heroes similar to Bob Burden's Mystery Men.

Razorhawk explained the formation of the team: "I had been thinking one night that there were a lot of heroes in this part of the country, and more were popping up. Geist and Watchman were a couple of heroes I became close friends with and I approached them about starting a team that would do charity work and could continue to do safety and crime patrols."

Razorhawk's secret identity, "Jack," was already a familiar face in the RLSH community. Jack is a former semi-pro wrestler who wrestled under the name "Jack T. Ripper." He began to explore his creative streak between practicing body slams. He gained experience working with spandex to create wrestling costumes for himself and his fellow wrestlers. After discovering the RLSH movement, he quickly set up shop with an online business named Atomic HeroWear, which offered RLSH, costumed activists, and cosplayers costume design and construction at very affordable prices.

Masks created by Jack are generally priced in the $40 range; patches bearing logos are around $10; a full-on suit is $100 to $150. You can add a cape for $50 to $100. Atomic HeroWear's first customer was Entomo, the insect-themed avenger of Naples, Italy. Dozens of orders followed.

When Jack thought of forming the GLA, he decided it was time to join the party and invented his own RLSH persona. He came up with Razorhawk, sporting a bold blue jacket with a screaming hawk logo and sometimes even a triangular mohawk shaved sharply as a wedge on his head.

"My original intention was that I could be an unmasked face that could handle media and charity sources, but I soon learned that I would make more impact with my own persona," Razorhawk said.

The trio of heroes looked to expand enrollment. RLSH were few and far between at this point. Many of the early teams were mostly Internet-based, since the distance between members wasn't convenient for quick meet-ups. Rochester is about an hour and fifteen minutes from Minneapolis, and Milwaukee is about six hours.

Soon more RLSH began to appear in Minneapolis. There was Legacy, Mr. Mystery* and Shadowflare.

Shadowflare was a member of the shadowy activist group Anonymous, another example of a movement or group influenced by writer Alan Moore; the Guy Fawkes masks they use as symbols originate from his graphic novel *V for Vendetta*. In that story, a masked individual carries on a secret war against a corrupt government.

The turnover rate for RLSH is pretty high, and soon these early recruits dropped out of the scene one by one, but more appeared to replace them: Arctic Knight, Blue, and Misery. Other early members include Brute, from Pittsburgh, who looked like Doctor Doom, and Firefox of Ann Arbor, Michigan.

Firefox was one of a small handful of RLSH to claim they had actual powers. In her case, Firefox claimed she had "shamanic superhero" powers. She describes herself as a "troublemaking revolutionary dedicated to shifting the dominant paradigm; I also have a knack for the wizardly arts." She moved from Ann Arbor to work with the park service in Utah, and it is there, she claimed, that she engaged in a supernatural showdown with skinwalkers.

Other members extended beyond the Great Lakes area. Death's Head Moth was an early member despite being in Virginia, and Nyx, a young woman from Kansas City who dressed as a ninja, was part of the roster. She soon moved to New Jersey to be with her RLSH boyfriend, Phantom Zero.

And although its greatest lake is Lake Okeechobee, the state of Florida enrolled three honorary GLA members: Amazonia, Superhero, and Doc Spectral, who acted as the group's "oracle." That term refers to someone who acts as RLSH tech support and emergency contact person.

A good starting point to explaining an oracle is the comic book character of the same name. In the Batman universe, Commissioner

---

* Mr. Mystery is hard to reach to team up with. "He is mysterious . . . just like his name implies," Razorhawk reports.

Gordon's daughter, Barbara Gordon, first gained popularity as Batgirl. In the story line *A Killing Joke* (Alan Moore again), Barbara Gordon is shot in the spine and paralyzed by the Joker.

Subsequent DC writers used this story to invent a new persona for Barbara Gordon: Oracle. Now in a wheelchair, she became tech support for Batman, relaying info to him while he was on the move. With high-tech computer gear, she was able to find information and maps, read classified files, hack into computer systems, and act as a communications coordinator.

Real life oracles are like a low-tech version of this. They find and provide information via crime maps and other sources but don't have the high-tech system-hacking abilities or the comic book dramatics.

"An oracle is like a long-distance spotter," Doc Spectral, the GLA's oracle, told me. "When Geist or sometimes another RLSH feels like they may need an extra something in the field, someone to keep Google handy for info on the fly, or just to know where they were last, in case something happens. Usually they supply me with an emergency contact number in the area, the local PD or a confidante."

The GLA had their first mission for Christmas 2008. They did some fundraising and bought toys for local charities. The Watchman raised money and delivered toys to the Gingerbread House, a charity that donates toys to low-income families. Doc Spectral and Superhero brought donations to Toys for Tots and a pregnancy center in Zephyrhills, Florida; Razorhawk and Geist brought supplies to People Serving People, a shelter in Minneapolis. The group was now officially in action and trying to live up to its motto, "Deeds not words."

When a couple of my friends told me they were taking a weekend trip to Minneapolis, I told them I wanted to ride along. I had some people I wanted to meet.

The Search for Dan Zamlen
St. Paul, Minnesota, April 18, 2009

"So," Razorhawk called over his shoulder, "is this the weirdest way you guys have spent a Saturday night?" We were walking through the woods, late at night, not exactly sure where we were. We had already almost slid down a cliff into the mighty Mississippi rushing below, heavy with the spring thaw. It was chilly and the woods were weird and playing tricks on our senses.

I had driven up to Minneapolis with my friend, photographer Paul Kjelland. I called Razorhawk on the way and he mentioned he wanted to search the woods for a missing college student, and that we would be meeting up with a new recruit, Celtic Viking.

"Wow!" I thought, visualizing some big burly guy of Scottish descent with an impressive red beard. "I hope he carries a battle-ax and a wooden shield," I told Paul as he navigated his car through the north woods of Wisconsin.

That evening I found the meet-up spot in St. Paul, near the University of St. Thomas campus. Celtic Viking, to my disappointment, did not look like a Viking at all. His floppy cowboy hat, gray flannel shirt, and knee-high boots were more consistent with an Australian bushranger. He was short and stocky and mumbled a lot. The three of us were all meeting for the first time. As we walked to the woods, Razorhawk laid out the story.

Eighteen-year-old Dan Zamlen was a freshman at the University of St. Thomas. On the night of April 5, 2009, he was at a party when he reportedly became upset about something and left, saying he was going to walk over the bridge to Minneapolis to meet some friends at the University of Minnesota.

As he walked on a trail near the Mississippi River around 2:30 AM, he talked to a friend on the phone. She said she heard him yell something like, "Oh my God, help!" before the call ended abruptly.

Search teams scoured the bluffs and banks of the Mississippi. Helicopters with infrared flew overhead; water patrol checked the shore. Friends and family searched everywhere. The university organized a block-by-block, door-to-door search. Over a thousand people searched for Zamlen. And on this night, I joined two RLSH in the search. Zamlen had been missing for twelve days already. We were entering the woods at 9 PM.

"You might wonder why we are doing this search at night," Razorhawk told me. "Well, that's part of all this. We're mystery men and we like to work under the cover of darkness."

We walked down a bike trail and followed a narrow path into the woods. Razorhawk and Celtic Viking both clicked on flashlights. Razorhawk explained that one theory he was mulling over was that Zamlen's disappearance might be no accident but the handiwork of the so-called Smiley Face Killers.

The Smiley Face Killers theory is questionable, considered by many in law enforcement, including the FBI, to be more conspiracy theory nuttiness than valid conjecture. The theory, proposed by retired New York detectives Kevin Gannon and Anthony Duarte, states that a group or gang of serial killers is picking off white college males and throwing them into rivers throughout the Midwest. The gang's calling card is a smiley face spray-painted somewhere near the murder scene, on rocks or concrete walls. Although some have embraced the theory, others dismiss it as coincidence of a common graffiti paired with inebriated accidents.

"So obviously we're looking for any smiley faces. If we find one, you know, it may offer some validity to the idea," Razorhawk said as we walked through the silent woods. The path dipped up and down and led us by several treacherous drop-offs. We took pictures of gang graffiti we found on a concrete wall by a drainage pipe for reference.

Razorhawk spotted some graffiti on a tree and, balancing himself carefully, edged down a cliff to get a closer picture. The earth gave way and he began to slide. Celtic Viking and I grabbed at his shoulders as he climbed backward up the hill. Back on terra firma, Razorhawk admitted it was highly likely Zamlen or anyone else out here without a flashlight could easily have fallen.

As we continued the search, which lasted about three hours, Razorhawk told me more about his adventurous life. He told me about the glory days wrestling as Jack T. Ripper, and how he met his future wife while on the wrestling circuit. There was a lot of drama between them, he said, but his manager knew that the two of them

Wrestling days: Razorhawk (right) wrestling under the name Jack T. Ripper against one of his dreaded opponents, Big Bob Travis, circa 1991. COURTESY OF RAZORHAWK

would be good together, so he insisted they work their issues out—literally and figuratively—in the ring.

They sat in a four-post wrestling ring and talked their feelings out long into the night. Not long after that, Mr. and Mrs. Ripper settled down, got married, and had kids.

Celtic Viking was pretty quiet but obviously excited to be on his first GLA mission. He would occasionally grunt in agreement or add a word or two and . . .

"Wait! Did you hear something?" Razorhawk said in a hushed tone. The three of us froze and strained our ears to hear. We heard some thrashing in the water.

"Ducks? Ducks, I think," I said.

"Yeah," Razorhawk said. "I'm getting a weird feeling, though."

Razorhawk has a strong interest in the paranormal and conspiracy theory, so his senses were kicked into high gear in the eerie woods. Our minds began to play tricks on us. We stopped a few times to evaluate weird sounds one of us had picked up—wind or squirrels or maybe forest ghosts. We called out "Helllllloo!" just to be sure, but there was no answer back.

At one point the path led us all the way down to the river. We stood on a muddy embankment. It was totally silent with the river rushing by. It was hypnotic. In the distance, we could see traffic on a bridge.

On our way back up to higher ground, Celtic Viking called out, "Hold up, what's this?"

Razorhawk and I came over to investigate where the Viking was shining his flashlight, into the hollow base of a tree. Wedged into a tree trunk, illuminated by the flashlight beam, was a metal army artillery box. We stared at it.

"I don't know if we should touch it," Razorhawk said. Celtic Viking grunted. Finally, curiosity overcame us, and the Viking carefully removed the box and opened it. It had some toy dinosaurs and notes scrawled in a child's handwriting in crayon. We put the box back.

Around 1 AM we decided to walk back to the cars. "My old lady is not going to like me being out so late," Celtic Viking said.

Razorhawk gave the new hero some advice: "I tell my wife not to expect me back until early morning."

Razorhawk and I got in his minivan, so he could drop me off at my hotel in Minneapolis. As we drove, he said he wasn't disappointed with the lack of evidence of the Smiley Face Killers or Zamlen himself. The fact that we made the effort, and the small chance the effort could have revealed something at all, was what this Real Life Superhero business was all about, he said.

The hoping and searching came to an end on May 1, 2009. Workers at the Ford Motor Company found a body in the river, and it was confirmed to be Zamlen. Cause of death was determined to be accidental drowning.

The Emerald Cowboy
Rochester, Minnesota, April 19, 2009

On the afternoon of April 18, 2009, the small town of St. Charles, Minnesota, was in a state of chaos. It was like a climactic scene in a comic book, but all too real. This peaceful village was thrown into panic when the town's main employer, North Star Foods, burst into flame. The meat-processing plant spewed black smoke that rolled down Main Street, shrouding the day in darkness. The town, population thirty-six hundred, was being evacuated, as the "flames edged dangerously close" to tanks of anhydrous ammonia in the plant.

"If the fire got to the tanks, it would be just like a bomb," said the St. Charles police chief. The blast would spread toxic fumes over the town, burning people's skin and lungs. People were loaded into school buses as firefighters from nearby cities did the best they could with a dwindling water supply.

Meanwhile, twenty-five miles to the north, in Rochester, Minnesota, a shadowy figure followed the news and monitored police scanners. This was Geist,* also dubbed "the Emerald Cowboy." When Geist heard that the city was being evacuated, he decided it was time to leap into action.

"I found a way to leave what I was doing and suit up. If they were trying to get all 3,600 residents out of town, I figured they might need some help," Geist recalled in an entry on his MySpace blog.

And so he adjusted his cowboy hat, tied on his green leather arm gauntlets and a green bandanna to cover the lower half of his face, slipped into a duster jacket, put on a pair of green-rimmed sunglasses, jumped in his car, and headed south as fast as he could.

Geist drove until he hit a roadblock. The smoke was visible in the sky. He informed the officer at the roadblock that he would like to volunteer to help. The officer instructed him to pull over and then completely ignored him. As time ticked by, Geist decided to bypass this obstacle and get straight to the source.

"Avoiding roadblocks and looking as if I knew what I was doing whenever I saw a city vehicle, I drove down the various hazy, deserted streets looking for anyone to help. It was a ghost town. Just

---

* Geist's name is often misspelled and/or mispronounced. It's pronounced GUYst and is German for "ghost." *Poltergeist* translates as "noisy ghost."

like those zombie movies where you see the downtown with parked cars, but no one at all on the streets," Geist wrote.

Geist was eventually directed to a disaster command center, set up in the baseball field in a city park. He was waved over to someone in charge, who was giving orders over a phone. "He got off the phone and told me that if I wanted to, I could relieve the highway patrolman who had directed me to the command center," Geist wrote. After helping direct traffic for a while, and seeing there was not much else for him to do in the empty city, he headed back to Rochester.

"All in all, I'm glad I went. I went there to find out what I could do and the answer at that time was: not too much," Geist concluded on his blog.

He reiterated this when I met him in person in Rochester. Paul dropped me off at Silverlake Park, where I found Geist sitting in his car and reading developments on the St. Charles fire in the newspaper.

"My efforts turned out to be somewhat useless, but whatever," he told me after I climbed into the passenger side of his car. "I did come right across the fire at one point, so that was interesting. But you know, and other RLSH will confirm this, if the cops or fire department are going on something, they don't need us messing around. They are the experts and you don't want to screw up what they are doing."

Geist's plan was a rolling patrol. He wanted to show me a few points of interest, including areas he patrolled. It was a rainy, gloomy day. Geist's windshield wipers squeaked back and forth as we headed toward downtown.

Rochester is a city of about ninety-nine thousand people, two hours south of Minneapolis. It is perhaps most famous for being the home of the Mayo Clinic.

"The building on the horizon there is called the Assisi Heights; it's been a convent for nuns for about a hundred years or so," Geist said, pointing to a large building on a ridge of the outskirts of town. "After a cyclone hit Rochester in the 1880s, the nuns convinced the

Mayo family to start a clinic here." He maneuvered his car into a valley of strip malls. Geist punctuated his talking with chewing gum, changing the pace of his chewing as he thought things over.

"I do have a destination in mind. I'm going to see if a homeless acquaintance of mine is hanging out on South Broadway. I don't know if he'll be out in the rain," Geist said as we cruised past electronics stores, shoe stores, pizza chains, and gas stations. He said the homeless man's name was Thomas.

"I saw him holding a cardboard sign, asking for food, money, whatever," Geist said, then chewed on his gum for a moment. "So I went to Burger King, got a value meal, and gave it to him. The first time I encountered him it was a pretty fierce blizzard. I gave him a ride to a homeless shelter downtown. Thomas is a great guy. He was injured doing construction work, had back problems, and lost his connection with work and society. He slipped through the cracks. He's having a difficult time trying to find a way to be part of society again. He's found a way to get by. He's not a drunk, not insane. Not totally disabled."

Geist pointed to the median where he had first spotted Thomas, a small triangular slab of gray concrete, a small island in the middle of a tangle of streets and litter and highway off-ramps. It looks especially depressing in the rain.

"When he can't get enough money to stay somewhere or when the homeless shelter is full, which happens frequently, there's an overpass down there." Geist pointed ahead to a concrete and steel highway bridge. "Even during blizzards he's slept down there, which is something I don't even want to think about doing. I mean, you're from Wisconsin, right? You know how cold it can get."

Our next stop was Kutzky Park, a small park near a stream with a bridge over it. We walked toward the bridge. He pulled a flashlight from his jacket and we leaned down, balancing on some large rocks, to peer underneath.

"A homeless woman was killed under this bridge," Geist explained. "Someone dropped one of these boulders on her head while she was sleeping. It is unsolved, although I think police believe it was another homeless person. That's the word."

A couple of bored-looking teenagers sat at a picnic table, smoking cigarettes. They looked at us for a moment, but even the sight of Geist could not cure their boredom. Geist waved and said hi and one of the teens nodded slightly in return and then turned his attention back to his cigarette.

"People see me and I see them and, whatever, it's usually not like ooh, look—it's Geist!" he told me.

I asked him if the Rochester police had noticed him.

"A little bit. I've encountered them a couple times. The first time was when I was drawing attention to an unsafe crosswalk. This crosswalk, it was featured in a letter to the editor. Someone wrote in and said, 'My family is trying to cross this unsafe crosswalk and my kids and I waited there, and it has a light and we pressed the button, but cars keep driving through, going too fast over a hill.' I went out there and looked at it, and said, yeah, this is not safe. And so I helped some people cross the street safely. I mean, I do draw attention," Geist laughed.

"And then three police cruisers show up, wondering what the hell I was doing. I explained it all to them, and one of the officers was like, 'Yeah, well, uh, you might want to write a letter to your city councilman instead of doing this,'" Geist said, imitating the officer's voice.

"I was like, 'Yeeeeeah, well . . . I won't.' I said, 'Well, unless you tell me otherwise, I guess I'll go now.' The officer said, 'OK, be careful crossing that crosswalk now,'" Geist recalled, laughing. "So the cops kind of have a sense of humor about it, and I try not to take myself too seriously. It helps, I think, when I acknowledge that I look unusual."

We headed across town, where Geist showed me a house where a murder had recently occurred. We cruised around a neighborhood. The rain had picked up, and Geist's windshield wipers worked hard to keep up with it.

"I mean, this seems like a nice neighborhood, but in the past few years, it's been the scene of frequent drive-by shootings. Among this neighborhood are rival gangs—Bloods and Crips. One unusual aspect of Rochester, I'm told, is that it's not like the north side is the Bloods and the south side is the Crips or that the Latin Kings are in the east. There are some gangs here and there all over, so rival gangs live right next to each other."

The rain had left the streets deserted. We headed toward the river—Geist had one more spot he wanted to show me. We got out of his car and he pointed to a large neutral gray square painted on a concrete wall near a bridge. Geist keeps a bucket of paint in his car and paints over gang graffiti whenever he sees it.

"In the morning there is a girl's synchronized rowing team that practices here. The gray patch up there, it was some . . . uh . . . pretty vulgar graffiti. These young girls, they don't need to be seeing that all the time. So I thought, I'll just jump down and paint over that. It's a lot bigger than it looks from here! I could stand there on the platform and my head would not reach the top of the thing. So I had to climb down and, you know, try not to fall in the water, paint over it, and get back up. That is a case for a grappling hook or something like that."

Geist would later have a pretty awkward experience getting stuck in a similar spot. After spotting a "swastika and a Gangster Disciple's star," he dropped himself down from the bridge platform with a couple nylon ropes.

"I even thought to myself, 'This is kind of dumb, but I'm a super-hero, dammit! It's my job to do something foolhardy,'" he recalled in a blog post. After painting over the graffiti he tried to climb back out but couldn't make it to the top of the embankment.

"I paced the small platform and tried to shake it off. My doubt grew and grew."

Geist tried to climb out again and injured his hand in the process. "My brain raced—what to do, what to do?" Eventually, with no local confidants available to help him, he decided to call the police nonemergency number. Minutes later, multiple fire trucks began to arrive on the scene. The responding firefighters decided it would be safer to call in a fireboat, which chugged up the river, threw a life jacket to Geist, and brought him onboard.

"I'm thinking, 'Holy crap, what a fiasco I've created,'" Geist recalled.

Back on shore, Geist says he had a "good chat" with a responding officer, who didn't charge him. He did take a picture of Geist, which was likely passed around the station. Geist says he learned important lessons from the incident, like being properly prepared for a mission. "I hope that will be the end of embarrassing stories I have to report," he concluded on his blog.

We headed back to Silverlake Park so I could meet back up with Paul. I would see Geist again soon, but for now he headed back into the rainy streets of Rochester, looking for gang graffiti to paint over, impromptu traffic directing, or anyone that needed the assistance of the Emerald Cowboy.

GLA Meet-Up
Minneapolis, Minnesota, June 27, 2009

In early June 2009, I got an e-mail from the Watchman. It read, "Tea, The GLA is planning a patrol for June 27 in Minnesota. Would you be interested in accompanying us? Honestly, I'm asking you for selfish reasons. You see, I have been wanting to get over there and meet my teammates for many months but the timing usually doesn't work out. This time it isn't timing but finances which prevent me from making the trip. However, if I could get one or two people to join me and assist with gas money, it may be possible for the three founding members of the GLA to finally meet in person. . . . What say you?"

I said I was in.

The Watchman pulled up at my house on the afternoon of June 27. It was the first time I had seen him out of costume—he was wearing his black army pants, a black nylon shirt (the type that swimmers wear), and glasses.

The Watchman and I hit the highway and tried to make some serious time—we were supposed to rendezvous with Razorhawk, Celtic Viking, and Geist at 9 PM at the statue of Mary Tyler Moore in downtown Minneapolis, six hours away. I had a lot of time to chat with the Watchman.

As he drove, he fondly recalled a story from his youth. It was Christmas Eve and his family's van had broken down at the side of the road. A Good Samaritan pulled over to help. To the amazement of the kids, the kind soul happened to be stout and sported a white beard—a Santa Claus in street clothes.

The man drove the Watchman's father into town to buy a timing belt, and when they returned, the Kris Kringle–like citizen had brought candy for the kids. The Watchman never forgot that act of kindness.

We also talked about the inner politics of the RLSH community, which are often tumultuous and full of drama. He told me the story of how he had tried to help start a nonprofit entity called the Heroes Organization. Some showed interest in the idea, but others were nonresponsive or apathetic or said it wouldn't work. The lack of participation left the project in a coma, and this had obviously irked the Watchman.

After a pit stop for gas and a fast-food dinner, we got back on the road. We got on the topic of body armor, discussing some of the vigilante types like Nightwatch who had head-to-toe protection. The Watchman laughed it off and said he didn't need that level of padding.

"I've got the most important thing covered," he said, taking the wheel with one hand and knocking with a hollow thud twice on his crotch, revealing he had been wearing a support cup the whole time. "As long as I've got them protected, I'm all right," he laughed.

We got a little lost and ended up in St. Paul, but got back on track and eventually spotted the trio of Minnesota RLSH near the Mary Tyler Moore statue. We found a nearby parking garage, which would also have to double as the Watchman's phone booth. He looked in his rear-view mirror and carefully put in his contact lenses. Then he adjusted his mask and goggles and slid into his trench coat. We strolled out of the dim garage, and the Watchman got to meet his teammates in person for the first time. They posed for pictures together, and then we headed out to what would be close to six hours of walking around downtown Minneapolis.

This experience was significantly different from previous patrols. Up until now I had joined RLSH in patrolling mostly unpopulated areas where encountering other people was rare. This meet was in the heart of downtown Minneapolis on a very busy night. The weather was warm and a lot of events were going on. There was a gay pride fest, a couple of sporting events, and a concert in the park. The streets were packed.

I began to observe some common responses to seeing RLSH walking down the street.

"Hey! It's a little early for Halloween!" yelled an inebriated man, sticking his head out of a party bus parked near a bar.

Down the street, two women (who with luck had a designated driver for the evening as well) were yelling, "Wooo hooo! Superhero dudes!"

One of the women followed up with, "Who are you, Batman? Wooooo!"

The RLSH got some high fives and cheering and sometimes nonsense—they got called "space ninjas" and things shouted from cars that were indecipherable.

Geist had a good approach to talking to people on the street and was calm and disarming. He explained briefly who they were and what they were doing, that they weren't crazy and didn't have super-powers. He tried to field questions and explain what RLSH were all about. A lot of people were interested, and some were obviously disappointed they weren't crazier.

"You mean you don't think you have superpowers?" one guy asked before walking away, dejected.

We passed an elderly gent near the light rail station, busking and smiling widely. He was banging furiously on some bongos, and when he saw the group he studied us carefully, his beat slowing to a whisper. As the RLSH walked by he tapped out a quick drum roll and sang out, "Vigi-*lantes!*"

But the response RLSH actually like to get is people recognizing them by name. Geist and Razorhawk had racked up some media by this point, so several people on the street recognized them. The weekly paper *City Pages* had featured a cover story on local RLSH with a dynamic illustration of Geist on the cover, his bolo snares flying into action. The team had been on the local evening news* and featured in reports on CNN and FOX, among other news sources.

"You're Geist, right?" one guy on the street said, pointing at Razorhawk, then he looked confused. "No, you're Geist! Who are you?" he said, pointing at Geist, and looking back at Razorhawk.

Even a police officer, riding with a group of three other officers on horseback, waved and called out, "Hi, Geist!"

"Man, I need a horse," Geist said as the horses clacked down the street.

"Well, you are the Emerald Cowboy," the Watchman agreed.

The team had collected a meager supply of canned food that they wanted to donate to People Serving People, so we walked over there. The guy working in the lobby had obviously encountered the RLSH before.

"Hey superheroes," he said, barely looking up. The heroes dropped off the food and the clerk shook their hands.

"Thanks, and have a good night," the clerk said, smiling slightly. "Stay out of trouble."

There was only one instance where we thought there might be a problem. We were walking down the street when we saw two

---

* For this report, the news team decided to shuttle Geist, Razorhawk, and Shadowflare to a specific location. The RLSH crowded into the back of a news van and Geist revealed he was carrying a large cattle prod-style Taser in his coat. "That would have been some interesting footage if it went off by mistake," Razorhawk recalls, laughing.

women who turned out to be a lesbian couple, arguing loudly and pushing each other.

This brings up what I believe to be the most problematic aspect of being an RLSH: what situations actually warrant intervention and how does one identify them? There have been several times I've been out on patrol when the posse has had to stop in silence and strain ears.

"What was *that*?"

In one case I was on patrol with the Watchman and new recruits when we heard loud shouting. We took off running down the alley only to discover the shouting was some terrible, off-key karaoke singing drifting through the window of a bar.

This situation was another example—the couple, probably intoxicated, were yelling angrily and pushing each other. Then one would walk away, turn around, and try to hug the other one. They would hug and then push each other away. It was hard to tell if they were coming or going. Were they actually fighting? Was it a mating ritual? Was it just fooling around? We decided to investigate from a safe distance.

We split up and walked down both sides of the street. There was more arguing and walking away and then walking back. By the time we got down the block, though, the women had their arms around each other and were strolling down the street. They noticed us.

"I'm really digging these outfits you got going on," said one of the women. She had on a tank top and a backward baseball cap. "Hey, do you know where the Gay 90s is?"

Razorhawk said that the club was the direction we were heading and that they should walk with us. The woman talked with the guys about what the RLSH stuff was all about as her girlfriend walked quickly and angrily farther and farther ahead. She ignored her name being called, and eventually the woman apologetically said she had to go catch up with her and ran off. We kept patrolling.

The Watchman dubbed me with my own RLSH name for the evening—Camel Man. This was because I had volunteered to carry a backpack filled with bottles of water. As Camel Man, I got to swing into action and help someone for a brief moment. We encountered a group of train-hopping homeless travelers who were flying a cardboard sign that read "Spare any random acts of kindness?" They were from Florida and were train-hopping, squatting in abandoned buildings, and dumpster-diving for food. I handed them several bottles of water.

We decided to head back on our final leg of the patrol. As we walked back toward our meet-up spot and the parking garage, we passed a smooth-looking guy with a couple of well-dressed ladies accompanying him for cocktails at a table outside a bar. One of the women spotted the RLSH and stared at them, her mouth agape. "Whaaaaat the fuuuuck!" she drawled.

The man looked over and smiled, then turned back and casually explained it all, "Those are superheroes, girl. Superheroes in town tonight." She looked at him like he was crazy.

By now it was past 3 AM and we were exhausted from walking around downtown for six hours. We parted ways with the rest of the GLA; the Watchman and I entered the mostly deserted parking garage. We had a *Spinal Tap* moment trying to find his car—we walked in one giant circle, then went up a level and walked the big circle again. Then we went up another level and walked in a circle, then went down a level and walked in a circle again. We had no idea where the Watchmanmobile could be.

"I bet this never happened to Batman," the Watchman said in a defeated voice. I laughed—the superhero and the reporter, outwitted by a parking garage. Then I remembered a sole landmark, a wall near the car that had had several spaces marked for "Compact Cars Only." We found a lot attendant and offered this puzzle piece, and he pointed us in the right direction.

The Watchman drove for a couple hours, back across the border into Wisconsin. We decided to pull into a truck stop, recline the car seats, and sleep until the Watchman had enough rest to make the rest of the return drive. We were tired enough that we passed out for a couple of hours despite the carseat beds. Bright summer morning light woke me up. I stumbled into the truck stop bathroom and splashed water on my face, then got a large coffee in a Styrofoam cup. When I returned to the car, the Watchman was awake and ready to drive. He drove and we reflected on the previous night's patrol and his Great Lakes Alliance teammates. The patrol had energized him about his team and his superhero mission.

We returned to Milwaukee early that afternoon. I spent the rest of the day in bed—my legs were killing me.

THE SECRET CITY

Civitron flanked by Beau Shay Monde (left) and Basilisk. MIKE PECCI

KER-blam! I was in a fight with a superhero. If this were a comic book, the panel would be filled with motion lines and starbursts. I swung with my right fist in slow motion, trying to connect with my opponent's face. In a smooth motion, he deflected my punch with his forearm, which was protected with a plastic arm gauntlet. I swung with my left fist and was again knocked away effortlessly. I could see my reflection in his sunglasses, framed in white plastic. He smoothed out his red and white spandex shirt, adorned with a letter *C* with a flame shooting out of the top, then stepped back into a fighting stance.

My opponent was Civitron and, luckily for me, our combat was not a battle royale to the death. Rather, we were sparring at Rebelo's Kenpo Karate, in New Bedford, Massachusetts, where Civitron had trained under sensei Joseph "Kenpo Joe" Rebelo on and off for more than ten years. And we weren't alone.

The dojo was packed with a dozen other RLSH, crowded into the studio room, striking and grappling, a multihued whirlwind of leotards and capes and combat boots. Rebelo and Civitron had teamed up to present this workshop as part of a three-day RLSH conference called Superheroes Anonymous. This was the third year for the annual event, which takes place in rotating cities sometime early in fall.

After previous conferences in New York and New Orleans, Civitron volunteered to host Superheroes Anonymous: Year 3 (SA3) in New Bedford. The itinerary included workout sessions, workshops, a patrol with the Guardian Angels, and an awards ceremony and dinner. I exchanged several e-mails with Civitron and Superheroes Anonymous founder Life, telling them I wanted to participate fully in the conference's events and learn the superhero arts. They were welcoming, so I booked a room in a cheap New Bedford hotel.

This martial arts workshop was one of the weekend's first events and my introduction to many of the key movers and shakers of the RLSH movement. Zetaman had flown (by plane, of course) all the way from Portland, Oregon, bringing along a suitcase filled with bulky blue plastic armor. Nyx, dressed in a gray leotard and a red dust mask, had driven up from New Jersey with her RLSH boyfriend, Phantom Zero. She was sparring with Zimmer, a wiry guy in gray spandex with the binary code for the letter *Z* running down his shirt.

Kenpo Joe, in his early fifties, was shouting orders to the RLSH on proper defensive and counterstrike maneuvers in a loud, animated voice. He was a hefty man with a walrus mustache, hyped up like he had just slammed a six-pack of energy drinks. He revealed that he is also a lifelong comic book fanatic, talking about recent Green Lantern and Batman story lines and clearly reveling in his surreal position as instructor to a class of students who looked like they had stepped out of his comic book collection.

Superheroes Anonymous

Superheroes Anonymous started in October 2007 when student filmmakers Ben Goldman and Chaim Lazaros decided to make a documentary about Real Life Superheroes. They were among the first people to realize there was potential in the RLSH story beyond the joke-of-the-day news blurbs that had been the sole media coverage up until that point.

"From the beginning I saw individuals with good hearts and there was a misunderstanding—the way they were being portrayed was not inspirational at all. It was silly and misunderstood, and I said this is a positive that could do so much good. It's so incredible, the story is amazing, and I want to be part of it," Lazaros explained.

Goldman and Lazaros decided to organize a conference that year that would allow them to capture interesting footage of heroes working together in New York City. Almost all the heroes attending were meeting each other for the first time, and they worked together doing a charity event, picked up litter in Times Square, and held a superhero-themed dinner party.

Motivated by the success of year one, they planned a second outing in 2008. Lazaros decided to adopt his own RLSH persona, Life, a reflection of his real name, Chaim, Hebrew for "life."

If this was a narrative device or a publicity stunt, it quickly evolved beyond that. Soon Life was putting on his shirt and tie, vest, domino mask, and fedora—the classic noir detective hero look—and hitting the streets even when the cameras weren't rolling. His main focus was handing out food and supplies to the homeless of Queens and Manhattan and trying to make a personal connection with them. Ben Goldman was also dubbed with an RLSH name—"Cameraman"—due to the video camera constantly planted firmly on his shoulder.

Superheroes Anonymous grew into something bigger than a documentary project. They began holding meetings and workshops in different cities in addition to the big annual meet-up. They began looking into nonprofit status.

"We've already met with lawyers on developing nonprofit status," Civitron, who leads the effort for the New Bedford chapter, said. "The funny thing is, they were really disappointed that they wouldn't be representing crazy people who thought they had superpowers."

Life sees this as a logical progression, as he told me in an interview in New Bedford. "Superheroes Anonymous is a collective," he explained. "It's designed to support each other, to meet each other, to learn from each other. Anyone who wants to become superheroes, we support them in that mission."

Life said he was happy to pass the idea on to others who would help develop it. SA3, for example, was Civitron's show, he told me. "I'm more of a guest here (at SA3) than an organizer," he said. "And that is what I've always wanted, to help create a movement."

I arrived in New Bedford a day early so I could walk around and settle in. New Bedford is a beautiful New England town: narrow streets, a harbor full of fishing boats, a museum dedicated to the town's former status of "whaling capital of the world." But, Civitron told me, New Bedford also has a dark side. The city has a long tradition besides whaling: smuggling.

It was John Walsh of *America's Most Wanted* who popularized New Bedford's nickname, "Secret City." In a 2006 episode, he explained that the name referred to the strong "no snitching" street rule in New Bedford; he detailed three unsolved homicides, casualties of gang rivalry between the west and south sides. It was not long after this episode aired that a man decided he would attempt to be the heroic defender of the Secret City.

Civitron refers to himself as an "instrument of the people," a sentiment reflected in his name choice. Civitron's real last name is Civatrese, and his similar-sounding heroic name, he explains, combines the Roman *civi* (of the people) and the Greek suffix *-tron* (instrument). He is a tall, dark, handsome, athletic man of Puerto Rican and Italian descent. He has a very warm, calm, Zen-like personality, a Kermit the Frog in a movement often overshadowed by Oscar the Grouches.

Civitron says he used to work as a counselor and currently works in a day program caring for autistic patients. He refers to his girlfriend, Jennifer, as his partner. She is a biology student and seems supportive of his superhero mission, appearing at his side for several of the weekend's events. Civitron has a strong support system in general. His mother is very proud of him. He's a rarity in that many RLSH never tell their families about their secret lifestyles. Several of Civitron's friends took the RLSH idea out for a spin— there was Green Sage and Kismet and Beau Shay Monde, but as with many RLSH, the novelty soon wore off and they returned to their normal lives.

Another supportive figure has been his sensei, Joseph Rebelo. Civitron says he first met Rebelo in a comic book store and fondly describes him as "a character," which has added meaning when it comes from a man who patrols his neighborhood clad in a red and white superhero costume with a flame motif.

When I spoke to Rebelo, he was enthusiastic and proud of Civitron and his colleagues.

"His actions make others aware that they can act heroically, too," says Rebelo. "Helping a food pantry, picking up litter, distributing food and clothes to the poor—these are actions that so many people have given up on. You hear so much about not being a snitch, about not getting involved. There's a famous quote from Charles Barkley, 'I'm not a role model.' Civitron is saying the opposite of all that— that he *is* a role model. He wants to be involved and do something positive."

At the end of my first day in New Bedford, I got a call in my hotel room from Civitron. After some discussion, the RLSH agreed it was acceptable for me to join them at a preconference meet-and-greet, an informal pizza party at Civitron's house. Civitron told me that Dark Guardian of New York City, along with his new girlfriend, would be rolling into town soon and by coincidence checking into the same hotel I was in. He said I could catch a ride with them.

Not long after that I got the call and met Dark Guardian and his girlfriend, Daniele, in the parking lot of the hotel. As with most of the RLSH I met that weekend, the experience of meeting Dark Guardian felt strange, since I had seen a lot of video footage and pictures of him online, and here he was, in person, firm handshake and thick New York accent and all.

Dark Guardian takes what he does as an RLSH seriously, some say too seriously. The videos I had watched, shot by Life and Cameraman, documented Dark Guardian's bold approach. Fed up with drug dealers in Washington Square Park, he would approach them, clad in black and red motorcycle pants and leather jacket and a spandex shirt with a DG logo on the front, and tell them to leave the park. Sometimes he shone a flashlight in their face or yelled at them through a bullhorn.

We found Civitron's modest townhouse on a narrow, quiet street. Jennifer answered the door and cheerfully led us into the party. It was a behind-the-scenes look for me, as the RLSH casually milled about making small talk, drinking beer, and munching from a stack of pizza boxes. No one was in costume, and so I stood looking around the room trying to visualize which RLSH costumes went on whom. I easily recognized Zetaman, a Hispanic man with a goatee, and Knight Owl, who was sitting next to Amazonia.

Knight Owl had been visiting family in Ohio, on leave from his job as a firefighter and EMT for a private contractor in Iraq. He had driven straight through Ohio to New Bedford and was now kicking back with a beer. He and four other thrifty RLSH were sharing a single hotel room near the harbor. I would meet Knight Owl a few more times down the road, and I often refer to him as the "most normal" RLSH I've met. He is clean-cut with a straitlaced career.

But Knight Owl has a secret. Whenever he would get leave from his job, he wouldn't join his work colleagues in partying in exotic places like Bali. Instead he'd take a trip to random places—New Bedford, Vancouver, London, San Diego—to dress as Knight Owl and join his RLSH colleagues in patrolling their streets.

After talking with Knight Owl and Amazonia, I introduced myself to a couple, a tall, husky man and an attractive young woman. They introduced themselves. The man was very verbose, and it took me a minute before his voice rang a bell.

"Hey!" I said, suddenly making the connection to a YouTube video I had seen. "You're Phantom Zero! And you must be Nyx." Phantom Zero had created one of the first heavily circulated RLSH video messages, in which he introduced himself, speaking through a white plastic face mask with a hood shrouding his head. The video was recorded in 2008 and has over 130,000 views, inspiring legions of other RLSH to document themselves.

Phantom Zero seemed surprised and slightly alarmed that I recognized him. Very protective of his and Nyx's anonymity, he regarded me warily but politely from a distance until he warmed up to me.

Surrounded by paper plates and pizza crusts, Civitron and Jen had assembled some friends to help them crank out a last-minute detail—the SA3 conference package. After the party wound down, I rode back to the hotel with Dark Guardian and spread out the contents of the package—maps, info on New Bedford, and a detailed itinerary for the weekend. Looking at it reminded me that the following day would be a big one.

SA3: Day 1

At 6:30 the next morning Zetaman, Daniele, and I piled into Dark Guardian's car. We drove to a seaside park and followed a trail marked by the Superheroes Anonymous logo duct-taped to a fence. We met up with the rest of the RLSH, and Dark Guardian led us through a workout session: a series of squats, pushups, running, and shadow boxing.

After the workout, we returned to the hotel lobby dining room to take advantage of the continental breakfast. I also took advantage of being with Dark Guardian and Daniele in a casual setting and asked how they had met. Daniele told me they had met online and, although she was surprised by his superhero persona, she got where he was coming from. Daniele found her new boyfriend's super-antics appealing.

"I practice martial arts and work in social work, so a lot of what these guys are doing I've been doing a long time," she told me, between bites of a bagel.

We began to wonder out loud what was taking Zetaman so long to arrive at breakfast, when he appeared in the doorway of the dining room, dramatically clad in his bright blue Zetaman costume, spandex and plastic body armor and a long cape, with a letter Z blazed across his chest. Several of the hotel guests stopped their conversations and stared at him in confusion.

"Uh . . . hi, folks," he said to his audience. He sat down at our table, looking a little embarrassed. "I thought we were supposed to be dressed up!" he said, looking around.

In the afternoon we drove over to Rebelo's dojo, located on the third floor of a warehouse filled with studios, for the SA3 workshops. As we waited for Kenpo Joe to show up in the parking lot, carload after carload of RLSH in their superhero gear began to arrive. About a dozen RLSH had travelled to New Bedford for the conference. Civitron was joined by his two New Bedford allies, Recluse and Basilisk. Recluse was an imposing figure—he wore a spiky rubber mask, a beat-up, dirty trench coat, and a shirt with a spider crudely painted on. Keeping in theme with his name, he was quiet and kept to himself—an outsider in a group of outsiders. He stood in a corner of the gravel parking lot, observing the group silently.

When I met Basilisk, I was deeply disturbed that the man was out doing crime patrols. He later told me that he was autistic. He was sporting a trench coat, a hood, and goggles and spoke to me in a very slow, deliberate voice. He told me that he had made an unsuccessful attempt to join the police academy and so he had become an RLSH. His mother (who he referred to as "Supermom") acted as his wheelman, tailing him slowly in her car while he went on foot patrol. That slightly eased my concerns until I met his mother and found that she was handicapped and had difficulty moving around. I was certain any encounter with crime by that duo would be a disaster.

In addition to the assembled superheroes, we had picked up another entourage—a small fleet of French journalists. There was a writer, Aurélia Perreau, and her photographer, who were there with a French magazine. Coincidentally, a separate crew of two cameramen was there from a French TV newsmagazine.

Throughout the rest of the weekend, the French photographers were constantly running, climbing, ducking, swooping, sticking cameras in people's faces, stepping into traffic, and doing gymnastics to get interesting footage, often with cigarettes dangling from their lips. They made a strange spectacle even stranger everywhere we went.

Dark Guardian had the slot for the first workshop and demonstrated methods to deflect an attacker. He asked that we pair up and try them out. I decided to be brave and pair up with Recluse. We practiced the defense moves, throwing punches and slapping each other's arms. I could just see Recluse's eyes through the rubber mask. After some small talk about New Bedford, I got him to open up about his RLSH activities.

"When I first started I was doing patrols in one of the worst neighborhoods, the South End, a lot of drug dealers, a lot of gangs, and I got injured doing that. When I started I thought it was like the comic books, apparently," Recluse told me. "I don't know what I was thinking. I tried to stop three people from breaking into a house and I got thrown off the porch and landed on my shoulder, so I learned a lesson there." Since then, he told me, he had been taking a more careful approach, usually patrolling in plain clothes in a vehicle.

Recluse at SA3. TEA KRULOS

Dark Guardian's workshop was followed by a slideshow on basic CPR procedures presented by Knight Owl. Kenpo Joe rounded out the workshops with more self-defense techniques, which led to me sparring against Civitron. Afterward Civitron gathered the group outside to discuss the day's next activity: a patrol with the New Bedford chapter of the Guardian Angels.

Many things differentiate the RLSH from their comic book counterparts. One of them is often lengthy discussion and decision-making to move them from point A to point B. The RLSH debated whether or not to wear their costumes for the patrol (they decided not to) and who would ride with whom.

I jumped in Civitron's car with Amazonia, Zetaman, and Rune-bringer squished into the backseat. We were leading a caravan of five cars. Inevitably, the caravan got split up by traffic lights, so Civitron pulled over to try to coordinate the drivers by phone. While we were waiting, we saw a woman in a shabby floral print dress struggling with an overflowing burden of laundry in a splintering plastic basket. She was slowly dragging along.

In an inspired moment of Real Life Superheroism, Zetaman decided to spring into action. "Hey, how far away is the meet-up spot?" he asked Civitron.

"A few blocks up that way," Civitron pointed.

"I'll catch up," Zetaman said, leaping from the car. "Ma'am, do you need some help carrying that laundry?"

The woman was surprised and apprehensive. It could have been Zetaman's over-enthusiasm to help with such a mundane chore, or maybe random acts of kindness were a rarity in her life. Zetaman assured her he didn't have an ulterior motive and grabbed an armload of beach towels. We got back into caravan formation and arrived at the meet-up spot, leaving Zetaman and his good deed behind us.

Team-Up with the Guardian Angels

"So this is the Justice League?" said one of the Guardian Angels, smirking, as the two groups shook hands. Clad in red berets, army boots, and Guardian Angel T-shirts, the eight members of the New Bedford chapter greeted their strange step-cousins, the RLSH.

The RLSH and the Guardian Angels have crossed paths before. They've walked the streets together in New York, Minneapolis, and Salt Lake City. The main difference between the two groups is that the Angels are more organized, almost like a military group. They have a screening process—interview, application, criminal background check, and self-defense and emergency response training. Although some RLSH teams have certain requirements, many do not.

One thing the two groups are starting to share is a mixed response from law enforcement. Although the Guardian Angels have won awards and recognition from New York City mayors, presidents, and other world leaders, their reception has been mixed at times.

The New Bedford Guardian Angels had recently had a small controversy themselves. Gerald Pinto founded the chapter in 2009, inspired to hit the streets after a burglary crime wave.

New Bedford mayor Scott Lang wasn't keen about their arrival. "New Bedford doesn't need the Guardian Angels," Lang told local news. "New Bedford needs its citizens to stand up, be responsible, be accountable and help us with information we need to prevent crimes or solve crimes."

In response, Angels founder Curtis Sliwa headed up to New Bedford to join the Angels in a New Bedford parade and to talk with local citizens to rally support. "Maybe the mayor and the elected officials should be walking with us to see all the positive response that we're getting as opposed to the negative response that they've initially given our effort," Sliwa had told local news along the parade route.

Pinto gathered us and paired us up in a long line two people wide. I was paired up with Zetaman, who had caught up with us. We stood behind Amazonia and Zimmer, with two Angels behind us. Pinto showed us hand signals indicating "stop" and "continue walking," and we were off. We marched down the street, stopping on occasion so Pinto could stop and talk with curious residents and hand out candy to children. It was a nice, sunny afternoon.

Only Amazonia seemed to have had a bad feeling while we were on the street. She turned to me and Zetaman suddenly and told us in a quiet panic, "I got a bad feeling. A really, really bad feeling. Keep your eyes open." She looked around nervously. "If I tell you to get down on the ground, don't ask questions, just do it." Zetaman and I looked at each other in confusion. Amazonia had actually seemed on edge a few times over the weekend. She freaked out at Zetaman later because the flash of his camera reflecting against a window startled her, and someone reported to me that they had seen her hit herself in the head with her billy club. Amazonia was the eldest RLSH at the conference—she's actually a grandmother, but not old enough to feel uncomfortable in a black spandex tunic, goggles, and elbow and knee pads.

We didn't encounter whatever Amazonia's omen was about, and after forty-five minutes of patrolling we parted ways with the Guardian Angels so we could rush over to the official SA3 dinner. Civitron had reserved a large private room on the second floor of the Waterfront Grille. It had giant picture windows overlooking the harbor. The sun was setting on the fishing boats and empty lobster traps stacked on the docks outside, a postcard perfect view.

As drinks were served, a brief awards ceremony took place, hosted by a sharply dressed Dark Guardian, looking very Bond-like in a suit and tie. Dark Guardian made short speeches giving accolades to his fellow RLSH and presented awards to Life, Cameraman, Civitron, and Zetaman for their help with Superheroes Anonymous.

Our waitress was a young woman named Mary. She found me in a corner soaking in the scene, and asked if I needed a drink.

I lowered my voice. "Do you know anything about these people in this room?" I asked.

"Well . . ." she started in a wonderfully thick Boston accent, "my manager was saying something about'm wear'n caa-stumes . . ."

"Yes," I said. "They are all superheroes. I mean they dress up like superheroes and patrol the streets."

"Shaddup!" she whispered, smiling, and covering her mouth. She peeked wide-eyed over her shoulder.

"Who . . . ," she began to ask.

"That's Runebringer. And that fellow next to him is Civitron."

"Geddoudahere!" Mary said, laughing. "Oh my gawd, now I've heard everything. Don't people throw rocks at 'em or something? That's whad I'd do if I was a kid and saw them." She eyeballed me.

"So why're you heyah? Hey wait—are you one of them superheroes, too?"

"No," I said. "I'm writing a book about them."

"Oh yeah?" she said. "That's pretty neat. I only read romance novels, though. Love 'em. You ever write a romance novel, I'll read it," she said, then completely dismissed the topic and headed to a table to bus some empty glasses.

I walked to the downstairs level of the restaurant where I spotted the French journalists sipping cocktails on the patio. They had been banished from the awards dinner as the RLSH did not want their exposed faces on film. I joined their table, and we began to discuss our subject matter.

"The Real Life Super Heroes, they, eh . . ." Aurélia paused, searching for the word, "they are crazy?"

I thought about Amazonia's bizarre behavior earlier on the patrol with the Guardian Angels. "Yeah, some of them are crazy." But I also thought of guys like Knight Owl and Civitron, pretty normal-seeming guys with a somewhat strange hobby. "But this is America," I told her. "We do all sorts of weird stuff here—hot dog-eating contests, Elvis impersonators, toddler beauty pageants . . . so I don't know how crazy it is in the grand scheme of things."

Aurélia frowned and scribbled in her notepad.

SA3: Day 2

After the awards dinner, several of the RLSH kept the party rolling at a bar called Crawdaddy's, staying all the way to last call. They joked around and had fun like any group of people. Civitron grabbed Life's hat and did a Michael Jackson impersonation. Zetaman tried to hook Knight Owl up with a lonely girl sitting at the bar. A toast was made to SA3.

The next morning, Civitron excused the hungover heroes from the scheduled early morning run. "Good morning, superheroes!" he sent out in a mass text message. "I'm just waking up and I'm pretty sure you are, too! Take it easy this morning. Recover . . . please."

Civitron had one event planned for the afternoon—a food drive and hip-hop performance by his friend Tem Blessed in a building next to a café downtown. The RLSH were all in attendance and dressed in their full gear.

I found Zetaman and Dark Guardian doing some impromptu advertising for the event by holding a Superheroes Anonymous sign on the corner outside.

"I had some kids threaten to kick my ass earlier. I told them they should come on down to the hip-hop concert," Zetaman told me. One of the French journalists was trying to get a shot of him and walked into the middle of the street while the unfriendly traffic zoomed by.

"Hey! You're in the middle of the street, man, there's a green light!" Zetaman shouted as cars whizzed by, honking their horns.

"Zetaman . . . saving lives!" Dark Guardian laughed.

Back at the food drive, I saw that donations had begun to stack up. Scavenger told me she was about to make a delivery of ten care packages she had made. Scavenger, from Waterford, Connecticut, was clad in a black corset, tights, and a face mask, her hair intricately split up into braids. Her outfit looked more like it came from a fetish dungeon than a superhero closet. The care packages were filled with toiletries like soap and razors and neatly wrapped by hand in decorated cloth bags. Scavenger had found the address of a nearby men's shelter, Market Ministry, and wanted to walk over to deliver the packages to them. She gathered Amazonia, Zetaman, and Zimmer to join her, and soon the French journalists were running down the street after us.

We found the shelter, and the heroes and journalists squeezed into the shelter's small office. The shelter manager smiled politely but was clearly taken aback by the sudden appearance of the four colorfully clad individuals bearing gifts and their camera-toting entourage. One of the cameramen stood on a chair to get a better shot, shouting to his colleague in French.

Zetaman, appearing annoyed at the commotion, fell back to the hallway. "This is too much," he said.

We returned to the food drive, which was wrapping up. I helped Civitron carry some of the bags of food donations, a couple dozen grocery bags' worth, to his station wagon.

I asked him if SA3 had met his expectations. He said it had. "I'll be satisfied in the end if I'm just perceived as doing my part," he told me. "I like being real and living my truth."

After the event, a contingency of RLSH decided that dinner at a café and some mini-golf would be a good way to wind down for the last evening of the conference. Nyx and Phantom Zero agreed to let me ride along with them. I got into the backseat of their car and looked through the couple's collection of gear sitting on the seat—a fake skull, a skull cane, Phantom Zero's mask, and Nyx's knee-high vinyl boots.

We got stalled in traffic at a steel bridge, slowly swinging open to let a boat pass. While we waited, Phantom Zero took the opportunity to tell me a story of kindness from superhero strangers. He said he had once found himself temporarily without a place to live.

"During this period where I was homeless and in this limbo, Geist offered to send me money—over a hundred dollars—and Zetaman offered to buy me a bus ticket to stay at his house," Phantom Zero said, looking at me in the rearview mirror. "And at that moment in time, I hardly knew either of them. In a way it's awesome they would have done that for me, but in a way it's also messed up because there are so many people that lie or cheat or steal. And I could have been one of those people."

After dinner we went to the indoor, glow-in-the-dark Monster Mini Golf. Inside, everyone's phones went off at once. Civitron had sent another mass text: "Thanks to everyone for all your hard work! You're awesome!"

After the mini-golf, I split ways with SA3. The group had one more event planned for the next morning, a litter pickup at the beach, but by then I was already heading out of the Secret City.

COMING OUT OF THE
PHONE BOOTH

Zetaman. PIERRE-ELIE DE PIBRAC

We all have dual personalities. There is the side we show off, our public persona, and then there is a side of us we try to keep to ourselves.

Imagine this: you come home from work on a day that could be described as normal. You pull into the driveway of your house and carry a bag of groceries in through the kitchen door. Your spouse yells a greeting from the living room and says he has something to show you. Your spouse's strange behavior lately crosses your mind—he's been working late a lot and seems to spend a lot of time absorbed in something online. In general, you can feel an air of secrecy surrounding him.

You walk into the living room and stare in confused silence. Your spouse is standing there, hands on hips and clad from head to toe in bright blue plastic body armor, a utility belt, a cape, and a pair of goggles.

This is what happened to Zetaman's wife, Alison.

"I was like, wow, this is really weird," Alison recalled. "I didn't know what the costume was for. I figured it was probably just a phase." In hindsight, Alison realized Zetaman had been trying to drop hints for some time.

"He brought it up three or four times. He would bring it up randomly, saying, 'Did you know there is a guy in Great Britain [Angle Grinder Man] that dresses up and runs around?' And I was like, 'Huh, that's weird.' And then a week or two later he said, 'Did you know there is a lady in New York [Terrifica] that goes around to bars and makes sure women get home safe and protects them from strange men?' and I was like, 'That's kind of cool.'"

Satisfied with Alison's reactions, Zetaman felt he was ready to take a step dubbed by some RLSH as "coming out of the phone booth." It doesn't always go well.

Once Alison realized that Zetaman hadn't in fact been working late but was instead patrolling Portland looking for crime, she was upset.

"Truth be told, I was really pissed off," she told me. "I had all of these thoughts: Is he going to be accosted, mugged, beaten? Am I going to see him again if he goes out by himself? It made me nervous that he was doing this by himself and it made me angry."

Alison describes what followed as a "big, big argument." Realizing her husband was unwilling to abandon his superhero lifestyle, Alison decided, "If you can't beat 'em, join 'em." She dubbed herself Apocalypse Meow and began joining Zetaman on his patrols.

COMING OUT OF THE PHONE BOOTH

"I figured, well, if he's going to get knifed, then both of us will get knifed," Alison laughed. "This is certainly not how I thought I would spend time with my husband, but I suppose it's as good a way as any."

The couple formed a team of RLSH from Portland and Seattle named the Alternates. The team raised money for charity walks, did foot patrols, and handed out food and "Zetapacks"—bags of supplies like toiletries and socks. Alison began to host a weekly RLSH-themed Internet radio show, *Meow and Friends*. For the moment, the two were happy building an RLSH life together.

Some RLSH can't bring themselves to step out of the phone booth, and it becomes a major dilemma.

Shortly after I met the Watchman for the first time, he told me that he had established contact with a new Milwaukee RLSH, MoonDragon. Sporting a blue wooden dragon mask and a full-body spandex suit, MoonDragon's goal was to patrol his neighborhood on Milwaukee's south side. I met up with him one evening at sunset to walk around the neighborhood. MoonDragon had left his flashier costume at home and was wearing a blue hooded sweatshirt, a ski mask with lightning bolts on it, and black army pants.

He was no stranger to crime, he told me. He pointed out a McDonald's where he had worked as a teen that had been robbed at gunpoint, and he recalled a tense shouting match he and his family had had with the Latin Kings, who were constantly tagging their garage and loitering in their yard.

"I'll be having a beer with my friends and I'll get frustrated with myself, and I think—I should be out there right now," MoonDragon told me as we walked through an alleyway. He told me, to my surprise, that no one knew his secret—not even his fiancée.

"I suppose I'll have to tell her someday, but I don't know how," he told me.

I imagined a scenario. MoonDragon's fiancée gives him a kiss, then heads out to the grocery store. But, oops, she forgot her list, so she returns home to find the man she will soon marry adjusting the utility belt of his bright blue supersuit, a dragon mask resting in his hand.

Awkward.

Although I couldn't see his face because of the ski mask, I could tell from his voice and body language that keeping the secret from his fiancée weighed on him.

MoonDragon met up with the Watchman and me a couple months later for an uneventful patrol on the south side. It was the last time we would see him. The MoonDragon disappeared as quickly as he had arrived on the scene. The Watchman and I talked about it and agreed he had probably hung up the cape at the request of his fiancée or to prevent her from finding out his secret life. Or perhaps MoonDragon is still prowling the streets and none of us are the wiser.

Sometimes coming out of the phone booth goes surprisingly well. A man from the Bay Area who was disguising himself in a red plastic mask and motorcycle gear calling himself Night Bug decided he would make a somewhat public coming out to his wife at a screening of an RLSH documentary titled *Superheroes* at the Roxie Theater in San Francisco.

"I had no idea—I had heard nothing about it," Night Bug's wife, who would soon adopt the persona Rock N Roll, told me. She says she began to like the characters represented in the documentary, and she noticed some oddly clad audience members in the front row of the theater. "I thought, 'Wow, we have some RLSH in the front row, how cool.'"

After the movie, director Michael Barnett got up to lead a Q&A with the Bay Area RLSH in attendance. Night Bug chose that moment to excuse himself to go to the bathroom.

"I was like, are you kidding me, dude, the Q&A is about to start! I said, 'OK, hurry up!'"

The Q&A rolled along but her husband did not return. Not dressed in normal attire, anyway.

"I was thinking, 'Is he OK? Did he get sick? Did he get mugged?' How ironic that would be?" Rock recalled. "Then, here comes this guy walking in from the back of the theater, and he walks right up to the front and hugs Motor-Mouth, who goes, 'Oh, hey, here's Night Bug.'" Rock looked the superhero over.

"The funny thing is I saw him in his mask and everything and I was like, 'Hey, that guy is cute.' How weird is that?" Rock recalled, laughing boisterously. "I raised my hand and said, 'What you guys are doing is really cool. You're putting yourselves out on the line. Someday I hope this is so common that no one is surprised to see you guys in costume walking up and down the street.'"

After the Q&A was complete, Rock headed to the lobby, concerned about the fate of her husband. She looked around to find a male volunteer to go in the bathroom and investigate.

"Then I heard his voice, but I turn around and it's Night Bug, talking to Michael Barnett," Rock says, laughing again. "I'm not a quiet person, you know, but I felt like I had the wind knocked out of me and I was speechless. It all started clicking in my head, then he came up to me and said, 'Hi. I bet you have a lot of questions.' I told him, 'Yeah, that is the understatement of the millennium!' My first thought was, 'How long has he been doing this? Geez, how did I not see this?' But my second thought was, 'I want to be involved. How do I get into this?'"

Some people not only tolerate the idea, they are attracted to it.* There is a term for someone who pursues a relationship with an RLSH because he or she is attracted to the superhero status: a "cape chaser." According to a definition on the wiki at www.reallifesuperheroes .org, credited to Phantom Zero, cape chasing is "the action of seeking romantic partners within the RLSH community."

Although this term sometimes applies to a woman who likes a man in spandex, cape chasers are most often male RLSH who dog-pile onto the relatively few single female RLSH who join the movement. These female RLSH are often shocked by their aggressive wooing by cape- and mask-clad Romeos.

---

* By "attracted" I'm referring to romantically, not as a sexual fetish. There is some precedent for the latter. The Transformational Warriors from New York City, for example, dress as superheroes and host workshops on spicing up relationships.

When Nyx first became an RLSH, there were very few women. "She's an attractive young woman and she gets hit on by a lot of RLSH guys," Phantom Zero told me at SA3. "Most of them have fantasies of having a superhero girlfriend."

Phantom Zero and Nyx met online. Nyx was being stalked online aggressively by another RLSH, Phantom Zero told me, not wanting to name the individual. He said that he forwarded her some tips and resources for dealing with online stalkers.

"I said, 'Here is some information. Do what you want with it,' and then—and this is the most important thing I did—I left her alone after that."

Phantom Zero wanted to help Nyx, but didn't want to appear like he himself was cape chasing. The two RLSH continued to talk and they fell in love. Unhappy with her life in Kansas City, Nyx packed her bags and moved to New Jersey to live with her superhero boyfriend.

Although things worked out well for the couple, cape chasing is often used as a derogatory term. It indicates a person heavily into the fantasy elements of being a superhero, someone who posts cheesy lines or lewd comments on social media or asks another if they'd like to be "in a relationship" even though they are hundreds or thousands of miles apart and have never met. It is frowned on by many RLSH as inappropriate, unprofessional conduct.

"Basically, it's similar to 'office relationships' and trying not to poop in your own nest," says Silver Sentinel, whose wife, Golden Valkyrie, became an RLSH after meeting him. "Once the relationship goes south, confidentiality and personal secrets are not likely to last . . . and this is a community that loves its secrets."

Most RLSH I talked to described a mix of pride and concern from their significant others.

"I was proud of him, because it was a nice thing to do," Alison said of Zetaman's big reveal, "but it made me nervous." A few RLSH told me their significant others viewed it as a nice, constructive hobby as opposed to something seedier like playing poker or going to strip clubs.

An RLSH from Gainesville, Florida, named Citizen Smoke told me his girlfriend (whom he referred to as "M") "made a few 'be careful' comments, but no more so than, say, a bail bondsman's wife might." Citizen Smoke told me he did patrols and in one case dressed as a homeless man to do detective work on a carwash he suspected of being a drug front. (It wasn't.)

"She's been very supportive," Citizen Smoke told me. "She went to a blood drive with me and asked if she could come along next time I hand out care packages."

One thing Alison, M, and maybe MoonDragon's fiancée must wonder is, "Why?" Why is it that of all the billions of people on earth, my significant other is one of a relatively tiny group of people who create their own real world crime-fighting superhero personas?

One person I spoke to, science researcher, writer, and child therapist Andrea Kuszewski, might have an answer. She wonders, could it be they were born that way? Is there a "real life X gene?"

I first encountered Kuszewski's work when I saw several RLSH were reposting an article she had written on their social media. The article was titled "Addicted to Being Good? The Psychopathology of Heroism" and explored the personality of a type of person Kuszewski calls an "extreme altruist" or "X-altruist."

"The term 'X-altruism,' or extreme altruism, is a specific cohort of people that embody the 'superhero personality,'" Kuszewski told me. "However, this type of person is not necessarily what you would imagine when you hear the word 'altruist.' This personality type is not always peaceful nor the most pleasant person to be around. They can be argumentative, rebellious, break all the rules—but all for the sake of good. They buck the system, challenge authority, and stand up for the underserved—not for fame, recognition, or glory, but because it is the right thing to do.

"These people are the trouble-makers, the whistle-blowers. But these are the most valuable types of heroes, and the most important ones to support, because they have the highest potential to do extremely good work for the betterment of society."

One of the most surprising things, Kuszewski explains, is that X-altruists actually have a lot in common with sociopaths. "Sociopaths are also rebellious and rule-breaking, impulsive and defiant, yet they have little expressed empathy, while the X-altruist has an abundance of it. This one feature of expressed empathy makes all the difference in the distinction between X-altruists and sociopaths.

"The traits that allow the X-altruist to be highly sensitive, yet quite fearless in times of crisis, are ego resilience and flexible detachment. This means they are able to set aside their emotions when the tension is high and important work needs to be done; this allows them to problem-solve without emotions shutting down that cognitive pathway.

"The sociopath, on the other hand, lacks these two traits, which makes it necessary for him to totally detach from emotions, in order to preserve the ego from harm. When this happens, they exhibit no empathy. While their motivations are quite different—the X-altruist is driven to protect others, while the sociopath is driven to protect himself—trait-wise, they are quite similar."

So, I wondered, that classic line where the villain tells the hero, "We aren't so different, you and me." That is a scientific fact?

"This is actually true," Kuszewski says, "but that one difference is a pretty important one."

She also says that heroes of the X-altruist type are something our world needs. "Society absolutely needs heroes. We say we want people to be peaceful and obedient, but that's not how progress is made. Following the rules all the time makes us, as a society, stagnant. Some rules can be broken, some should be broken, and some need to be broken. X-altruists may break the rules and challenge authority, but if everyone always followed the outline and never questioned the status quo, there would never be any advancement in this world."

Superhero Secrets

If coming out of the phone booth to your spouse or significant other is a difficult task, revealing the alter ego to parents, family members, and coworkers is often seen as impossible. Mothers worry too much, especially when it comes to things like walking through a tough neighborhood with a Taser and a bulletproof vest.

"At first my mom hated it—she just didn't want me to get hurt," Urban Avenger, an RLSH from San Diego, told me. He's a member of a crime-fighting team called the Xtreme Justice League, a group that patrols and does things like hand out missing person and crime suspect posters. "She's always been overprotective and thinks I'll get shot or stabbed out there. She got really upset when she found out and was crying and stuff."

Coworkers are also kept in the dark. The last thing RLSH want to do is to show up for work to find that their secret has spread in water cooler gossip and that they are the laughingstock of the company.

The Watchman experienced how terrifying and tense this situation can be after he appeared on the local six o'clock news. The show's producers asked him if he would prefer to have his voice digitally altered, but he decided against it. "I didn't think it would seem honest or convincing. It was already strange enough I was wearing this outfit," the Watchman rationalized. It was his distinct voice—slow and reflective, with a predominant Wisconsin accent—that busted him. A coworker recognized the voice immediately and the next day at work confronted the Watchman at his desk.

"I know who you are," she told him.

"If someone busts you out, I always think it is best to be honest and admit it," the Watchman told me, adding that the coworker agreed to take a vow of secrecy. "I explained it to her and the response was mostly positive. She still asks me about it once in a while."

His brother also saw the report and called him. "What the hell was that all about?" his brother demanded. "I explained it and his reaction was, OK, I think it's weird, but it's your thing." His brother also agreed to keep the secret.

One coworker knowing his secret was stressful, but after a story appeared about him in the *Milwaukee Journal Sentinel*, the Watchman found himself in a nightmare work situation. A coworker had been reading the paper at lunch and came rushing back to work with it.

"He walked in the room and yelled, 'Hey look everybody—Milwaukee has a superhero!'" The man sat down to search for more stories of the Watchman online while his coworkers crowded around behind him to get a look. The Watchman eyed them nervously from across the room, certain he would be discovered any second. A work-related distraction diverted everyone's attention for a moment, and the Watchman decided to take the opportunity to appeal to his coworker, still looking at pictures of the Watchman online.

"I said, 'Hey, keep quiet, that's me.' He started looking back and forth at me and the picture of the Watchman on his computer screen and he didn't believe me. He said, 'There's no way it's you. Nice try.'" The coworker still looks at him with a hint of suspicion in his eye.

The Watchman media had also launched a Watchman witch hunt of sorts. A week after the incident at work, the Watchman was out on patrol when a group of people having a party on their porch spotted him and began shouting in disbelief. They said that they were so convinced that their roommate was secretly the Watchman that they had searched his bedroom and car while he was at work. They were certain they would dig up the Watchman's costume hidden in his closet or the backseat of his car. Now their roommate sat on their couch playing video games while the real deal stood before them, listening to their story and laughing along with them.*

Because of bad situations coming out of the phone booth, many RLSH are extremely protective and paranoid about revealing details of their lives. I have had to swear to many RLSH that I not only won't reveal their true identity (which I felt would be anticlimactic anyway) but in some cases wouldn't reveal anything about their day jobs, the name of the towns they live in, and even the color of their cars.

---

* My friend Groschopf became a prime Watchman suspect, due to being roughly the same height and having similar facial hair. His boss asked him if he wanted to talk about it at one point. Even a picture I took of Groschopf and the Watchman standing together was not enough to squash rumors.

If their lifestyle is a secret within their homes, they are careful to stash their costume and gear in the back of the sock drawer, under the bed, or in the trunk of the car. If the home setting is more relaxed, they might have a corner of a room or a den set up as a low-rent superhero HQ, proudly displaying their costume, pictures, and framed newspaper articles. But even if this is the case, the shield of secrecy goes up once they step out of the house. Sometimes they have confidants, and this angle is very much true to their comic book counterparts—they seek advice from people they've shared their secret with: martial arts instructors, pastors, reporters, the guys at the comic book shop.

My own friends had some fun with this.

"You're like Jimmy Olsen," one of my friends laughed, referring to Superman's photojournalist pal at the *Daily Planet*. "No, technically you're more like Lois Lane," a wise-cracking friend corrected, referring to Superman's reporter colleague and love interest.

Despite the veil of secrecy, I did end up learning a lot about the Watchman over many months. Like a lot of RLSH, once he starts talking, it's hard to get him to stop. I heard all about his family, their joys and sorrows. But despite this, there remained secrets. I'm still not really sure what his day job is, other than it's a second-shift office job. He would call me regularly during down time. Once in a while, I'd hear a voice on a loudspeaker, like at a school or hospital.

Sometimes he'd put his hand over the mouthpiece, have a short, stressed, muffled conversation with someone, then return and say, "Ah, I got to go. Something's come up." The Watchman told me he wanted his day job to remain a secret, and so I let it be and never asked what had come up. It could be a world-threatening disaster or a work meeting about casual Friday policy for all I know.

I met the Watchman's wife and kids at a birthday party grill out at his house. I wondered what the Watchman's wife thought of the RLSH business. The Watchman told me he had retired from his first round as an RLSH before he met his wife. Then he heard about the growing RLSH movement and wanted to join back in. He took a wise approach—he decided the best thing to do was to have an upfront, honest discussion with his wife before he even suited up for the first time. He warmed her up by talking about charity events and children's hospital visits.

"She thought it was an interesting idea and was supportive," the Watchman told me. But when he began to do patrols, her support turned to leeriness. It led to a discussion where she asked him not to patrol.

She was particularly upset when the *Milwaukee Journal Sentinel* article came out. The website's comments section, which can be rabidly hysterical and highly insulting, had comment after comment about how the Watchman was an idiot and would surely be shot dead and die a gruesome death bleeding out on the street.*

The Watchman reassured his wife that his patrol techniques were safe, and they reached a compromise that if he hit the streets he would do it with a group. The timing was good—a few new Milwaukee RLSH had begun to appear on the scene.

"There are times she is understanding and supportive and other times she tells me, 'I don't know why you have to do this.'"

The Watchman's wife is comfortable enough with the idea that she has let their children join him on a mission—his annual Christmas toy drive. First his sons and later his daughter—code names Danger, Wonder Boy, and Guardian Girl—went through the ritual of creating costumes and superhero personas.

"They think it's fun—Daddy has a secret they can't tell anyone. They're the reason I do this. I want them to know the world isn't perfect and everyone needs to do their part to make it better," the Watchman told me. I heard his words echoed by every RLSH parent I spoke to.

---

* This article appeared during a divisive, heated election for the governorship of Wisconsin. The comments section had several comments from Democrats speculating that the Watchman was a symptom of shoddy policy by Republican candidate Scott Walker, while Republicans blamed the appearance of the RLSH on Democrat candidate Tom Barrett.

Other RLSH have brought their kids along for the ride. DC's Guardian marched in the Fourth of July parade with his wife and kids, Jetstorm and Soundwave, a nuclear family of superheroes. While I was at SA3, I met Civitron's six-year-old son, who had adopted two separate personas, Kid Civitron and Mad Owl. He worked a craft table for kids at the food drive/hip-hop show and on other occasions helped his dad pick up litter and hand out bottles of water on a hot summer day.

"Something I say all the time is that I'm not really Civitron alone," the elder Civitron told me. "Civitron is a creation of everybody in my life who helped me get to this point." He cites Jennifer, his mother, and his son as inspirations for him to be a hero.

It'll be interesting to see how this generation of superhero offspring grows up—if they follow in the legacy of their X-altruistic parents or if they rebel, embracing a hedonistic, selfish lifestyle.

They might even grow up to become supervillains.

A TAPESTRY OF EVIL

"Unmask is the word. Unmask him." —Street Shock

The sinister Lord Malignance of Colorado.
COURTESY OF LORD MALIGNANCE

Bring Me the Mask of Shadow Hare

"You're not going to believe this next story," the anchorwoman told the audience of Cincinnati's Channel 5 news on the evening of April 27, 2009. She was arching her eyebrows and wrinkling up her forehead, a smirk playing around the right side of her mouth.

109

Shadow Hare patrolling Cincinnati.
CAROL RUCKER

"He walks our streets wearing a mask and even a cape. Tonight we're introduced to the man who calls himself Cincinnati's superhero . . ." The camera then cut from the anchor's desk to the bemused face of a reporter, standing elsewhere in the studio. He had the look of someone who has something incredible to tell you, something you just aren't going to believe.

"He calls himself the Shadow Hare," the reporter began, incredulously. "He patrols the streets of Cincinnati to try and stop crime and clean up the city. And he's not alone . . ." The camera then moved to footage shot on street level, showing the man known as Shadow Hare marching down the street with his team: Dark Demon, Tyr, and Silver Moon—the Allegiance of Heroes.

Shadow Hare was the stereotype that would haunt the RLSH, what every snarky newscaster has dreamed of under that lacquered helmet of hair. He was young, slight, scrawny, and squeaky voiced. He was dorky and delusional. He wore an ill-fitting black spandex costume with a crudely rendered rabbit ghost face on the chest. He sometimes patrolled on a Segway scooter.

The video of the report quickly went viral. It was picked up on CNN and websites like TMZ and became the water cooler talk of Cincinnati for days. Morning drive radio DJs made jokes and even created a hip-hop theme song for the RLSH.

Overwhelmed by the popularity of the story, Channel 5 did a follow-up a couple days later. As they reported on Shadow Hare's newfound success, the anchor and the reporter burst into laughter.

"We kid because we care," the reporter said, stifling his laughter.

"Heh, yeah, wekidbecausewecare," the anchor muttered sarcastically. "People really do seem to support him," she added, shrugging with her hands and gesturing hey, what a crazy world.

The Shadow Hare report, like most media pieces, received a wide mix of responses in the comments sections. Some predicted his doom, others cheered him on.

"Who cares how he dresses? At least he is trying to do something positive for the benefit of someone other than himself. Society could use more people like this," one enthusiastic fan posted. A few future RLSH cited the report as their first exposure to the RLSH movement, so they owe their origins to the mysterious Shadow Hare, who disappeared shortly after the reports.

Many speculate that the media attention was too much. Others think it was something else Shadow Hare inspired: a bizarre new sub-subculture or anti-movement, an online rogues' gallery known as the Real Life Supervillains (RLSV).

In the comic books, superheroes and supervillains are part of an endless cycle like the chicken and the egg, so it isn't surprising that RLSV appeared to try to become the counterparts of the RLSH.

Since a group of actual RLSV would be shut down quickly by law enforcement, the interpretation of villainy in real life is benign. They are a group of individuals, perhaps a couple dozen at any given time, who show how varied reactions to the RLSH story can be. Some people hear about the superheroes and are inspired enough that they start collecting superhero gear to give it a go themselves. Others are mostly indifferent or dismissive.

And then there is the rare individual who spends his spare time practicing his maniacal laugh.

After the Shadow Hare report, a swarm of Internet villains appeared to mock, taunt, challenge, and insult him. There had been a couple of attempts prior to this. In a 2008 YouTube video, a man identifying himself as Dark Horizon mocked the RLSH.

He appeared to be broadcasting from his basement den in the video, surrounded by candles. He was dressed like a cross between the Invisible Man and a cartoon spy with a trench coat, fedora, sunglasses, leather gloves, and pantyhose stretched across his face.

"Some may say we are living in a time of hope. A time where the heroic actions of a few are making the stand against the forces of evil," Dark Horizon reflected thoughtfully in the video. "These same people see good in the world and how it rises above everything else. Well, I say everything that stands will eventually fall. And I say evil is stronger now more than ever, and its time has come to show its face and demonstrate its powerrrr."

He went on to call out several RLSH by name, referring to Amazonia as a "scary beast of a woman" and threatening to crush Geist "like an insect."

Dark Horizon didn't appear again after the video, but he correctly predicted there would be others like him. "There are many villains who will appear and become known," he growled in the video.

He was right. The Shadow Hare video was the catalyst that burst the supervillain dam.

There was the fiendish High Noon Tortoise, for example, who made a YouTube video threatening to jaywalk and loiter every day at noon until Shadow Hare unmasked himself.

"Slow and steady wins the race, Shadow Hare!" the Tortoise bellowed in the video.

Dr. Sadistique set up a MySpace page; his first status update was "Plotting the demise of Shadow Hare!"

Both villains claimed they were from Cincinnati, and Ohio was in fact the first hotbed of supervillain activity.* It was home to Sword Kane, who did a second-rate impression of the Joker. Since Batman is popular with the RLSH, it's not surprising that the Joker is popular with the RLSV.

---

* After Ohio, the states of Washington, Florida, and Utah have the highest population of RLSV.

Sword Kane created YouTube videos challenging Shadow Hare. His MySpace had a screen with a photo of Shadow Hare marred with Joker-style smiley face vandalism with "Vote me for Cincinnati's Official Bunny Kicker" scrawled above in scratchy red writing. Sword Kane's major act of villainy was sending out a MySpace bulletin that read, "Click here to see video evidence of RLSH behaving badly."

Intrigued, I clicked on the link and watched as my computer got stuck in a loop of Rick Astley singing "Never Gonna Give You Up." I had been rickrolled. The RLSV strikes again.

After the initial pranksters had their few minutes of fun and disappeared, those who remained became a fan club for people who didn't like RLSH or simply enjoyed embracing their inner villain.

Executrix, another Ohio RLSV, described herself as a "hero/villain hybrid." She mocked some RLSH and got along well with others. Her villain side adopted a punk rock persona with streaks of purple hair and a dust mask with an X on it; her hero side organized a zombie crawl to benefit the Little Victories Animal Rescue.

She became friends with several RLSH online and even began Internet dating one of them, but she also hung with a naughty new crew of villains—Tiny Terror, Street Shock, and Gravestar. All of them had been inspired by Shadow Hare.

"These people claim to be heroes, but honestly they do very little that is heroic," Gravestar said when the trio called into Apocalypse Meow's Internet radio show *Meow and Friends*. "We want to unmask [Shadow Hare]," Street Shock added. "Unmask is the word."

Ruthless Organization Against Citizen Heroes

The report on Shadow Hare also inspired a Seattle man to hear the call of the supervillain and call himself the Potentate. Depicting himself sharply dressed in a suit, with a smoldering volcano Photoshopped for a head, he formed the satirical "meta-villain" group ROACH, the Ruthless Organization Against Citizen Heroes.

The Potentate's secret identity is a video producer who works on commercials and music videos. He says the satirical supervillain group was started for a farce. "I saw the video of Shadow Hare and I thought, 'If this guy can claim he's a superhero, then there's no reason I can't claim to be a supervillain.'"

He soon filled the ranks of his evil army with a motley gallery of villains. The skull-faced and trench coat–sporting White Skull, a San Diego schoolteacher, became second in command. Calamity, sporting a half moon–shaped head made of duct tape, shared his villainous philosophy on a blog, musing on the meaning of heroism and villainy like an evil Buddha. He delivered this message to RLSH in a blog post: "You tell yourself you have done a good job, yet all you see is hatred in the eyes of those you've helped. They hate you for helping them . . . they want to struggle. Perhaps humanity can only be truly realized through suffering . . . so why help? Why help them?"

One ROACH I hit it off with was Agent Beryllium, a petite, geeky girl with a pile of wavy red hair (or sometimes a blonde wig) and a mischievous smirk. She is wickedly funny, smart, with a touch of social anxiety. She told me that it was what she perceives as flaunting a super-ego that turned her off to the RLSH. When she found out about ROACH, she enthusiastically sent in her villain resume. She modeled her character as a goggle-sporting, time-traveling evil-doer who had shot back in time to warn ROACH about the RLSH.

"At the turn of the millennium, something embarrassing happened," Beryllium wrote on her blog. "Grown men and women began styling themselves as 'Real Life Superheroes,' parading through the streets at night to 'rescue' people, and demanding recognition for their efforts in an ever-expanding network of vanity sites, MySpace profiles, YouTube channels and blogs. Learning how to be a good citizen was no longer just a part of growing up—it was suddenly a goddamn superpower."

When I found myself in Agent Beryllium's home territory, "Jet City" (more commonly known as Seattle), I suggested that we meet up. She invited me to join her, the Potentate, and two other ROACH members at their "West Coast headquarters."

When I arrived in the Capitol Hill neighborhood in Seattle, I realized that the villain headquarters was in fact a gourmet hot dog restaurant called Po' Dogs.* Inside I found Agent Beryllium perusing a menu. She smiled and pointed out the wallpaper, which had a design featuring handguns, and villainous-sounding creations on the menu, like wasabi egg roll hotdogs.

"This is the perfect hangout spot for villains. We love it here," she told me energetically.

The Potentate arrived with his young daughter in a car seat. "Aw, who's gonna grow up to be an evil genius and take over the world? Yes, *you* are!" Beryllium cooed at the smiling baby.

I told the villains that while I was in town I'd be meeting with one of Seattle's RLSH, the Irishman. They laughed.

"Damn!" Beryllium smirked. "I just invented a new torture method—whiskeyboarding. I guess it'll be useless against him."

We ordered hot dogs. As we spoke about ROACH, the Potentate told me how he was half amused, half alarmed that people had taken his joke so seriously. There were RLSH who absolutely hated him and a few "villains" who had taken his satire a little too literally and were eager to join the war against superheroes.

"I mean, it says right on the site that we're a satirical organization," he said, shrugging in disbelief. The last two to join our party were Aluminum Chef and Fatal Phyllo, a couple and real life chefs who were friends of Beryllium's and had created evil chef personas to join ROACH. Aluminum Chef was wearing his toque and chef's jacket with the ROACH logo on the lapel.

With the villains assembled, I asked them about one of their more controversial moments. The Potentate had posted a picture on the ROACH blog of DC's Guardian posing with his young daughter,

---

* When I returned to Seattle eight months later, I met Agent B again briefly for coffee. This time it was at the "ROACH Estrogen Headquarters," a cupcake shop.

also dressed as her superhero persona, Shockwave. The caption to the picture implied, in so many words, that the picture was creepy and that DC was a pedophile.

Outrage over this post was high and led to a group of DC's Skiffytown teammates posing as villains and starting their own villain group as an attempt at an anti-anti-movement or a sub-sub-subculture. I call this group the Creature Feature crew, because that is the name of the Internet radio show where they congregated on air each week. They included a guy who spoke in a fake British accent and called himself Krampus, Agent Mixsae (the one who was so concerned about Skiffytown getting mixed in with vigilantes), and Mr. Jingles, a fake profile for another Skiffytown member.

"The blog post was in poor taste," the Potentate admitted as we chewed on our gourmet hot dogs. "But I mean, we are supervillains, so what do you expect?"

After lunch I jumped on a bus with Agent B and Aluminum Chef so they could show me the famous Pike Place Market. As I got on the bus I got a call from the Watchman, interested in my West Coast adventures. I showed the villains the name flashing on my phone.

"Yes, but who watches the Watchman?" Aluminum Chef said in a stern voice as the two villains burst into a fit of giggling. These villains struck me as not being evil or particularly terrible. They were just geeky and liked to goof around.

Enhancing the Tapestry

During the year following the Shadow Hare video, the villain alliance grew. More people joined ROACH; others remained "independent villains." Like the RLSH, they developed their own terminology. The word "arch" became both a noun (that's my arch, Phantom Zero) and a verb (I hate Phantom Zero; I'm going to arch him). The word "capes" became a sneering insult for RLSH. The RLSV created their own month-long holiday, Übermas, celebrated with sinister greetings throughout December.

Just as there are many interpretations on what it means to be a superhero, villains had a wide range of ideas, too.

The Overlord, a villainess from Portland, Oregon, viewed the RLSV idea as a form of performance art. Her blog began to fill up with villainous art, philosophy, and recipes. A gay supervillain calling himself the Lavender Leopard (or "Lav-Leop" for short) created a blog viciously criticizing RLSH fashion. In one entry he quotes Nyx on her desire to help people, then says, "Well, isn't that sweet. It's too bad she has to make those same people suffer by looking at her horrid taste in 'uniforms.'" He titled another entry "Ninjas: The Fashion Functionally Retarded of the RLSH."

A new breed took their role as RLSV more seriously and devoted considerable time online posing as their villain personas.

Lord Malignance of Denver, Colorado, went so far as to construct a "Hall of Villainy" in his lair that included framed photos of Rupert Murdoch, Dick Cheney ("former vice president and dark lord of Haliburton"), and his "minions" Ghost of Nixon and Bob the Minion.

Dressed in a bronze-painted mask, sunglasses, and a lab coat, Lord Malignance often appears with his pet shih tzu, Comrade Cocoa, by his side. Lord Malignance embraced his fellow villains, saying that they were creating a "rich tapestry of evil."

A duo of villains who emerged as genuine haters of the RLSH were Malvado, who referred to himself as "the most hated villain in America," and the foully named Poop Knife. They are both from the Gainesville area of Florida. These villains began a pretty intense operation of trolling personal information and finding ugly RLSH behavior to spotlight, sharing this info through a villains filter on blogs and Internet radio shows.

There were a lot of ripe targets, and of course the angry, out-of-control tirades the villains received from their hero counterparts only egged them on to insult them further.

One of the RLSV's favorite victims to troll is Master Legend, the highly eccentric RLSH who runs around the Orlando area in silver body armor and an army helmet. Although he receives a positive response from his neighbors for his vigilant patrolling and from homeless people he hands supplies to, he is despised by RLSV. They point out his publicly displayed love of chugging beers and his tall tales, delivered in a twangy southern drawl, about crime fighting. He claims he has metaphysical powers and is actually an incarnation of the archangel Metatron.

Master Legend's pontificating drew the ire of RLSH and RLSV alike. In one forum post he condemned RLSH who wanted to do voluntary security at a gay pride parade and dealt out other harsh moral condemnations.

When RLSV would mock Master Legend* and tell him this behavior would hardly be considered heroic, he would often become irate and threaten them with a tour of "Fist City" or tell them to "Go run and get a Popsicle from your mammy." This, of course, only encouraged more intense trolling and criticism.

RLSV as Criticism

Master Legend wasn't the only one drawing criticism. Sometimes the idea of the RLSH in general was taken to task. I interviewed about fifteen people who claimed to be Real Life Supervillains. Although some were in it purely as a joke or to fulfill some villainous cosplay, some styled themselves as serious critics of the RLSH. I began to encounter the same criticisms over and over.

The first and foremost among these criticisms is that the RLSH are in it for an ego boost and to revel in media attention.

One of Shadow Hare's nemeses, Tiny Terror, mentioned this to me right away. "Shadow Hare is riding the waves of fame because the news had a slow day and now he's gobbling up whatever attention he can get."

RLSV say that these egotistical heroes are seeking glorification for things that many people do every day. They cite the volunteers

---

* "Master Legend is like Fred Phelps mixed with Dog the Bounty Hunter," Agent Beryllium told me.

who organize charity events, help the homeless, and participate in community block watch groups without costumes and media spectacle.

"Every day citizens go about their lives and help people," Lord Malignance says. "To say that one must put on a costume to inspire others is to seek to elevate themselves ('Super') at the expense of ordinary people. If one wanted to fight crime, become police. If one wants to help the hungry, work in a soup kitchen. The reason they are superheroes is ego, and ego alone. Look at the history—these heroes only operate with a self-promoting media intent in mind. Or as Villains like to point out, 'If a superhero gives a sandwich to someone, and they didn't film it or brag about it, did it actually ever happen?'"

Another key villain criticism is that RLSH who are patrolling and fighting crime are not adequately trained to take on criminals and are thus putting themselves (and by extension their families) and innocent bystanders in jeopardy. Here the villains are taking an odd role reversal. They say they are the voice of reason and that the heroes are the menace.

"It is the ones that perceive themselves better or in higher standing than the law who I have problems with," Poop Knife, who also goes by the alias Jebediah Von Deathbread, told me. "Going up to a large group of armed drug dealers is extremely stupid. I could care less what happens to either party in this encounter. It is the bystanders who are at risk from the vigilante's foolish actions. Those bullets that miss their target go somewhere. This is not a comic book world, kids."

"It's the fame before common sense and safety," Lord Malignance agrees.

Supervillains in Real Life

Despite all of this evil Internet chatter, supervillains have yet to appear in the real world to do battle with RLSH, kidnap their girlfriends, or pull off any high-stake heists. The fact that a mentally unstable person could be lured into this world and take a fatal approach is something that concerns RLSH and fun-loving RLSV alike.

There is some precedent for real life villains. Consider colorfully nicknamed gangsters like Machine Gun Kelly or Joey "the Clown" Lombardo. Serial killers like the Zodiac Killer are as terrifying as anything in fiction.

There was a comic book connection, although the perpetrator had no affiliation with the RLSV, in the tragic scene at the Aurora, Colorado, premiere of *The Dark Knight Rises*. With dyed orange hair, body armor, and a gas mask, James Holmes entered the Century 16 movie theater, unleashed tear gas, and shot audience members, killing twelve and injuring fifty-eight. Holmes allegedly told police he was "the Joker."

RLSV denounce such behavior and, for now at least, are content to just squawk on the Internet.

Occasionally I got a dramatic e-mail, like this one from Dr. Unknown: "The RLSH should know their deep desire for a villain has come to pass. A villain who will do more than mock them and make stupid YouTube videos." Dr. Unknown went on to claim it would be the year of the supervillain, and then I heard nothing from or about him again.

The closest example of something happening in real life took place in May 2010. Zetaman and Apocalypse Meow woke up in Portland to find their tires slashed; someone had printed off the ROACH logo and placed it on the windshield. It wasn't actually ROACH, however, just some neighborhood hoodlums who had put two and two together and decided to play a mean prank on Zetaman.

"I know I expect more class, intelligence, and cleverness from any member of ROACH when dealing with heroes," the Potentate wrote on the ROACH blog. "If I find out it was someone affiliated with us (again, highly doubtful), sorry pal, but you'll be left swinging in the breeze, and that breeze is going to be swinging in the direction of the law."

RLSH reaction to their online villain counterparts varies. Some are amused and even strike up friendships. You know your street cred as a friendly superhero is good if even villains have only nice things to say about you. Other RLSH refuse to speak of or even acknowledge the existence of RLSV.

"Basically, if there were such a thing as an online RLSV who did something to harm civilians, I'd call the FBI at once," Geist told me. "And any true criminal would know this before they flaunt some sort of Internet identity."

"I agree with some of the critiques offered by RLSVs and disagree with others," Treesong says on the subject.

"Yes, some of the self-promoting RLSH are just hungry for attention. And yes, some of the crime fighters are ill-prepared for their work, either in attitude (too brutal), or training (no self-defense), or gear, or all of the above.

"But should we judge the potential of a movement by its worst examples or its best examples?

"The whole 'superhero' angle can be odd and surreal at times, especially to people who aren't personally drawn to it. But if it's an archetype that inspires both RLSH and their allies, and it gets attention for the good work that they do, then what's the harm in being a little surreal?"

Many RLSH choose to not let RLSV get under their skin and simply ignore them. "I have the perfect device for getting rid of Real Life Super Villains," an RLSH named Victim wrote on an online forum, posting a picture of the power button on his computer. "Once I press this there is no proof they even existed."

Excelsior! RLSH Captain Sticky (left) with Stan Lee at the 1975 San Diego Comic Con.
ALAN LIGHT

Richard McCaslin, also known as the Phantom Patriot, before his Bohemian Grove raid in 2002. COURTESY OF RICHARD MCCASLIN

Strange collaborators—
Treesong, left, is a liberal pagan
while Crossfire the Crusader
is a conservative Christian.
COURTESY OF CROSSFIRE THE
CRUSADER

An artistic interpretation
of the Fox, a mysterious
environmentalist who
pioneered "monkey wrenching"
techniques in the late 1960s
and 1970s. DAVID BEYER JR.

The Skiffytown League of Heroes in the nation's Fourth of July parade, Washington, DC.
J. JASON GROSCHOPF

Razorhawk leading a search expedition for a missing college student in St. Paul. PAUL KJELLAND

Geist, the Emerald Cowboy of Rochester, Minnesota. PAUL KJELLAND

Assembled RLSH at the SA3 conference in New Bedford, Massachusetts. TEA KRULOS

Miss Fit (foreground) and Rock N Roll practicing martial arts in Los Angeles. GREGG SIMPSON

Left to right: Mutinous Angel, Motor-Mouth, and Hellpool of Oakland's Pacific Protectorate.
PIERRE-ELIE DE PIBRAC

RLSV ROGUES' GALLERY

The Potentate, leader of ROACH. COURTESY OF ROACH

Malvado, "the most hated villain in America." COURTESY OF MALVADO

Agent Beryllium, Real Life Supervillainess.
COURTESY OF ROACH

Blackbird surveying the streets of Milwaukee. PAUL KJELLAND

Operation: Sidewalk Chalk. PAUL KJELLAND

The Challengers and Junior Challengers at their annual Christmas charity toy drive.
LACY LANDRE/THIRD COAST DIGEST

The New York Initiative, 2012. CHRIS LEES

Zimmer demonstrates his "North Star" light deterrent. TEA KRULOS

Assembled heroes at HOPE in San Diego. TEA KRULOS

Urban Avenger, of San Diego's Xtreme Justice League. GREGG SIMPSON

Left to right: Cheshire Cat, Miss Fit, Blue Angst, and Emerald Fáel at a fundraiser for St. Jude Children's Research Hospital. GREGG SIMPSON

New York's Chaim Lazaros aka Life interpreted into a movie poster as part of Peter Tangen's Real Life Super Hero Project. PETER TANGEN

Peter Tangen's portrait of Thanatos. PETER TANGEN

Inside Thanatos's "work locker." COURTESY OF THANATOS

Interviewing Phoenix Jones and Purple Reign at a café in Seattle. LUCIEN KNUTESON

Unmasked: Phoenix Jones after the Pepper Spray Incident. PETER TANGEN

THE MAN IN THE GREEN SKULL MASK

Thanatos. EVA SIU

Many RLSH don't have a very memorable origin story. They're bored and see a news report circulating online and decide it's something cool that they want to try out. After some cruising around the Internet, they find the RLSH forums and begin to join in.

Thanatos's story is different. Before he began dressing in a trench coat, a fedora, a skull and crossbones patterned tie, and a bright green skull mask, before he had even heard of the RLSH, Thanatos was already doing what he does now, minus the costume.

Thanatos hands out supplies and befriends an element of society in Vancouver that has often been swept under the rug, the type of element governments try to round up and hide when they host the Olympic games—the homeless, the drug addicted, the prostitutes, the downtrodden.

One day, the man who would become Thanatos was making his rounds handing out food and supplies when he ran into a young Vancouver police officer who scoffed at his efforts.

"Hey, man, you're wasting your time," the officer told him. "These people only got one thing to look forward to: death."

Those words stuck in the back of Thanatos's mind. When he heard about the RLSH movement, they came back to haunt him. He decided to make his image a parody of the Grim Reaper and to help people out so that they might actually look forward to seeing death.

Olympic Meet-Up: Day 1
February 22, 2010

I knew something had gone wrong. The customs official at the Vancouver airport had directed me into an intimidating warehouse-like room with concrete floors and rows of fluorescent lights. A line of grim-faced customs agents scrutinized passports and turned luggage inside out. I was the only Caucasian waiting in line, towering above families of Asians who looked like they had all of their worldly possessions in tow—trunks and huge old suitcases and even laundry baskets filled with stuff. I was called forward and approached a young Asian woman. She had not a trace of good humor in her face.

"What is your business in Vancouver?" she asked me, as I handed her my beat-up passport.

I tried repeating the story I had told the first customs agent in the airport. I said I had some time off work, I had always wanted to visit Vancouver, and I was going to hang around a few days and soak up some atmosphere of the 2010 Winter Olympics. This was all true, except I was omitting a key detail—I was also there for a meet-up of RLSH, organized by Thanatos.

My story had not worked for the customs agent. He thought I was a suspicious character. Maybe it was my black leather jacket or my uncombed hair, but in any case he sent me into the deep scrutinizing department, and I could tell my story wasn't flying here either.

Did I have tickets to the Olympic games? No, I admitted, but maybe I'd pick some up. Did I have a place to stay? Yes, I said, perking up, pointing to a stack of pages printed off and stapled together, marked with notes. This was great, I thought. This stack of papers will clear my entrance into Canada.

"See, this first couple of pages is my flight and bus itinerary," I explained. She read the itinerary carefully, then flipped the page. "And this is my receipt for the hostel I booked for the weekend, and a map of how to get there from the airport." She flipped the page.

"This is just a map of Vancouver I printed off. I marked my hostel here," I said confidently, pointing to a section of Vancouver named Gas Town.

"And Mountainview Cemetery? Why is that marked?" she asked, her suspicions rising again.

"Well," I said, "I have an interest in old cemeteries." Although this is true, I had a different reason for marking the cemetery. This is where Thanatos traditionally invites the media to meet him for interviews. The reporters walk through the graveyard, silent except for the croaking of ravens, until Thanatos appears from behind a tomb to greet them.

She flipped through a couple more pages, more maps of Vancouver, then she stopped. Something had caught her eye.

"And what is this?" she asked, pointing to an itinerary labeled "Vancouver meet-up 2010 schedule of events" with Thanatos's skull and crossbones logo on the top.

Oh boy, I thought. Her eyebrows pinched together as she read the list.

"Who is Knight Owl?" she asked. "Who is Thanatos? What is this 'undercover walk around?'"

I took a deep breath.

What followed was one of the longest interviews I've done on the subject of the RLSH. Did these people think they had superpowers? Was I a Real Life Superhero? And again, who was Thanatos?

I explained that Thanatos was just an ordinary citizen of Vancouver, that he was a Vietnam vet in his early sixties with a family. I told her that he had a strange hobby of wearing a green skull mask and handed out supplies to the homeless as well as collecting things like drug paraphernalia to turn in as evidence against drug dealers.

"So why does he need a costume to do that?"

"I don't know," I admitted. "I think it is somewhat comparable to performance art—he wants people to see him and see what he's doing and talk about him."

She began asking me how I had met these people and if there were teams and a lot of other questions. Then I noticed something— she seemed more relaxed and I could see a smile in her eyes. That's when I realized she was no longer asking questions for official business, but because she was curious. I went with it and answered her questions as best I could.

When all her questions had been answered, she went to speak with a supervisor. I sighed and looked at the clock. I had been stuck here more than an hour. Then she returned and told me I was free to go.

"Good luck," she said in a friendly tone. I left the airport and stood squinting in the bright winter afternoon sun of Vancouver.

Main and Hastings

After I unloaded my luggage at my hostel, I decided to go for a walk. My choice to stay in Gas Town wasn't random—I picked it because it was close to an area I would be visiting several times over the week. Main and Hastings is also known as the "poorest postal code in Canada" and is an area Thanatos visits often. I began walking up Hastings. I wanted to check things out by myself first.

As I walked, the gravity of Thanatos's mission overwhelmed me. The area looked like it had been hit by the apocalypse. I approached a block filled with a mass of homeless people—there were probably close to a hundred—outside a row of abandoned storefronts. One of these storefronts had been converted into a can recycling center, and a long line of weary, beat-down people stood outside. They had shopping carts stuffed with trash bags full of aluminum cans. They waited for their turn to cash in their stockpile.

The crowd had attracted a makeshift junk bazaar on the sidewalk. A few people had laid out wares for sale, odds and ends like VHS tapes, shoes, an extension cord. One man walked up and down the block trying to sell some packs of AA batteries.

I put my hands in my pockets and walked slowly through the mass. The smell of weed and stale beer permeated the air, and the ground was littered with burning cigarette butts and discarded wet clothes. Pigeons flapped around and dive-bombed at garbage.

Many of the people showed obvious signs of drug addiction—unnatural thinness, unhealed sores, unhealthy skin, a general catatonic look.

I walked until I reached the corner of Main and Hastings. I stood nonchalantly and watched more groups of homeless and junkies buying and selling drugs and just hanging around. One woman sat on the ground, her head resting in her hands. It was a desperate horde of people. I turned and began to walk back to my hostel. I had only one word to describe what I had just witnessed: hopeless. As I walked, I reached for my phone and called Thanatos.

He told me that, in a rare departure, I would not be meeting him at Mountainview Cemetery but would meet him at a café for lunch. He was with Knight Owl, who was on leave from his job, traveling from Iraq, and Motor-Mouth, who had bused up from

San Francisco. I got directions from the front desk at my hostel and jumped on a bus. During the bus ride I was deep in thought, staring out the window at the displays of Canadian and Olympic flags everywhere I looked.

I walked into Reno's Cafe and easily recognized my party sitting in a booth by the window, even though none of them had their full superhero gear on. Thanatos had on his skull and crossbone tie, duster jacket, and cowboy hat, but not his mask. He looked like a cowboy.

When I slid into the booth next to Knight Owl, I felt an odd sensation, like I was scripted into a Tarantino movie—it was like a scene where random guys get together to discuss a heist they are going to pull.

Thanatos shook my hand from across the table. He had a kind, weathered, bespectacled face, and his gray hair was pulled back in a ponytail. He smiled at me, revealing a broken tooth. Motor-Mouth, working on a club sandwich, acknowledged my presence briefly and then immediately returned to the long thought he was sharing. His name is quickly understandable since he seems to verbalize his entire stream of consciousness.

Motor-Mouth, a comic book fanatic and a punk rock aficionado, had bleached blond hair, mutton chops, and a lip ring that bounced back and forth as he talked. His costume switches up but frequently includes a leather jacket and balaclava.

Often referred to as "MM," Motor-Mouth has a distinctly California style of speaking, punctuating most sentences with "Know what I'm sayin'?" or "Right, guy?" He uses the word "basically" a lot, sometimes several times in one run-on sentence.

"He talks nonstop, but he has a big heart," Thanatos told me later.

Motor-Mouth, leader of a team called the Pacific Protectorate, would later tell me of a team highlight in a breathless hour-long storytelling session. Oakland was aflame with riots over the trial of a police officer who shot an unarmed man named Oscar Grant. The officer claimed he had accidentally grabbed his firearm instead of a

Taser, and was charged with involuntary manslaughter. A riot was brewing and soon broke out in the streets of Oakland.

Motor-Mouth and his teammates Citizen Change and Hellpool arrived on the scene, ducking between burning dumpsters to attempt some do-it-yourself crowd control.

"There was a crowd of approximately 100, 150-plus people there, right, so we kinda ran in front of the protestors, right, and a guy in front of us—obviously a native of Oakland—ended up saying something like 'Goddamn it, I got to get my fuckin' drink on' or something of that nature, he had a ten-speed bicycle and tried bum rushing the door of the bar on the corner there and ended up shoving people out of the way—my memory is foggy to all the details—but the guy who wanted the drink tried to rip the door open but it was bolted shut but the guy was like 'Fuck this shit' and he stormed around to the side of the bar with his ten-speed bike and basically started slamming into the glass, from the angle we were at—we took less than three seconds, we took a look at the guy, saw what he was doing, looked inside and the bar owner was like looking outside with other patrons, and you could see the look of terror on their faces, you know what I mean?"

He went on. "So that is when me and my guys were like 'Fuck this shit' and we got our weapons ready and I ended up just taking point lead again and basically cracked my electric knuckles and the crowd backed up. Citizen Change ran around me and flanked my right side and Hellpool had a couple of sticks and we just stood there and held our ground, basically . . ."

Motor-Mouth talked on at the diner while Knight Owl, seated across from him, tried to follow along, nodding occasionally and sipping coffee. He was a familiar face to me, as I had met him a few months before at SA3.

I sat and pondered these three individuals—so very different in many ways, and yet united here in Vancouver, at their own expense, to work together on a secret mission to help the homeless.

We discussed our first mission, set for the early evening.

The Olympic Tent Village, located close to Main and Hastings, was set up by activists as a shelter and advocacy protest to spotlight Vancouver's homeless problem. They commandeered a parking lot, owned by a developer who planned on turning the lot into a 160-unit condo building. The site had quickly filled with homeless people and young student activists who had organized a food tent and decorated the chain-link fence around the lot with political protest signs. At its peak, hundreds of homeless would temporarily call the tent village home.

Thanatos's plan was to stop by, say hello, and drop off several bins filled with food, blankets, and tarps that evening.

Thanatos dropped us off at Knight Owl's place to have some time to hang out and let the RLSH gear up for the mission. Knight Owl had found an efficiency apartment on Craigslist to sublet for the couple weeks he was in Vancouver. It was being rented by a couple who wanted to get out of town to avoid the Olympic-mania. Little did they know that their humble abode was now an RLSH HQ for four days. We dubbed it the "Owl Hutch."

Olympic Tent Village

A couple hours later Thanatos picked us up in his van to transport us to the tent village. We piled into the back and sat on a gurney.

"That's what I use to move dead bodies," Thanatos said.

He wasn't joking. At that time Thanatos had a day job that he was deliberately vague about. "You can say that I work in the funeral industry," he told me. He also revealed that part of the job sometimes involved cataloging the contents of people's pockets. One day he found the Thanatos card he hands out with his e-mail and phone number—he has his own Thanatos line set up—in the pocket of someone who had died of a drug overdose. He looked at it sadly over his spectacles under the bright morgue lights before adding it to the deceased's meager possessions.

After speaking to the people monitoring the entrance to the village, I helped Thanatos haul a giant tub filled with folded blankets and plastic tarps. Motor-Mouth and Knight Owl followed, carrying cases of water and bags filled with food.

Inside the camp was a different world. It was very dark. Dozens of people milled around, wrapped in blankets or sitting in front of their tents and eating stew out of recycled yogurt containers. A fire pit burned in the center of the rows of tents.

I walked around the camp with Thanatos. Even through his mask, I could tell he was upset by the sights in front of him. His voice shook with emotion. "No one . . . no one should have to live in conditions like these," he said, sounding both angry and sad. We left the village and headed back to the van.

Other RLSH help the homeless, but I think some of them only feel it at the level where they know it is the right thing to do, much in the same way they know recycling is the right thing to do. I could tell that for Thanatos it had a deeper meaning.

Thanatos has run into his fellow Vietnam vets on the street before. He told me, "I get very upset encountering any vet forced to live on the street, regardless of where they served. It's just not right they are treated like that and it makes me more determined to do something." Thanatos himself was eighteen and living at home in Santa Monica when he joined the army. "I went to 'Nam in '68, attached to military intel, special forces MAC V SOG," he told me.

Thanatos still dreams of Vietnam. In his journal he recalled a dream in which he was back in Saigon. He says he was relaxing with his fellow soldiers when he decided to go to a store to get a six-pack of beer and some Oh Henry! chocolate bars. He "hear[d] the sound of choppers overhead" and suddenly found himself in the middle of a firefight. He ran to take cover behind a car and noticed that the driver had been shot and blood was dripping onto the street. A grenade launcher ended the fight and woke Thanatos, covered in sweat, from his dream.

Olympic Meet-Up: Day 2

The next morning we all met by my hostel to take an "undercover" mission up to Main and Hastings. Thanatos wanted to lead us in there for a good, long look at the area. We encountered much of the scene I had witnessed the day before—long lines waiting to get into the Salvation Army soup kitchen, prostitutes smoking outside a methadone clinic.

Thanatos pointed out a police headquarters down the street that looked abandoned—there were a few homeless guys sprawled out on the front steps, their shopping carts parked in front of them.

We went into the Carnegie Community Center on the corner of Main and Hastings. Thanatos led us into the basement, where we passed tables filled with homeless people nodding off and old Asian men playing checkers. We got Styrofoam cups of coffee for sixty cents and went to the fenced-in courtyard. Thanatos watched the drug deals going down in front of him on the corner by the bus stop with a sad, concerned look on his face.

Our next stop was a meet-up point to pick up another member of our party—Victim. The spot was the beautiful Chinese gardens of Dr. Sun Yat Sen Park. This was a favorite spot for Thanatos to reflect, he told me; he often brought his wife and daughter along. After Main and Hastings, I could see the importance of the tranquility.

Victim, who had driven up from a Seattle suburb, is what is known in the RLSH movement as a gadgeteer, someone who creates inventions and acts as tech support. Victim, who works as an engineer, fit the stereotypical look—neatly trimmed mustache, hair pulled back in a ponytail, inquisitive eyes behind thick glasses, sensible clothing, his tone sometimes pedantic.

WHAT IS A GADGETEER?

Victim is an example of an RLSH tech support and device-building engineer generally called a gadgeteer in the RLSH

RLSH assemble at Victim's garage for a gadget-building workshop.
GREGG SIMPSON

world. He has worked on developing homemade bulletproof body armor for RLSH, calling the project "the armor initiative," and was able to get several RLSH to test his materials, different layers of plastics, by shooting them with firearms.

He has also posted advice and tutorials in "gadget building" sections of online RLSH forums. In one lesson he demonstrated how RLSH could construct "spiral wound polycarbonate forearm bracers" to protect their forearms, and blogged about other possible devices, such as a handheld light that would simulate red-and-blue police lights to frighten off criminals.

A little closer to home, Victim hosted a series of building meet-ups out of the workshop in his garage. RLSH from the greater Seattle area met up there to work on body armor and other inventions. White Baron and his associate Sir Bob, for example, constructed a portable rain barrel shower they planned on delivering to a homeless camp they had discovered in the woods.

Gadgeteers are small in number, but they show up here and there.

Artisteroi operates out of Florida and builds gadgets for Team Justice. "I have been a design engineer for a long time, but I deal mostly with creating drawings and programming. I had little chance to create anything physical," Artisteroi says. "Even when I did get to build, it was never for me, always for the boss or for a customer. It was kind of boring.

"When I got a request from RLSH to start building gadgets for superheroes, I jumped at the opportunity. I knew there would be little or no funding, but I didn't let that sway my decision to offer my skills up."

In the evening, Thanatos wanted to patrol downtown in an area overwhelmed with Canadians reveling in the stellar performance of their hockey teams. Thanatos figured the crowd mixed with alcohol could use extra eyes on it. We got about half a block into the patrol when two police officers on bicycles zoomed over to us.

"Hi there, fellas. What's with the masks here?" one officer asked. Thanatos, Knight Owl, and Motor-Mouth began to deluge the officers with particulars of the RLSH concept while the officers balanced, a foot on the ground, and listened patiently, looking concerned.

"I think it's the wrong time to do this with these masks," one of the officers said. He explained that people were still upset by an appearance by the anarchist group Black Bloc. As the Olympics got under way the Black Bloc, sporting ski masks, had joined a peaceful protest and caused chaos. As they had done in other protests, they rampaged in downtown Vancouver, smashing storefront windows and clashing with riot police.

"The crowd might get the wrong idea," the officer explained politely. "Especially if they're drunk, you might become the target yourselves."

Thanatos and Motor-Mouth decided to heed the officer's advice and do the patrol maskless. There were police and drunken revelers everywhere. We ran into a couple of guys wearing nothing but boxer shorts and winter hats, their bodies painted with the Canadian maple leaf. The crowd was celebratory but not overly rowdy or dangerous. Thanatos seemed happy about this as he ambled along like a cowboy, watching his countrymen cheering in the streets.

Olympic Meet-Up: Days 3 and 4

The last day of the Vancouver meet-up was an incredible day. I would say it was almost like an RLSH spiritual journey, a day of enlightenment. Instead of using peyote or meditating with sitar music, it was fueled by sleep deprivation and fast-food coffee.

The previous day had been uneventful. We had done a plain-clothes patrol of Vancouver's west side and stopped to talk to one of Thanatos's friends, a homeless Native youth named Dances. He didn't recognize Thanatos without the green skull mask, but when he identified himself, Dances was overjoyed to see him again.

I had already read about Dances in Thanatos's blog. "I explained what I was doing, and he said I had given him much to think about," Thanatos reported in his entry detailing his meetings with Dances. Many RLSH keep a blog or journal of their activities, but I found that Thantos's writings about the people he encountered on the street were the most emotional and interesting.

From the west side we had picked up Thanatos's wife, Lady Catacomb, and took a long drive to the US-Canada border. Thanatos was suspicious that a house he had found here was a meth lab. He says that it was being guarded by dogs with their vocal chords removed, a technique used by drug dealers to get the drop on intruders. He wanted us along as backup while he looked around for any sort of

evidence he could turn in. I was a little nervous about this mission—I wasn't sure how it would play out when a crew of costumed
oddballs took on Canadian meth dealers.

When we got there, it appeared that the meth house was a
self-correcting problem—nothing remained but a remnant of the
house's foundation, scraps of wood, and patches of charred grass. It
looked as if the house had burned down.

"Well, that's that," Thanatos shrugged. After the long drive back
into Vancouver, he suggested we all rest up. Death would come calling at four in the morning.

Thanatos picked me up just after 4 AM and we drove over to the
Owl Hutch. Thanatos was cheerful and talkative, reminiscing about
a music venue near my hostel, but my senses were dull from just
waking up. At the Owl Hutch, the RLSH were slowly moving and
assembling their gear. A Seattle RLSH, the Irishman, had arrived
late in the night. Irishman, named for his pride in his Irish heri-
tage, had a simple outfit of a trench coat, flat cap, and tartan scarf
to shield against the cold and disguise his face. Inspired by the film
version of *Watchmen*, he started patrolling with local RLSH after
punching out of his day job as a mechanic and locksmith.

Also joining us was photographer Peter Tangen. A Hollywood
movie poster creator, Tangen had an impressive resume including
the Spider-Man, Batman, and Thor franchises, and other movies of
all genres. After discovering the RLSH, he envisioned a project that
would transform them into faux movie posters. He set up the mag-
num opus of the project, a photo shoot in a Hollywood studio with
twenty RLSH, in September 2009.

"I felt a lot of media was exploiting and mocking these people,"
Tangen told me. "I felt like I had an opportunity to hand the microphone to the heroes and give them a chance to talk about what they
do. I think they really show the power of an individual."

After the shoot, Tangen adopted the role of informal publicist
and press manager to the RLSH, recommending and rejecting various media requests and offering advice on getting the most positive

spin on their media appearances. He also continued to build his collection of RLSH portraits whenever the opportunity arose.

We were all up at this hour because we were joining Thanatos on one of his handouts. About once a month, Thanatos wakes up early and assembles packages of supplies. On this morning he had gathered a bounty of cereal bars, water, and plastic tarps to help protect against the winter rain.

At first I was skeptical of this idea. Can you imagine being awakened on the street at four in the morning, possibly while you're under the influence of hard drugs, by a man in a green skull mask? But it turned out my skepticism was misplaced. Thanatos is nothing short of a legend on the streets of Vancouver. Many of the homeless are familiar with him and he is slowly and steadily meeting those who aren't.

He has a very careful approach to those he hasn't met before. He walks slowly to them, his hands in plain sight. He talks to them for a while, explaining who he is, and then asks them if they have a need for any of the supplies he has with him.

Thanatos has a route of places he stops where he knows he will find his people. We soon pull up to our first stop, where a man has set up camp in front of a sub shop. Thanatos said hello, calling the man by name. When the man looked up and saw who it was, he jumped up from his sleeping bag and gave him a hug.

"Thanatos! Oh yeah, bro!" he shouted. Thanatos stood and talked with him a few minutes, asking him how he was and if he'd been able to get enough food. He handed him a cereal bar, water, and a tarp. He wished him well and got back in the van.

Down the street Thanatos spotted a woman in the doorway of a shop, sickly thin, shivering. He had never seen her before so he got out and introduced himself, holding out some supplies as an offering. She told him her name was Carina and that she "could be better, could be worse."

When he returned to the van, he shook his head. "She had on a belt," he reported, "and there were a bunch of new holes punched crudely in it. She's getting thinner and thinner, starting to disappear."

We visited more and more homeless, camped out on the steps of a church, at bus stops, and on park benches. Thanatos found one of his regulars, William, camped out in his usual spot beneath a highway overpass. He crawled out of a nest of tarps and grungy sleeping bags and Thanatos handed him a bundle of supplies, bottled water, and a tarp.

"Thanks, Thanatos," William said hoarsely, shaking his hand.

Thanatos recalled that William was resistant to speaking to him at all when he first encountered him. "I keep a special eye on William," Thanatos wrote in a blog entry. "He is very defensive and paranoid but he has gone from 'you don't need to know my name' to 'my name is William.' . . . He has always said 'thank you' to the bundles."

The last stop was in an alleyway where Thanatos found a man with a shopping cart propping up a cardboard wall in a fire escape doorway, a thin protection from the outside world. Thanatos peeked over the top and talked to the man, dropping the supplies down to him.

ROSE

Illustrations by David Beyer Jr.

The comic on the following two pages is a story about a homeless woman Thanatos met on the streets of Vancouver. It is taken from a journal entry he wrote titled "The Rose of Pender Street," May 31, 2009.

After ten drop-offs, we got coffee and sat around and talked at a fast-food place. As we parked, I heard Thanatos tell his wife in a satisfied tone, "Ten more. Ten more today."

After the handout, Thanatos welcomed us all into his home, a small apartment he calls "the Crypt," to talk about the meet-up.

It was a fitting nickname. The first thing I noticed when I walked into Thanatos's living room was a full-size coffin propped up in a corner, adorned with a cow skull. This is Thanatos's work locker where he keeps all of his RLSH gear, masks, weapons, organizing materials, and a patrol log. The room also sported a small coffin set up as a coffee table and a sarcophagus being used as a computer desk. Plastic skeletons and a toy Godzilla waving a Canadian flag decorated the desk.

Thanatos is usually smiling or laughing about something. His sense of humor is radiant but very macabre. He'd fit great as an uncle on *The Addams Family.*

There were plenty of signs of a normal life in the apartment. Smiley face magnets on the fridge held a handwritten recipe for chocolate chip cookies. A poster of a kitten stretching in a yoga pose that read "I Can Haz Inner Peace" was tacked to the wall.

As Lady Catacomb made coffee, Thanatos took off his shirt to show off his extensive tattoos—he has over a hundred. "I just wanted to get one," he said, laughing, "and now I got 116. Whoops!" Some of the tattoos are fresh and colorful; others are worn and faded. He has a wide range of images, sailor- and biker-style pieces, as well as images from old horror and sci-fi movies. They completely sleeve his arms and cover his torso.

Taking advantage of being shirtless, Thanatos grabbed a pair of nunchuks from his coffin and showed off his skills, swinging them around in a Bruce Lee impersonation before we sat down to discuss the things we had seen over the last few days.

Earlier in the weekend, Lady Catacomb had admitted to some hesitation about Thanatos, saying, "It's a hard decision when you have a family," but she added that she "is very supportive and proud of him for doing good in the world." She often acts as wheelman, delivers food, and takes pictures during his missions.

After Vietnam, Thanatos met Lady Catacomb and the future superhero couple moved around Canada until they settled in Vancouver. They have a teenage daughter. She, too, has been supportive of her dad and plans to become an RLSH herself.

"She is planning on joining us," Thanatos told me proudly. "She has developed her own superhero persona and will be joining in later this year. She loves the whole idea."

Thanatos had a few brief final words for us. "You guys," he said, directing his gaze to Motor-Mouth, Irishman, and Victim. "Anytime you guys can make it up here, I could use the help, you can see that."

"You," he said to Knight Owl, "stay safe in Iraq."

"And you," he said to me, "tell the world about us."

Then he said he had one more surprise for us. A few days earlier we had been walking on the street and Thanatos pointed out a building that a keen eye would spot had been used as a backdrop in the movie version of *Watchmen*. He said he was pretty sure part of the set built for the movie still existed on the outskirts of Vancouver. After we left the Crypt, we set out to find it.

It was an exciting prospect for everyone; we were all fans of the graphic novel. Knight Owl says he chose his name because of his own nocturnal habits, but still embraces the *Watchmen* character Nite Owl. Thanatos has a style similar to his favorite character, Rorschach, and Motor-Mouth can cite the comic line for line.

After some random driving around, Thanatos remembered the location and we found the set locked behind a chain-link fence. We cruised around the perimeter and then got out of the vehicles to try to make out what part of the set it was. We debated crawling through a hole in the fence, but then Motor-Mouth spotted a worker near the gate.

We walked over to him and Motor began laying on his superpower. He explained, in many hundreds of words, that we were all *Watchmen* fans and wanted to go see the set for five minutes. The man, who I'm pretty certain didn't speak English, looked very confused at the torrential outpouring of words and nodded warily. We found a narrow entry in the gate and slipped through.

Knight Owl and Motor-Mouth could not contain their excitement and took off like kids entering an RLSH Disneyland. Inside, Knight Owl got his picture taken next to the front door of Nite Owl's brownstone, and we identified Rorschach's spartan apartment building. We got to walk into the Gunga Diner. The seats were gone, but the lunch counter and a picture of Mount Rushmore remained.

Parts of the set had been switched around or altered, probably so it could be recycled for use in a different movie or TV shoot. We saw a spot on the side of a building that likely had some of the famous "Who Watches the Watchmen?" graffiti, but it had been painted over.

After a lot of picture-taking, we walked down the silent street of the set, a surreal case of life imitating art imitating life.

It was time to part ways. We headed to the bus station, where I was boarding a bus heading for Seattle with the Irishman. We said our good-byes to Thanatos and company.

I thought about Thanatos on the bus ride to Seattle. I was impressed. It was clear to me that he didn't have any delusions of cleaning up Main and Hastings. That was impossible. But he believed he could give people a spark of hope or a simple gesture of friendliness. He was treating people with respect and dignity. He was showing compassion. And in these times, sadly, that simple act can be a superpower.

After I returned home, I got an e-mail from Thanatos updating about William, the homeless man we had met under the overpass while on his handout. Thanatos said a social worker found him on Facebook and relayed the message that William had gone home to family in Ontario.

"We have a program in Canada that will send people on welfare or the street back to their home," Thanatos explained to me. "William told the worker that a guy dressed as death named Thanatos had been helping him out the last couple years and if that was how he was living, then it was time to go home."

Those are the words of Thanatos—a heavily tattooed, costumed man, a friend to the homeless, and a true Vancouver street legend.

INTERNATIONAL JUSTICE INJECTION

Thylacine and Flying Fox, of Melbourne, Australia, handing out literature promoting veganism. COURTESY OF THE FAUNA FIGHTERS

Superheroes have been reworked to the nuances of cultures around the world, often leading to translations that are unique or might seem bizarre to English speakers.

In a Bollywood version of Superman, for instance, we see the Indian Man of Steel flying through the air with an attractive woman wearing Spider-Man's costume, minus the mask. The happy super-couple dances on clouds to Indian pop music, before flying to help a woman being mugged. One of Mexico's most popular comedies, *El Chapulin Colorado* ("The Red Grasshopper"), aired in the 1970s and '80s and starred an inept Mexican superhero.

In Japan, Batman starred in a 1960s manga comic, featuring some very Japanese enemies: a gang of robots, an alien-like mutant, and giant lizards that looked like they stepped out of a Godzilla movie.

As the story of the Real Life Superheroes began to spread through international media, foreign RLSH popped up in random places around the world. I would say many of these interpretations are the most colorful and quirky in the movement.

Here is a tour around the globe to meet RLSH on six continents. There are none in Antarctica to report . . . yet.

North America

In Canada I met Thanatos and Lady Catacomb, and at a later meet-up I was introduced to Anonyman, the teenage hero of Saskatoon. He organized a team of classmates named Saskatonian Help to work on humanitarian and charity efforts. I became aware of other Canadian RLSH, too—Paladin of Calgary, Spin of Toronto, and the Crimson Canuck of Windsor, Ontario.

One of the most unique RLSH is Polar Man, of Iqualiut,* a village of six thousand in the arctic climate of Baffin Island. Polar Man, dressed in a thick white and black outfit, mask, and white mining helmet, is a familiar sight on the frozen streets of Iqualiut, and by

---

* Polar Man is the RLSH found at the farthest northern latitude in the world, 63°44'55"N. The Fauna Fighters of Melbourne, Australia, are the farthest south at 37°48'49"S.

all evidence he is a cherished asset to the community. There is little crime to fight, so he spends his time shoveling snow for the elderly, proudly showing off his shovel-handling skills. He also reports reckless snowmobile riders, makes public appearances, and keeps his eye open for bullies.

In addition to Super Barrio and other early prototype social *luchadores*, Mexico has occasionally been home to its own RLSH. Vampireto, for example, lives in the Saltillo area of Mexico and has juxtaposed two concepts in an unusual way—a vampire-themed costume and his background in agronomy, "teaching people in rural areas how to better grow their food and improve their lives."

South America

Alma Fuerte (Strong Soul) patrols Buenos Aires, Argentina, dressed in a monk's cowl and mask, with a cross hanging around his neck. He says he feels his calling comes from God Himself. In a journal entry he said he was overwhelmed by the evil in the world around him. "I asked God why he did nothing. He said he needed someone brave, capable of keeping the faith, even under the most adverse conditions. Then I said, 'I am here, Lord!'"

NN (named after the Argentinian code for an unknown body, similar to "John Doe") is also from Buenos Aires. He introduced himself in this post: "Time to wake up, people. Buenos Aires stopped being a nice place to live, and it is a tomb nowadays. I don't pretend to be Batman or something like that, I'm not going to jump in the middle of a shooting or climb terraces, but I won't tolerate laissez faire anymore. My name is NN and I don't know about you, but I got bored being afraid."

NN also had the unique challenge of dealing with a dengue epidemic: "Dengue is a disease transmitted by a mosquito, if you get dengue once you can be cured, but twice you die," NN wrote. "The mosquito appears in ponds and places where people gather water. Everyone in Buenos Aires is under a little paranoia. I have been using all my free time and some night hours by cleaning the streets and places where garbage can gather water. I had to add a full mask to my suit so I don't get stung by the mosquito."

It's likely NN is the first RLSH to list "contracting tropical illness" as a reason for donning the mask.

O Gavião (the Hawk), from Rio de Janeiro, Brazil, openly embraces vigilantism. He shared a story about beating graffiti taggers vandalizing homes. "I surprised taggers in action by shooting objects I found on the street (stones, cans) against them to make them fall from the wall," O Gavião wrote to me. "Then I invested against them with my steel baton, targeting their arms and legs to make the most moral effect possible. With arms and legs injured it is much more difficult to climb on walls to vandalize and they feel humiliated in front of residents who have less fear of vandals now."

A much more lighthearted approach out of Rio de Janeiro is Heróis do Cotidiano (Everyday Heroes), an activist collective who wear similar outfits and are named for the skills they want to emphasize in life. The group is a quintet led by a professor of theater who calls herself Heroina da Escuta (Heroine of Listening).

An article in the Brazilian newspaper *O Globo* described the group's mission: "The collective does urban interventions and performance art to show that small heroics can be done by anyone. They've cleaned up the statues of Gandhi and [former Brazilian president] Getulio Vargas, collaborated with community, and helped with simple gestures such as paying attention to patients arriving at hospitals."

Europe

Great Britain

Like Canada, Great Britain has had a small but steady roll call of RLSH. One of the best known Brit RLSH is the Statesman of Birmingham, a large man with a handlebar mustache. He works as a banker by day and dons a domino mask and a spandex Union Jack–print shirt to do patrols and homeless handouts at night. He told his girlfriend he was out having late-night poker games, choosing not to come out of the phone booth and keeping his superhero identity a secret. He organized an early British meet-up in 2009 with Vague and Swift of London, and Barns of Glasgow. Statesman reports that they saw some action that night, helping police chase and corner "a crim" who was running through Trafalgar Square; they were hanging out when they saw two police officers chasing a man down. The RLSH quickly leapt up and joined in the chase.

"I'm proud to say that nobody hesitated. We were off after the getaway, pounding up the steps and away out of the Square . . . the police thanked us and asked us to wait until the van arrived to pick him up. We talked until they had him locked up, and I gave my details so that I could provide a statement. I'll admit to a little cheesiness here, cos I got to answer, 'Don't worry, it's what we do,'" the Statesman said in a forum post.

In 2011, Statesman found himself in his most hair-raising situation to date—diving into the Birmingham riots. The riots in England had started over a couple of cases perceived to be police brutality, and peaceful protests had flamed into rioting in several cities. In Birmingham, a police station was burned, store windows were smashed, and hundreds were arrested.

The Statesman decided to head into the thick of it to see if he could help. When he got into town, he found a line of police officers confronting a group of rioters thirty to forty strong, wearing hoodies and scarves around their faces. He also spotted a young Scottish couple who looked frightened.

"[They] stood behind the lines, loaded with wheeled suitcases and duffel bags. I approached them to see if they were okay, and they told me that this was their first night living in Birmingham; they were literally straight off the train, on the way to their first apartment together," the Statesman recalled. "They were scared; they had no idea how to get to the next train station—Snow Hill—which was located on the opposite side of the 'Hot Zone.'

"I explained that my name was the Statesman, and Craig [the young man] grinned and said that he'd seen me in the paper and recognised my mustache! We shared a laugh at that, which seemed weird with bottles starting to shatter on the road behind us. I took one of their bags, and led them off down a side road towards the other side of town."

After delivering the couple safely to the train station, Statesman next encountered a young man smashing a storefront window and decided to put him under citizen's arrest.

"I saw him do a brief double-take at my appearance. I grabbed his arms, forcing them back and down. He twisted, and we struggled. It is incredibly difficult to grapple someone down who doesn't want to be. My sleeve rose up, and he raked his nails down my forearm. I got his hands behind his back, and after a further struggle, he eventually gave up the fight. I zipped his wrists, tight over his sleeves."

The Statesman took the looter to a makeshift police station where the confused police held the superhero and the criminal. "After about twenty minutes, I was told to leave and they took my guy to a waiting minibus with a half-dozen sullen-looking figures inside." Exhausted, Statesman left, but he returned the next day to join a crew of volunteers working on cleaning up damage from the riots.

Another challenge Statesman faced was an aggressive pursuit by the British tabloids. After the *Sun* found out about the RLSH, they posted his picture and offered a cash reward for information on his secret identity. A former classmate revealed his name and the tabloid reporters hit the street to get surprised reaction quotes from his mother; they also outed his secret identity to his girlfriend. The article, done in traditional ridiculous tabloid fashion,* was a hit

---

* Sample quote from the Statesman's "mum" on doing his laundry: "I still do his washing even though he's a grown man, the cheeky little devil."

and the Statesman and subsequent RLSH (there is a five-member team named the Justice Union) face the uniquely British challenge of dealing with prying tabloid reporters.

Italy

Naples is well known for its ancient piazzas and churches, classic opera houses, and small, intimate restaurants serving pasta. There is another side to Naples, though, and that is the ruthless Camorra, the oldest criminal organization in Italy. The Camorra deal with drug trafficking, extortion, and racketeering and will mow down anyone in their way in a hail of gunfire. They've also severely damaged the environment, running a racket on garbage disposal in southern Italy. They bury trash in caves, under housing units, anywhere they can find room.

If there was ever an environment for a superhero, especially one with an ecological twist, Naples is it. And the man who heard this call is known as Entomo, "the insect man." He has a spandex body suit, a mask with small antennae decorating the eyes, and a catch-phrase in English: "I inject justice!"

"As you must already know, I live and operate in one of the most difficult cities ever built on Earth: Naples," Entomo states. "We're plagued by pollution, criminality, and corruption among politicians. Overall speaking, I must confess ignorance rules upon most people. This is not a fertile terrain for a man to grow up, dress the way I do, and watch upon the town."

He admitted to me, though, that actively fighting against the Camorra is not something he plans to do. "No, not at all. Camorra is not my battle. I just stop vandalism from 'casual' criminals and investigate on amateurish gangs. Plus, I'm an environmentalist, and everything I do is to promote respect for people and the planet itself. I can't fight 'that other' battle, and that is because it would need an entire one million man army to stop it. I'm just a masked guardian."

Still, reports of the insect man began to pick up in the Italian media, climaxing in a media blitz Entomo has dubbed the "Entomo-craze."

Inspired by the craze, several new Italian RLSH appeared on the scene, and Entomo recruited them into a team named I Rivendicatori (the Vindicators), one of the first foreign RLSH teams. Members included Dr. Presenza, Howler, Morte (Death), Giustiziere Anomino (Anonymous Executioner), Diavolo Azzurro (Blue Devil), and ItaliaNinja.

Entomo is also one of only a very few RLSH who claim to have some form of superpowers, which he describes as "paranormal faculties." He describes a strange kinship with insects and a psychic, information-gathering power he calls "the Parallelogram."

ENTOMO'S "PARANORMAL FACULTIES"
Illustrations by David Beyer Jr.

In a dossier-style report, Entomo explains that he had a near-death experience in 1982 and that it connected him to "a spiritual plane of existence involving insects and their collective consciousness—maybe the so called 'morphogenetic field of insects.'" The comic on the following page shows the powers he claims to have gained.

A. "Sharpened senses, reflexes and agility, augmented sight and hearing."

B. "Peculiar optical perception in aquatic environment (irises become green on contact with sea water)."

C. "Resistant immunitarian system."

D. "Special vocal properties like emulation and pitch-shift."

E. "I can emit a spiritual sense of social attraction or repulsion, like that achieved by ants with chemical pheremones," Entomo says, adding, "I've not yet mastered this quality as required, and sometimes it plays a disadvantage."

F. Entomo describes his "Parallelogram" ability as an insect method to "deduce an approximative tessellation of their animal opponents."

Razorhawk first met Entomo as one of the first RLSH customers to order a costume from his new business, Atomic HeroWear. "Entomo is a great guy. He really intends well. I think sometimes when his words are translated that they don't come out right, but he has some great ideas, and a great love of doing good. He will fight to the end to help save the world," Razorhawk reported to me.

Although he has some avid RLSH supporters, Entomo has had harsh conflict with others. Some of these RLSH are clearly annoyed by his claims of "paranormal faculties," his repeated mentioning of the "Entomo-craze," his tendency to speak with an authoritative voice to others, and his frequent predictions of doom for the RLSH movement. This has led to various RLSH trying to put him in his place, sometimes in blunt, harsh language.

"Entomo is an egomaniac," Zero told me. "He loves you if you agree with him, he curses you if you disagree. He stabs friends in the back. And he's full of shit. Claims to have powers."

Entomo often responds to these critics by saying they are "trolls" or "fakes."

"The sickness of the RLSH movement has reached a new stadium. Now, the so-called, self-proclaimed, delusional 'leaders' close threads with replies filled with American bad language and insults.

"How aggressive. They just believe to be 'badasses' by acting this way. Wow. They are tough. I suspect in a street fight they would succumb under their own weakness. And I pretty much know they never were involved in a REAL street fight, anyway," Entomo stated in a forum post.

Why take on the criminal culture of Naples and deal with drama within the RLSH community? What is the reward for Entomo at the end of the day? "There isn't one," the Insect Man told me. "You're alone with yourself at 5 AM, dead tired. And nobody claps the hands."

Finland

Laserskater found a way to take his roller skating hobby and turn it into real life superheroics. Inspired by a rare comic book titled *Skate*

Man,* he first strapped on his Rollerblades to start patrolling Helsinki in 1996, wearing a skimpy white half-shirt, white short shorts, and sunglasses.

"It is difficult to say when I started to be a real life superhero; at first my purpose was only to skate on the streets for my physical exercise," Laserskater told me. "However, while I was skating I noticed that opportunities to help people increased little by little. It was like a destiny for me. I couldn't help it and I liked it!"

And with that he was off, skating the streets of Helsinki and the nearby towns of Vantaa and Espoo. Laserskater says the crime rate is very low in these cities, so his patrols focus more on lending a helping hand rather than active crime fighting.

In 2003, Laserskater began to record a "book of good deeds." "For example, I am helping beggars and street musicians, guide tourists and take part in collections. Sometimes I have an opportunity to help guards or police and secure the general order. I do charity work, too." Laserskater logged 297 good deeds in 2009, broke his record with 580 deeds in 2010, and broke it again in 2011 with a reported tally as follows:

Final results of Good Deeds in 2011:
2011 (final results):
Helping beggars: 203 times
Tipping cafe waiters: 199 times
Tipping cafe bouncers: 29 times
Tipping street musicians: 148 times
Taking part in a collection: 4 times
Guiding tourists and other people: 8 times
Telephone help: 3 times
Depositing a lost property: 1 time
Other good deeds: 143 times

TOTAL: 738 good deeds

---

* Skate Man is an obscure influence for Laserskater. Only one issue of the comic was produced, by the short-lived Pacific Comics company, in 1983.

The Netherlands

Gorinchem is a town of 34,500 in the western Netherlands. Little do its citizens know that a ghost-faced crime fighter lurks among them. Gost Face (a spelling variation on the killer from the *Scream* movies) began night patrols and collecting frightening ghost-themed masks.

"Except for wearing a mask when confronting an offender, I don't really wear a costume. I think it's important to blend into the crowd, so I wear urban style clothing with a hood to complete the mask," Gost Face wrote.

He said he began doing RLSH-like activities when he was in high school. "I had been intrigued by superheroes ever since I was little and my mom and I went to visit our neighbor and I first laid eyes on her son's comic books." He says the pulp pages made him aware of the injustices going on around him. A night owl by nature, Gost Face began to go out at night to watch out for drunken misbehavior and check walls for gang graffiti.

Gost Face also demonstrates the major culture clash that has repeatedly reared its ugly head in the Netherlands. "I don't want to turn this into a racial thing, but in my country 70 percent, which is official numbers, of all crimes are committed by Turkish and Moroccan youths; third-generation Muslim children who destroy public property and sell drugs. They harass Dutch girls because they consider every non-Muslim girl a whore that they can touch and rape whenever they feel like it.

"The problem is that the Dutch government thinks that political correctness is much more important than public safety. They are cowards who are afraid that addressing the Muslim community about this problem will result in racial tension (they call us racist every time we mention their children's criminal behavior) and eventually a civil war between the Dutch and Muslim immigrants. And trust me, that is not far off."

Let's hope Gost Face is wrong on that prediction.

The Netherlands are also home to a unique man and machine duo collectively known as the Iron Lamb. A Dutch man began noticing a disturbing string of sheep mutilations in the meadows around the town of Zoetermeer. "In 2006 a sheep was set on fire with gasoline, and in 2007 two lambs were killed with hammer blows to the head. Another attack took place in 2009. A man was caught and confessed in 2010. He was sentenced to three weeks jail and a fine of 500 euros."

At first the man behind the Iron Lamb began patrolling the fields in civilian clothes with a camera. Netherlands has mask laws and he was afraid he would get into trouble for trespassing, so he searched for a creative approach to monitoring the fields.

"Then I got an idea from a source most of us draw inspiration from—a comic book. I read *Kingdom Come*, wherein Batman is an old, broken man. He doesn't go on patrol anymore, but uses remote controlled bat drones he controls from the batcave."

Seeing the first *Iron Man* movie further inspired him. "I decided I would build an Iron Lamb," he declared. "I now patrol with the Iron Lamb on weekends. It uses non-lethal weapons, has a camera, and uses warning equipment to make a possible crime more visible for everyone living close to the meadows."

After photos emerged of the machine, Iron Lamb critics dismissed the robot, saying it could not possibly be functional. "I was one of the people giving him crap on the whole Iron Lamb project," fellow gadgeteer Victim told me. "I'll still call BS on this unless we get a video. I think it's just a model."

Asia

Japan

Japan has something that could be considered to be in the same family tree as RLSH. They are known as "local heroes" and are created as mascots for companies or local government. They show off at martial arts demonstrations and perform shows designed to teach children lessons. Most are known only in the local area where they live, but some have become famous nationwide.

Chojin Neiger, for example, has a typical Japanese space robot look and has spawned comic books, radio, and television programs as well as a series of original songs.

Someone who jumped into the first early wave of RLSH was Red Arrow of Hong Kong. He looked like a Hong Kong knockoff of the DC superhero Red Tornado. He wears a blue cape and shirt with a giant red arrow and a blue mask concealing his face with a giant plush red arrow stuffed with Styrofoam attached to the forehead.

A video from 2006 documents him handing out candy at a school assembly, performing yo-yo tricks, handing origami swans to children on the street, and offering to shade pedestrians under an umbrella. In a second Christmas video he walks around handing out one hundred small gifts to "kids in poor places in Hong Kong."

In 2007 Red Arrow announced he was moving to the United Kingdom and disappeared until 2010, when he returned online and said he had been inactive for years but was returning to the scene, the giant red arrow on his head guiding his way.

One of the most popular RLSH in the world is not an American but the Beijing Bauhinia, also known as Hong Kong Flower. Inspired by the American RLSH and a 1965 Hong Kong film, *Black Rose*, featuring a Robin Hood–style heroine, Hong Kong Flower assembled a sexy costume and a mask.

She is frequently spotted in Hong Kong and Beijing (leading to false reports she was two different people), handing out food, supplies, and cash to the homeless. She sometimes also gives them a bauhinia flower, the flower of Hong Kong, as a calling card. The press picked up the story and began speculating on her secret identity, saying she might be the daughter of a powerful politician. She began picking up thousands of fans online who began sending her encouraging messages and fan art, including manga-style comics stories.

"Although I haven't solved the problem, at least I've caught the attention of citizens and government officials," the Bauhinia is quoted as saying in an article. "That was my goal, and besides, I've done more than some of the all-talking-no-action government officials."

An example of a manga comic starring Hong Kong Flower. ART BY TMAN TSE

Australia

Australia's most famed, colorful RLSH is the larger-than-life Captain Australia. Dressed in a style similar to Captain America, with an @ symbol on his chest, Captain Australia is gung ho on fighting crime in his city of Brisbane, as well as Sydney and Australia in general. He considers all of this an epic "quest" that he is on, as he explained in an e-mail interview.

"All my life, apathy has followed me like a dark cloud. I knew something was deeply wrong with the fabric of society, but I chose to do nothing about it. I vicariously directed those feelings out through movies, games, television without actually altering the world around me in any meaningful way.

"Society is slowly eating itself, but the cannibalism is reversible if we only step up and take personal responsibility for the world around us. That is the basis of my mission: I am on a quest to save the world."

Surprisingly, though, Captain has distanced himself from the main body of the RLSH movement.

I asked him to share what he thought of his fellow heroes. "I like the idea of teaming up with other like-minded individuals, but from what I've seen these folks aren't like me. I've researched dialogue they've engaged in and I'm generally a little troubled by the tone. You see, despite all evidence to the contrary, I am in fact actually completely sane and completely serious."

Captain maintains a website and answers calls for help he receives via e-mail—after a young man reported to him that his bicycle was stolen, the Australian hero took him to a local shop and bought him a new one.

I asked Captain Australia what he sees on the horizon for his heroics. "I honestly don't know. I am in it for the long term. I am on a Quest. But I don't have a map. My feet are on the path, I'm just going to keep walking and see what kind of a difference I can make."

In Melbourne, creative animal activist couple the Fauna Fighters donned pleather and rubber outfits to become Flying Fox and

Thylacine. The names are uniquely Australian—the thylacine, also known as the Tasmanian tiger (actually a marsupial), was declared extinct in the 1930s. Many members of the flying fox family call Australia home and are on the endangered species list. The Fauna Fighters don't call themselves RLSH, but they do say the colorful concept was an inspiration to them. They have called themselves "eco-vigilantes" and "Watchmen of the Animal Kingdom." They say their goals are to help find lost pets, collect supplies for animal shelters, raise awareness of animal habitats, and "fight the disgraceful practice of puppy farming and animal testing." They've also handed out literature on veganism and protested in front of stores that sell fur coats.

Their reception in the RLSH community was stormy after they got into long, ugly arguments on the Internet when it was discovered they were supporters of the Animal Liberation Front. The radical animal rights group has occasionally burned down buildings and caused property damage, leading them to be labeled as a domestic terrorist threat. The Fauna Fighters stuck by their decision to support the group, causing them to be RLSH outsiders down under.

Africa

There is one known RLSH in Africa named Lion Heart, who lives in Liberia. Dressed in a simple mask and street clothes, Lion Heart travels from village to village educating people about sterilizing water and preventing the spread of diseases, as well as warning about the trickery and dangers of human trafficking.

At age fourteen, Lion Heart made a trek from the country to Liberia's capital, Monrovia, to try to reunite with his family. "I made a vow with God," Lion Heart said in an interview, "that if he would bring me home, I would go help my people, help them live a healthier life."

Lion Heart teamed up with Peter Tangen's Real Life Superhero Project to raise over $3,000 (mostly from within the RLSH community) for a charity called Generosity Water to build a well in Liberia in the RLSH Project's name. The well will be able to serve three hundred Liberian villagers for twenty years.

Meanwhile, Lion Heart continues to travel and educate his people to try to save their lives. It's a huge challenge, even for a superhero—diseases from unclean water are the leading cause of death in Liberia.

CHALLENGERS, ASSEMBLE!

The Challengers on patrol in Madison, Wisconsin. HEATHER HAYNES

"I'm outside," the Watchman told me** when I answered the phone. I left my house and spotted the RLSH in his car in front of my house. He was wearing his new gear, the new costume that would become his signature look—a red rubber cowl, leather gloves, a spandex shirt (or hooded sweatshirt in cold weather) emblazoned with the Watchman logo, and his trench coat. Months had passed since our road trip to Minneapolis. We had stayed in contact, sometimes talking frequently, other times with months passing in mysterious silence. It was now a cool November night and the Watchman had called on me to join him on an unusual mission.

Operation Sidewalk Chalk

As I climbed into the Watchman's passenger seat, I found a plastic bucket filled with his children's sidewalk chalk. The Watchman had an idea for some public art for this evening.

"I came up with this idea after I read something Thanatos posted on the Heroes Network," the Watchman had told me earlier. Thanatos had gone out on the streets of Vancouver and created chalk body outlines, the type you find at murder scenes. Then he labeled them with societal ills like "apathy" and "substance abuse." Thanatos encouraged other RLSH to do the same, and the Watchman decided to heed the call.

Our first stop was to visit my friend, photographer Paul Kjelland. We decided the alley next to his house would be a good place to do a test run. For the first of several times that night I found myself lying on the cold concrete while the Watchman scratched a chalk outline of my sprawled body. Paul shot pictures and we watched as the Watchman lettered the word "Greed" into the outline. He stood up and dusted the chalk off his hands, his eyes on the outline and a satisfied look on his face. He turned to me. "Any suggestions where to go next?"

I led the Watchman to a heavily traveled pedestrian and bicycle bridge. After he traced me he asked what I thought the biggest crime issue in my neighborhood was. I told him it was probably crime and violence related to buying and selling drugs and drug addiction. It worked for him and he wrote "Drugs" in the outline.

We then headed downtown, stopping at Cathedral Square Park along the way. On the path of the park we did two outlines labeled "Gang violence" and "Domestic abuse." Homeless people watched us suspiciously from a nearby picnic table. As we walked away a homeless man, undeterred by the Watchman's strange attire, asked him for spare change. The Watchman apologized and said he didn't have any.

"I don't carry any cash with me on patrol," he explained to me as we walked away.

We headed to the busiest intersection of downtown Milwaukee. A white stretch SUV limousine with four wheels in the back pulled up at the stoplight. A tinted window descended and half a dozen excited women peered out.

"Woooooo-ooo! Who are you?" one of the women shouted.

"I'm the Watchman! I'm a real life superhero!" he yelled back.

"A superhero! That is so cool!" the woman yelled as the limo drove away.

"I think we (the RLSH) spend a lot of time on our patrols explaining who we are and what we're doing," the Watchman shrugged as a honking car rushed by.

Perhaps with the partying women still on his mind, he wrote "Alcohol abuse" in the next outline. It was traced on a river walk between businesses. A nervous-looking couple walked silently by, not wanting to capture the attention of the man lying dramatically on the sidewalk and the man dressed as some sort of superhero tracing him with chalk. A couple sipping martinis in a nearby bar stared at us intently.

The last outline was done in front of the *Milwaukee Journal Sentinel* building. A Milwaukee Bucks basketball game had just let out across the street and a large crowd quickly gathered on the corner. The Watchman had just finished lettering the "y" in "Poverty" when the walk signal turned on and the crowd began to cross the street and walk over the chalk outline. Some looked startled or confused by the outline and the masked man nearby; others seemed to have no reaction at all.

"Hopefully people see it. I guess I hope that if it wakes people up just a little bit, if it makes them think enough about it to make them change something for the better or prevent any of these things, then I think it was a success," he told me in the parking garage when we had completed the mission. "This is one of those cases where we aren't going to know if it does any good, but it's worth trying."

Blackbird Joins the Flock

A few months later I got a call from the Watchman. He was excited to report that he had been contacted by a Milwaukee man, a new RLSH who called himself Blackbird. Since MoonDragon's disappearance he had once again been the sole RLSH around town, and he was optimistic that the appearance of this new, like-minded mystery man could be an omen that recruiting a more localized team was on the horizon. Although the Watchman had pride in the team he had helped found, the Great Lakes Alliance, leaving his wife to watch the kids while driving six or more hours to Minneapolis each way for a meet-up was not in his superhero repertoire.

Blackbird, we would later find out, was a Batman fanatic, with a huge collection of Batman memorabilia. He loved other superheroes, too, but Batman was number one. "Because he is really an everyman. We're all victims, afraid, but he's not afraid. And the people we're afraid of, criminals, they're afraid of him. He's the ultimate badass. Even the Justice League relies on him, even though they have powers and he doesn't, because of his intellect. Plus he has the best rogues' gallery," he explained.

Blackbird had been operating without a persona for a while, he later told us, staking out different crime areas for surveillance and collecting gadgets like night vision binoculars and devices to enhance hearing. He read the article I had written on the Watchman for *Milwaukee Magazine* and felt compelled to adopt an RLSH guise and join him. The Watchman asked if I'd like to join him in meeting Blackbird and taking him on patrol for the first time.

On February 6, 2010, we met him in his south side neighborhood. It was near an industrial park, and the factory lights lit up the smoke-filled air with an eerie pink glow, like cotton candy dropped in a rain puddle. It was a quiet winter night with only the faint hum of the night shift in the background. We met Blackbird outside an abandoned bar and he greeted us with a low, soft voice. The streetlamp reflected off his mask, a beak and a pair of unblinking eyes staring us down.

Talking to Blackbird is unsettling—he is hard to see. His attire is all black—black pants, boots, hooded sweatshirt, leather coat. And his mask, a blackbird face, has a short, sharp beak and translucent yellow lenses with a slit eye drawn on. When he speaks you hear his voice, but you can't see his mouth or eyes. It makes reading facial expressions impossible and blending into shadows very easy.

As I learned more about Blackbird, I found him and the Watchman to be unusual teammates. The Watchman was a humble, conservative, suburban family man and Blackbird was a hip bachelor working in the fashion industry.

We set out for a long walk through the side streets and alleyways. After we walked through the industrial area for a while, the Watchman glanced at the clock on his phone, said, "Oh!" and stepped out of earshot to make a call to Geist and Razorhawk, who were also patrolling that night in Minneapolis with a new female recruit: Golden Valkyrie. She was a few days away from moving to upstate New York to join her superhero husband-to-be, Silver Sentinel.

I spoke to Blackbird about all the RLSH I had met until that point, but I kept one ear on the Watchman's conversation. This was a check-in call to make sure everyone was doing OK. The Watchman wasn't sure what to expect in Blackbird and wanted this lifeline in case he turned out to be psychotic. Despite the unblinking bird mask, Blackbird seemed like a nice, albeit fantasy-prone type of guy, and I overheard the Watchman telling Geist that everything was "going OK."

Blackbird led us to a small park where he had been staking out the street in front of the park. The street was poorly lit and close to a main drag of bars and restaurants. There had been several muggings and car break-ins recently, he told us. We hid behind some trees, watching the street and talking quietly for about forty-five minutes. There was no one out. After another loop through the neighborhood, we began to head back to our starting point when we noticed we had drawn the attention of the police. A patrol car crawled by us, then a second slowly passed, and then a third, which parked sharply in front of us. The passenger side window rolled down.

"What's with the masks?" the female officer asked. She gave us a wary smile. I think she expected that we would mention something about a late-night costume party. Her partner, a gruff-looking male, stared at us from behind the wheel.

"Uh, well . . . we're just walking around, keeping an eye on things," the Watchman said, stumbling over his words a little bit. The two officers looked at each other and then quickly got out of the squad car.

"I need you to take the masks off," the male officer said firmly.

"What, really?" Blackbird said.

"Yeah, really," the officer replied, growing irritated. "And I need to see IDs."

The two RLSH cooperated, removing their masks, their sweaty hair a mess. I saw Blackbird's face now. It was always a weird experience to suddenly see a masked face bared.

The male officer took our IDs back to the squad car to puzzle them out. The Watchman had the female officer's ear and started to explain to her the RLSH lifestyle, pointing out his volunteer hours and charity involvement, almost as a plea to recognize his sanity. She was friendly, and although I could tell she was still baffled by the whole superhero concept, she nodded her head and smiled and replied, "Well, Godblessya. Godblessya guys."

Her partner got out of the squad car. He wasn't smiling, but handed our IDs back and returned to the car without a word.

"Hey, can we put our masks back on?" Blackbird asked the female officer.

"Well, sure," she replied, still nodding, still baffled. "Sure, you can do that. Well . . . Godbless yaguys." They drove off.

The Watchman and Blackbird agreed it was a good sign to call it a night. It was the first time the Watchman had been stopped by police on a patrol. As we walked back to the vehicles to part ways, the Watchman and Blackbird discussed meeting up soon to discuss patrol techniques and focus on patrolling one particular area of Milwaukee.

Center Street

After a month of trading e-mails and phone calls, the two RLSH decided they would like to concentrate efforts on patrolling my own backyard, the neighborhood of Riverwest, and specifically an area with a lot of bars and small businesses around the main drag, Center Street.

I was thrilled at the idea of the RLSH patrolling my stomping grounds and curious to see how Riverwest would react. The neighborhood boasts an artistic atmosphere and a strong sense of community, which has always appealed to me and kept me as a resident for fifteen years. But like many of my neighbors, I was perennially frustrated by crime issues. Muggings and robberies are common; rape and murder are less frequent but not unheard of. Could the RLSH actually deter crime?

"Cleaning up a city has to start somewhere," the Watchman told me. "Riverwest is as good a place as any. I've been there, I've walked those streets. Plans are being made, people are coming together. We are setting something into motion that I hope will help, and it begins with Riverwest."

The first Riverwest patrol was set for March 13, 2010, just a little over a year since I had met the Watchman for the first time. I invited the two RLSH over to my house for a pre-patrol meeting at my kitchen table. We reviewed a hand-drawn map I had made of the Center Street area, and then spoke with Metadata, our oracle for the night.

Metadata, I later found out, was an art student from Atlanta, Georgia, who had fallen in love with the RLSH movement and began participating by offering her service as an oracle to anyone going out on patrol. She later developed a costume and performed other RLSH activities like handing out supplies to the homeless. She began dating (and later married) another Atlanta RLSH, the Crimson Fist.* As we spoke to her, she began pulling up crime data maps of the area on her computer and instructed us to call and check in with her at the top of every hour. We left my house and headed out into the night.

Our patrol plan consisted of one fixed point and two revolving pieces. A friend with a warehouse space on Center Street had agreed to let us up to the second floor to use the large picture windows as a surveillance station. Blackbird would take this spot, code-named the Bird's Nest. He remained up there, crouching in the darkness and watching the street with binoculars. Meanwhile, I would join the Watchman on foot, armed with flashlights, to walk a radius of about six blocks around Blackbird's location. Last, my friend Groschopf and two of his friends had agreed to cruise around in Groschopf's car in a slightly larger radius, keeping an eye on us and looking for activity. I dubbed them Team Cthulhu, since Groschopf had named his car after the ancient monster from the horror tales by H. P. Lovecraft. All three of our groups were in contact with each other with walkie-talkies. We set off. The gears of the patrol meshed smoothly.

We didn't encounter much except drunken revelers wandering from bar to bar. The only thing that looked slightly suspicious was two cars parked just off Center Street with two men talking to each other outside while the motors were running. Drug dealers? Loiterers? We staked them out from the shadows of a basketball court across the street, but it was impossible to tell. They drove off and we continued to walk.

---

* "Crimson" has become the clear favorite color among RLSH. In addition to Fist, there is a Crimson Crusader (Milwaukee), Crimson Catalyst (Chicago), Crimson Canuck (Windsor, Ontario), Crimson Tie (Asheville), Crimson Crow (two, in fact—one in San Bernardino, one in Bangor), Crimson Hawk (Tacoma), and Crimson Shadow (Salt Lake City). There is also a RLSV named Crimson Nematode.

After the bars closed, we signed off with Metadata, said good-bye to Team Cthulhu, and began to walk back to my house, where the Watchman and Blackbird's cars were parked. It had been another long night with no action. A jeep stopped in the middle of the street next to us. There was a group of four women in the car, and their interpretation of the Watchman and Blackbird's leather, rubber, and spandex attire was much different from what the duo had in mind.

"Hey! Where's the S and M party?" the driver of the jeep asked. "We want to go get our freak on!"

"Mee-yow, baby, looking kin-ky!" a woman purred from the backseat.

Blackbird shook his head. "No, no, that's not what we're about," the Watchman said. "We're just out here patrolling for crime, making sure people are safe, helping them out if we can . . ."

"Who are you supposed to be?" the driver asked.

"I'm the Watchman."

"Blackbird."

"Well, that is really nice of you guys," the driver said. "That is really cute. You know, I might dress as Wonder Woman some night and join you." The jeep drove off, and the sound of giggling faded into the night.

Over the next year the RLSH patrolled Riverwest at random intervals. I joined them when I could, and if I couldn't, they would report to me how a patrol had gone by e-mail or phone call.

The strangest thing I have to report on this period of patrols is that we found very little to talk about. Crime continued to take place in Riverwest, but despite long patrols in the night, we never encountered it.

The highlight of one patrol was finding a man vomiting into a garbage can in the alley next to a bar. We stopped to see if he was OK, and he stared at us in disbelief, slurring an incoherent question. His buzz-killed friends exited the bar, also confused by the sudden appearance of the superheroes. They told us it was the puking man's bachelor party; they were about to get in a cab with him to get him to his hotel safely and make sure he brushed his teeth in the morning before he got married.

Community Superheroes

I wouldn't say the RLSH were a complete failure in Riverwest, though. Like the larger RLSH community, their shining moments have come from active community participation.

After a posting on a Riverwest Neighborhood Association mailing list, a couple of volunteers from the neighborhood joined the RLSH on foot patrol. One family invited the Watchman and me over for dinner to talk about crime in the neighborhood. The kids were a little disappointed that the Watchman didn't show up in his signature red cowl—he was concerned he might freak out the neighbors. After dinner the husband offered to act as an oracle and extended an invitation for tired RLSH to crash on the couch after a long night of patrolling if necessary.

The Watchman even got his first cry for help, in the form of an e-mail from a frustrated neighbor, which he forwarded to me: "RE: Superheroes! Help my block!" the e-mail read. "I live at [address deleted]. I am becoming increasingly more and more frightened of my neighborhood. The house at [address deleted] contains some shady characters that seem to attract even more shady characters. Could you patrol down my street?"

But like Thanatos's meth house in Vancouver, the issue was attended to before the Watchman could swoop in—I walked by a couple days later and saw that the house had been boarded shut and affixed with orange warning stickers by the city.

The Watchman's reputation grew, and he was getting recognized frequently on the street. One night we walked by a club with a burly bouncer standing outside, his arms folded.

"'Sup, Watchman?" he said, nodding, as we passed him. Another night we were standing at a corner when a man in a passing car yelled, "All right, Watchman! You're my hero, man!" Other times people yelled random things like "Power Rangers!"

Some friends of mine organized a weekend festival of music and workshops and suggested that the RLSH lead a superhero-themed community walk. About a dozen people created homemade superhero costumes and joined the Watchman and Blackbird in walking around Riverwest for an hour.

My favorite moment of the evening was passing a porch full of kids who were waiting in anticipation to see the superheroes. Their parents had read about the walk online and told the young ones to keep an eye out for a parade of superheroes. They were staring bug-eyed when they realized it wasn't a joke.

"They've been waiting out here all night for y'all to pass by," their mom said, laughing and telling her kids to wave at the group.

There were other small victories, too. That winter we tried out a different method for the Watchman's annual Christmas toy drive. We set up the Watchman and Blackbird outside a local business, Fuel Cafe, with a large cardboard box for donations. They had a special guest, Citizen, an RLSH from Chicago, sporting a spandex mask somewhat similar to Spider-Man's except yellow, with a fedora and a brown leather coat. He looked like a cross between something from Marvel's Silver Age and a pool hall hustler.

It was freezing cold, but a couple of media mentions brought in a steady stream of people who donated toys and art supplies for two local charities. At one point, a fire truck pulled up. One of the firefighters jumped off and stared at the Watchman with a serious look on his face.

"I know you're the Watchman, but who are these guys?" he said, pointing to Citizen and Blackbird. Two other firemen headed inside to get coffee. He stuffed a twenty-dollar bill in the collection jar, said, "Keep up the good work," and jumped back onto the fire truck.

Blackbird had another arctic adventure that winter. One morning after a blizzard, I got a call from one of my editors, Jan Christensen of the *Riverwest Currents*.

"I got a job for your superheroes," she told me. Another of her writers had been snowshoeing along the Milwaukee River, one of the borders of Riverwest, when she came across a homeless man. He asked her if she had heard any weather forecasts, wondering if the snow was going to let up.

I looked out my window. Giant drifts of snow were piled up, burying cars and blocking off the streets. It was 18 degrees Fahrenheit outside. I knew the Watchman would be stuck in the suburbs, so I decided to call Blackbird.

That night Blackbird picked me up, blasting the electronic beat of Daft Punk in his car. He was wearing his Blackbird outfit, minus his face mask—he had replaced that with something more weather-sensible: a scarf.

We parked on the street near the river valley. We had come up with some items—a hat and gloves, a jacket, wool socks, and a blanket, and stuffed them into an old duffel bag. We waded through waist-high snowdrifts toward the river. Once we got there, we couldn't find a path so decided to walk on the frozen river. This freaked Blackbird out. "What if we fall in?" he asked, and then we heard a noise in the woods.

"What was that?" he said, and took a pair of night-vision binoculars from his coat pocket. He scanned the coast. It was very quiet—just the breeze and the occasional sound of tree limbs snapping in the cold.

Down the river, we found the camp. Embers were still glowing in the fire pit. A couple of beat-up chairs, a bucket, and a tarp were nearby.

"Maybe he heard us and he's hiding behind a tree," Blackbird suggested. He began to scan the trees with his binoculars.

"Hey, man, if you can hear us, we're not cops or anything! We're just a couple guys from the neighborhood that want to make sure you're OK!" I yelled.

No answer. We left the duffel bag near the campfire, and made the long trek back to Blackbird's car.

Blackbird returned the next day to take a look at things in daylight. When he arrived at the site he discovered not one but three people camping in the woods. They were sitting around the fire pit and he joined them. They told him that this was their base camp; their shelters were buried deeper in the woods. They were thankful for the clothes we had dropped off, but they were proud people. They told Blackbird he was welcome to visit, but that they could fend for themselves.

The camp became a regular stopping point for patrols. Sometimes the RLSH would trek through the woods just to say hi; sometimes they brought supplies like food or insect repellent as a gift.

Meet the Challengers

The Watchman and Blackbird, like RLSH in other cities, experienced a short-lived media blitz in the local press.

Media interpretations, as always, varied drastically. The *Milwaukee Journal Sentinel*'s video portrayed the RLSH as optimistic do-gooders, with encouraging quotes from citizens of Riverwest they met along a patrol one night. The *Onion AV Club*, on the other hand, posted a write-up along the lines of Spider-Man's newspaper editor nemesis J. Jonah Jameson: the post was titled "Will Somebody Please Help Us Unmask This Dopey Riverwest Superhero Guy?"

REALITY BITES

Both Blackbird and the Watchman shot test footage for two possible reality shows produced by the same company. We'll call it Company X. The production company stopped in Milwaukee when it was making its first run at a reality show, intensely trying to win what the Watchman dubbed the "Space Race."

Company X was trying to pitch its show to one cable station, and a competing production company was also trying

Blackbird. PIERRE-ELIE DE PIBRAC

to package an RLSH show and had a different cable station on the line, potentially interested. Once the two companies became aware of each other, they began a mad dash to sign every RLSH they could find to contracts, and began flying around the country to shoot test footage.

Company X stopped in Milwaukee in part because, its spokesperson told me, it liked "the whole angle of you being like Jimmy Olsen and the Watchman being like Superman." The company led me around Milwaukee and got some footage of me on the street, trying to act journalistic and giving some witty quips about how mysterious the Watchman was. Later that night, the crew met up with the Watchman and frog-marched him around a busy, bar-filled intersection over and over to film him interacting with intoxicated revelers.

"I found they kept deciding where we would go and who we would talk to and they kept asking me to say certain things rather than just following me in what I would normally do," the Watchman told me, clearly irked by the session.

Then the Space Race fizzled out. After the intense pursuit of the RLSH, there was a sudden, cold silence, and everyone assumed the show ideas had both been dropped into the shark tank.

Then suddenly Company X was back with a new concept for an RLSH reality show—a house full of superheroes, like the classic reality prototype *The Real World*. Blackbird was drafted for this concept, and flown out with eight other RLSH to an undisclosed location in New Jersey, where Company X had all sorts of unrealities waiting for them.

These included actors hired to act as vandals for the RLSH to pursue. After the RLSH actually caught one of the "vandals" an alarmed producer ran over and admitted that the RLSH had caught an actor and asked that they let him go. Other ploys included trying to hype love interest between the sole female RLSH and two of her "costars" and setting up an obstacle course that would end badly for an obese RLSH.

A pilot episode was created but the show has gone on permanent hiatus.

In any case, the media attracted a stream of new RLSH recruits. There was a teenager from Riverwest who called himself Charade. He looked like a young Barack Obama and wore a glittery Mardi Gras–style mask, a padded vest, and combat boots. A man from the suburbs, Crimson Crusader, wore a red hooded sweatshirt with matching red pants and a domino mask. A leather jacket had his symbol, a red crucifix, on the lapel. One of Blackbird's friends dubbed himself Nightvision and dressed in green spandex, a black mask, and goggles. Rounding out the newbies was Electron, who lived ninety miles away in Madison but occasionally made the trek to join his brethren.

Now six strong, the assembled RLSH were quite a sight marching down the sidewalks of Riverwest. They agreed that they should forge a new team, the first Wisconsin-specific alliance of RLSH.

"The name I keep coming back to and like the most is 'the Challengers,'" the Watchman said in an e-mail he sent out to me and the crew of RLSH. "It has a feel to it like comic book teams like the Avengers or even lesser-known teams like the Outsiders. It makes us sound like the underdogs, and we certainly are. I really like the multiple meanings behind it. One of the main things we are doing is challenging people. We challenge ourselves to be better than we were. We challenge other people to step up and do more. We challenge people to stand against crime, to give more to those in need. We challenge police and politicians to do their part and lead by example. We challenge people to care."

The first official meeting of the Challengers was held in Blackbird's cluttered living room after a patrol, the group wearing their costumes minus the masks. They sat around Blackbird's pool table, discussing future goals.

The team continued to patrol Riverwest and other Milwaukee neighborhoods, did supply handouts to homeless, and participated in charity events. They helped unload pallets for the Veterans for Peace food bank, and participated in a comic book art–themed event, Motionary Comics, that benefited United Way.

I participated in one last event with the team before a hiatus, the Riverwest 24 bicycle race. The Riverwest 24 was set up by neighborhood activists as an endurance challenge for solo riders or teams to complete as many laps of the race route as possible in a twenty-four-hour period. The annual event is also meant to boost community ties and make the streets safer because of the large number of bicyclists—the race has upward of seven hundred participants. In addition to the regular route, bonus checkpoints were set up every hour. These would put the riders through their paces doing odd challenges. The organizers asked me if the local RLSH might be interested.

The Watchman and Blackbird participated two summers in a row. The first year, a group of volunteers lined bicyclists up and had them put together their own superhero costumes, then stand in front of a video camera with the Watchman and Blackbird to answer questions about what it meant to be a superhero.

For the second year, bicyclists had to choose between Path A or Path B. Path A led to Blackbird holding a sign that said "Wrong way, turn around!" Path B led to the Watchman and Crimson Crusader, who made the cyclists recite an oath about staying vigilant for the safety of others, swearing them in as temporary members of the Challengers for the duration of the race.

Some 150 racers were challenged and sworn in at the checkpoint, making it the biggest RLSH team ever assembled, at least for the remaining seven or eight hours of the ride.

BROOKLYN'S EX-SUPERHEROES

Z, also known as Zero (left) and Zimmer, 2010. JAKE BAGGELEY

One of the most iconic stretches of land in Manhattan is Washington Square Park, where a steady stream of tourists, musicians, chess players, and millions of everyday New Yorkers enjoy the urban greenspace.

At night you can sometimes find a seedier element—drug dealers. They hang out around the park benches or hover around the
corners, offering up a smorgasbord of black market substances to
people passing by.

One spring night, a group of drug dealers was sitting around
the park, business as usual, when they were confronted by a posse
of oddly clad concerned citizens. About a dozen RLSH, led by Dark
Guardian, marched into the park following the direction of an
RLSH named Citizen Smoke, who was dressed in street clothes and
acting as a scout.

The RLSH shone flashlights on the drug dealers. Cameraman
made them aware they were being filmed. Dark Guardian held a
bullhorn and shouted through it, ordering the dealers to exit the
park.

"No more drugs in the park! This is not your park!" The RLSH
then stood their ground, staring the dealers down, hoping they
would pack it in and retreat.

The drug dealers might have been confused by the posse in
goggles, masks, combat boots, spandex shirts, and hockey pads, but
they weren't afraid. The dealers shouted back, cursing out the RLSH
and threatening them. One of the dealers lifted his shirt and pointed
to a gun tucked into his waistband. Stress levels were high.

After a tense standoff, the RLSH fell back and retreated from the
park. The Washington Park Mission is described with mixed reactions from its participants. "He had balls, but he didn't have a plan.
It was poorly planned, poorly executed," said Zero, who was along
that night, a guest from out of town. He would soon be moving to
New York himself. "His plan was to go into the park and yell at the
dealers through a bullhorn. That was it. It could have been the pre-
lude to a war. The whole group was nerve-racked."

Dark Guardian's take on the mission was different. "We had two
goals," he told me. "The smaller one was to disrupt drug sales, which
was a success. It was such a success that their higher-ups came by
and yelled at them for letting us disrupt them and steal their spot.
The big goal was to make a statement to them and the public that

selling hard drugs out there will not be tolerated. I feel we had some success."

This was not Dark Guardian's first foray into Washington Square Park security. Dark Guardian was in fact one of the first RLSH to try to create an RLSH "community" or "movement."

Dark Guardian

Dark Guardian started doing safety patrols and handouts to homeless people around 2003. "When I first started, there was nothing like the modern community, just a few people talking about it online. Only a small handful of people were actually doing it."

One of his New York City superhero colleagues was Squeegeeman, a man in a bright spandex outfit who exclaimed, "Squeegeegreetings, citizens! I have squeegee-vowed to fight the crime and grime of New York City!" He even made a mock run for president in 2008, soliciting the public's "squeegee-vote."

DG took the RLSH concept more seriously. One day, while hanging around Washington Square Park, he was inspired to take on a new mission. "I noticed consistent and very open and brazen drug dealing and a lot of dealers. I watched a guy selling drugs as a mother walked by with her kid in a carriage. I started scoping things out and reporting the dealers to police. It hit a point where I decided I had to step in and since then I've been proud of the results."

The new task was an intimidating one. In a video captured by Cameraman, DG boldly confronts a grizzly bear of a drug dealer who towers over him by more than a foot. "Ahh, Carmello. He is definitely a scary guy. He's been arrested over fifty times and even shot in the head, but he is still out there. I'm not going to lie and say I wasn't afraid but I overcame it, stood my ground, and pushed him out of the park," Dark Guardian remembered.

The information on Carmello was provided to DG by the NYPD, when they asked him to come in to a precinct house for a talk. "They appreciate what I do, but they don't want me or anyone else to get hurt," DG told me. He was warned but not deterred.

The Forming of the NYI

Despite having a crew backing him up that spring night, DG often worked alone, or with just a couple other people, like Life and Cameraman from Superheroes Anonymous. In 2009 he began to get some company. The first New York City team—the New York Initiative—was forming.

The NYI name draws a comic book parallel—there is a Marvel Comics story line that crossed over several titles, including *The Avengers*, in which S.H.I.E.L.D. launches a superhero-led team in each state, a program dubbed the "Fifty State Initiative."

RLSH teams had already been attempted, but in most places they shared the common problem of distance—members were located cities, if not states, apart from each other. The NYI was different in that they visualized the core of the group being not only teammates but also roommates. As the talk of the idea got more serious, a small group began planning to move to Brooklyn.

The original NYI roster was a longer list. Nyx had moved from Kansas City to New Jersey to be with her boyfriend, Phantom Zero. She expressed an interest in joining the NYI but pretty shortly stopped going to meetings. Scavenger, of Waterford, Connecticut, signed up but disappeared shortly thereafter.

Death's Head Moth was going to move from Virginia and a young British man named Lionheart was going to move from London, but both of their plans fell through.

New York's resident RLSH, Dark Guardian, attended the first NYI meeting, but he soon had a falling out with the group. "We just had different ideas and opinions on some things," he told me, referring to arguments over patrol methodology and personal drama.

RLSH have a pretty rocky history of getting along together, which seems strange at first given the very specific thing they have in common. But the movement attracts people with strong personalities, and egos often clash, sometimes causing dramatic exits over the smallest details.

They had some other support. Wolf, a Toronto detective and founder of Wolf's Detective Agency, would come down to visit, and

Victim, the gadgeteer from Seattle, began working on armor for the group; he mailed them samples.

But essentially the group started off as a gang of four—Zero, who moved to the city from Philadelphia; two of his friends from Detroit, Lucid and Tsaf; and Zimmer, the RLSH from Austin, Texas, whom I first met at SA3.

The quartet moved to a tiny apartment in a fairly rough-around-the-edges neighborhood in Brooklyn named Bushwick, close to another neighborhood called Bedford-Stuyvesant (Bed-Stuy for short). This small apartment was home to a big idea—a group of people who would live and work together and dedicate their spare time to fighting crime.

Z, also known as Zero

When I first established contact with Zero he was calling himself simply by the letter Z. The Z stood for Zero, he told me, and explained this was his interpretation of having your feet on the ground—neither plus nor minus, just at that neutral integer. He views the numeral zero as the symbol of a Zen existence.

He had shortened the word to one letter because there was an RLSH in Michigan already using the name Zero. This Zero was, by all evidence, mentally disturbed. He had posted a lot of insults and threats, including a threat to a RLSV, saying he was going to drink his blood. Z didn't want anyone confusing the two Zeros.

After the Michigan Zero changed his name to Eclipse, Z fleshed out his name to the full four-letter word. And for some it really was a four-letter word. Z had built a reputation as a sharp-tongued, argumentative, tough-toned person who seemed more critical than supportive of the RLSH.*

---

* When Z switched to Zero he handed his Z persona on to a friend in Indiana. "Being Z isn't about being a superhero," the new Z told me in a tone consistent with his predecessor's. "It's not about tights and being recognized for your deeds. It's about making a difference, whether people notice or not."

"I can be abrasive. I can be a complete dickhead when I'm trying to get a point across. That doesn't discount what I'm saying."

I would see Zero's visage, decked out in gear I would describe as steampunk Batman, pop up on the RLSH forums and MySpace, berating others and offering advice on a regular basis. His eyes squinted behind a modified gas mask, surrounded by mismatched black body armor. He described his gear as a "poor man's Iron Man suit." It was an intimidating look.

He had a strong dislike for RLSH seeking media attention and, at first, refused to speak to media. His first response to a query from me was, "Normally I wouldn't even be talking to you because I think media—you either have to accompany me on a mission or do something with a charity, but I know you're writing a book and I know that's more important than some guy writing a newspaper article. I think it's important that you see some of the fakes that exist inside of this community."

Zero says he didn't like the RLSH concept in general from the beginning. "I don't really relate to the whole superhero thing. I rarely wear the mask," he told me. He would later abandon the mask for good. He was more inspired by an idea to start an altruistic version of something like Fight Club, he told me. He wanted to move away from the spandex-clad RLSH imagery.

"I used to straight up hate the [RLSH] term," Zero told me. "I'm still uncomfortable with it as it refers to the self as both 'super' and 'hero.' The term has caused some massive problems and misunderstandings."

Along with his colleague Night Bug (of San Francisco) he developed an alternate term to RLSH: X-ALT. They derived the term from Andrea Kuszewski's article on "Xtreme Altruists."

"I think that by offering a new term to those who want to work parallel to the RLSH without being pigeonholed by it, we can open a door to people interested in the work but not all the bells and whistles," Zero explained. The term caught on, and soon newcomers to the movement found they had the choice of referring to themselves as "RLSH" or "X-ALT."

Zimmer

Like his teammate Zero, Zimmer also says his biggest influence isn't the comic book world; he relates more to the *Matrix* films. In Austin he studied science and technology, writing occasional online articles on new inventions and trends. His spandex shirt is gray and has the binary code for the letter *Z* rolling down one side of the front. His interests include practicing parkour, the activity of running and jumping around urban structures, and computer hacking.

"I think computer hackers probably have a lot in common with the RLSH, but probably not everyone in this community sees that." Zimmer has attended a couple of hacking conventions, including one in Austria, where he gave a presentation on RLSH.

Zimmer is also unique in that he is one of the first openly gay RLSH, and he says this contributes to certain aspects of his RLSH life. Zimmer is his real first name, and he doesn't wear a mask to conceal his identity because it's too much like "hiding in the closet."

He says one of his influences is the Lavender Panthers, a group of twenty or so people who patrolled San Francisco in the early 1970s, armed with chains and billy clubs. They cruised around the bars looking to protect people from gay bashers. The group was founded by Reverend Ray Broshears after he was severely beaten outside his gay mission center. In Austin, Zimmer had helped form a team called the Lone Star Defenders and had become president of the Heroes Network forum, a key online resource and hangout spot for RLSH.

Like Zero, Zimmer's strong personality sometimes brought him into contention with his RLSH colleagues. They related on one level, but there was also a steady stream of conflict.

I talked to Zero and Zimmer several times and then asked about spending a few days in Brooklyn. Zero sent me a text: "I talked to everyone, and you're clear to stay here at the NYI apartment. Not sure how you'll keep up with us, though. We patrol on longboards." I looked at an old skateboard-inflicted scar on my knee and thought the text over.

A month later, I was at the airport to catch a plane to New York. The check-in attendant smirked at me. "Did you make this luggage yourself, sir?"

"I did," I admitted, looking down at a large cardboard box with two holes punched in the top and an old purse handle threaded between them. "There's a big skateboard inside," I told her.

"Oh, my," she said. "You be careful now!"

Arrival at NYI Headquarters

It was hot, steamy, and crowded in New York, and I made my way on the subway to my stop. I got off at Broadway Street in Bushwick, a neighborhood with a mixed reputation—some parts of the neighborhood had seen renewal, but this stretch on the border of Bushwick and Bed-Stuy was pretty gritty.

I walked down from the subway platform into a crowded street of pawnshops, bodegas, laundromats, barber shops, and doughnut shops. I walked through the noisy, graffiti-covered streets until I was standing in front of a towering apartment building.

After we exchanged some texts, Zimmer arrived and led me up several flights of stairs until we arrived at the NYI HQ. The apartment held a tiny kitchen and bathroom, a small living room, and three bedrooms. Tsaf had her own bedroom, and so did Zimmer. His room was furnished with a desk stacked with piles of books on technology and computer programming. Lucid and Zero shared a room, each with a modest foam mattress on the floor. Lucid was apparently rarely around, often gone a week or more at a time. They also had a punching bag and weight set wedged in a corner of the room.

A fifth resident of the apartment was Lucy, a cat the team had found and rescued while out on patrol. When they found her she was barely alive, but she was now healthy, purring, and rubbing against a pile of body armor.

The living room of the apartment was dedicated to the NYI and impressed upon me how serious the lifestyle was to them. A workbench set up to work on masks and gear was covered with tools, leather, pads, and other materials. There was a large dry-erase board dedicated to keeping track of NYI goals. Behind the workbench was a map of the subway system and a mirror, which had a handwritten note taped to it. It read, "What can be broken, must be broken."

On the workbench was a large box that had been shipped to them by Victim. He had sent them a selection of sample squares of polycarbonate plastic, instructing them to test various weapons against them to see how effective they might be in body armor.

"I had to carry that thing ten blocks from the post office," Zimmer told me. He showed me one of the squares on the workbench that had a couple of dents in it—the NYI had attacked it with knives, a hammer, and various blunt instruments.

Shelves throughout the room held a supply of gear—protective arm gauntlets, walkie-talkies, flashlights, batons, binoculars, a decorative battle-ax, volumes of books on martial arts and crime fighting. Zero's old mask, cloth covered in safety pins, was draped over a foam mannequin head and stared at me with blank eyes. A row of black, upside-down roses was tacked around the perimeter of the room as a morbid decoration. A sole window looked down to a small, beat-up courtyard between apartment buildings.

Later Zero would show off the NYI's weapon collection in more detail. He handed me a collection of blunt-force weapons from an umbrella stand of pain—a cane and a couple of ax handles with the ends wrapped in duct tape that could be used as clubs. He showed me some stun knuckles, which zapped loudly, intimidating with their high voltage. He also had some spiky medieval-looking hand guards, a Chinese import that looked like something a Mongolian warlord would probably brawl in.

Despite the ferocity of this collection, none of the armory ever made it out of the apartment building, I was told. New York has very strict weapons laws and almost nothing in the NYI's collection was street legal. Not wanting to get charged, they decided to leave the weapons at home and use strategy and martial arts training instead.

Zimmer led me up to the roof of the building, where some of this training took place. The rooftop looked like a comic book scene, with the lights of Manhattan visible in the distance. Up here the group held sparring sessions, running, jumping, kicking, and punching at each other to hone their skills. Zimmer also used the rooftop to practice parkour.

The next morning I met Tsaf briefly. She was on her way to work.

"I'm glad you met her," Zimmer joked later in the day. "I was worried you were going to start thinking I made her up."

Tsaf had a Zen-like, reflective quality to her, and I could tell she was a quiet person who enjoyed her privacy. She was a woman of few words. When I asked her what her life was like prior to the NYI, for example, she had a one-word answer: "preparation." I later found that her name was an acronym, which stood for The Silent And Forgotten, the people she wanted to stand up for and help. She pronounces the name "saff."

In the afternoon, Zimmer and I were on our laptops, trying to lift a signal in the hallway outside the apartment, when Zero came home. There were no pictures of him without his mask at that point. I had spoken to him on the phone, and so I was very curious about what his face might look like. I was imagining some horrible scar from a knife fight, or maybe tribal tattoos. One RLSV, Lord Malignance, had speculated that he probably had filed his teeth into fangs. But he seemed like a normal enough guy. He was tall, athletic, carrying his longboard with him. When he's not at his day job or leading NYI patrols and missions, he concentrates on creating art, writing, and recording music.

The previous day Zimmer had taken me to one of his favorite hangout spots, a hacker collective with a warehouse space called NYC Resistor. Their goal is "to share knowledge, hack on projects together, and build community," according to their website.

When we were leaving the space, someone told us we should return the next evening to attend their inaugural "Show and Tell" night. We made the impromptu decision to head over there with

Zero. About fifteen people had gathered, showing off contraptions like robotic arms, a self-balancing unicycle, and a portable UV light. Then Zimmer took the stage and explained who the NYI was and demonstrated one of his signature tech inventions, the Northstar. This nonlethal device consists of a powerful cluster of LED lights attached to his chest with backpack straps. Wires lead to a large battery inside the backpack. A flip of the switch can illuminate the sky or temporarily blind a criminal. The backpack also contained potentially useful items like a first aid kit, CPR mask, and handcuffs. The audience was very curious and somewhat puzzled. Then Zimmer called Zero up.

Zero took the stage. "Uh . . . hi," he said, opening up a metal suitcase-shaped box, pulling out his arm gauntlets and strapping them on. "These are stainless steel," he said, clanging them together for effect. "And these straps are actually truck ties." Then he pulled his most recently created mask from the box. It was metal and black with a zigzagged, sharp-toothed smile painted on it, like a cartoon shark. White dots formed a pattern around the rest of the face, and strings of wound electrical tape hung like dreadlocks from the top. Zero turned on a bright LED light attached to the side of the mask and shone it onto the audience. The mask resembled the alien in the movie *Predator*, which one audience member noted, saying, "Is there a missile launcher built into your shoulder, like in *Predator*?"

Zero answered some questions from the curious audience about the NYI. One person even approached us after the show and tell was over to ask if he could sign up for tech support, carefully writing down his e-mail address.

Very shortly after we stepped off the subway in Bushwick, about a block from the NYI's apartment building, a police squad car rolled around the corner and came to an abrupt stop next to us.

"What are you doing?" was the first thing one of the officers asked us as he climbed out of the squad car. He looked at us suspiciously, then instructed Zero to put the metal case with his gear in it on the hood of the squad car and open it slowly.

"What's this?" the officer asked, holding up a stainless steel arm gauntlet. He was white and his partner was Middle Eastern.

"Skateboard pads," Zero said nonchalantly, as if the officer was boring him.

The officer then asked for our IDs. Addressing the three of us, he said, "Let me ask ya—youse guys got any drugs on ya?"

We told him we didn't. The officer looked closely at me as he was collecting IDs. I think he was trying to see if my eyes were bloodshot or dilated.

"I got a buddy that looks just like you," he said turning to get in the squad car. "That guy loved to smoke weed."

"OK," I said, glancing at Zero and Zimmer. I wasn't sure what the insinuation was. There were a couple minutes of silence while the officer was running our IDs, but then his partner continued the line of talking.

"The reason we're asking," he told us, "is the only reason people of your . . . uh . . . skin color come into this neighborhood is to buy drugs."

"We live here," said Zero impatiently. "We live a block away."

"What?" the officer said incredulously as his partner rejoined him, handing back our IDs.

"In fact, we're thinking of starting something like a community block watch or safety patrol," Zimmer added.

"Block watch!" the white officer said, and let out a hearty guffaw.

His partner smiled. "Nah, furgedaboudit," he said, sobering up. He looked at us intently. "Look, the guys in this neighborhood will shoot you and no one will ever know who did it. There's a strong no snitching rule on the streets here. You'll be shot dead and that will be that."

Zero and Zimmer nodded their heads but didn't say anything.

In fact, the NYI had developed a distrust of police. While careful not to paint the entire NYPD in a broad stroke, Zero pointed me in the direction of a recent series of reports in the *Village Voice* that reported on NYPD officers being pressured to not record crime data accurately. Tapes were being secretly recorded by an officer in the 81st Precinct in Bed-Stuy, not far from the NYI HQ.

"[The tapes] reveal that precinct bosses threaten street cops if they don't make their quotas of arrests and stop-and-frisks, but also tell them to not take certain robbery reports in order to manipulate crime statistics," the report said.

The team had personally experienced being ignored by officers when they tried to report a hit-and-run. The officers drove off, oblivious. The NYI had come to the conclusion that the police couldn't be trusted to respond in Bushwick.

The police, after finding that we weren't in fact holding drugs, let us go, but not before issuing further warnings, telling us to stay off the streets at night. The talk from the police brought my level of nervousness up a notch, because the plan for that evening was to get out on the streets of Bushwick to go on what the NYI calls a "bait patrol."

The Bait Patrol

Later that night I was sitting in the living room while Zero worked over the punching bag in his room. "Ever hear these guys?" he asked, indicating his stereo. "They're called 50 Tons of Black Terror." He bounced from foot to foot, releasing a volley of jabs and crosses on the heavy bag. Left! Right! Left, left! Right! He ducked and wove and punched some more. He hit the bag so hard that the session left deep marks on his hands.

After finishing his punching session, Zero sat down across from me and began strapping on his arm and leg braces and a crude protective apron of butcher mail under a brown leather vest. I asked what he feels when he gears up like this before a patrol.

"It depends who is around. I know you've seen people gear up like this before. It's almost a holy, sacred feeling to me. We all prepare for patrol in our own ways," he told me.

Zimmer was putting together his gear and getting into his spandex Zimmer shirt. He had black jeans with knee pads sewn in, calf-high canvas shoes, and the Northstar.

Tsaf was in her room meditating, Zero told me. Soon she would be carefully applying makeup and getting into a slinky dress and opera gloves—tonight she would be the bait.

The bait patrol is a controversial patrolling technique that the NYI embraced as a way of flushing muggers, rapists, and gay bashers out of the shadows. One of the NYI members, usually Tsaf wearing a skirt and carrying a large but empty purse, acts as the bait. They walk on a predetermined route trying to look natural and oblivious but staying in contact with the rest of the team. Tsaf "focuses on staying alert," she told me, while a second person follows the bait on foot, about a block behind. The other members cruise around in front and back of the bait on longboards.

Longboards are heavy-duty skateboards, designed not for tricks but for high-speed cruising. The NYI found them useful not just for covering more ground at a faster pace but also for their stealth and dual makeshift use as a weapon—a shield for defense, a heavy club for offense.

The team moves the bait around, zooming around on the longboards, checking in with their walkie-talkies. If an assailant takes the bait, the team moves in to make a citizen's arrest.

"Bait patrol is not a common, every-patrol type of tactic," Zero explained to me. "We don't use it to drum up problems just to have something to do. It's a specific tactic for areas where there have been specific patterns of crime—muggings, sexual assault—that we tailor the operation to fit."

I had brought my recently purchased longboard to join the NYI, but a series of technical problems made the patrol short-lived.

Things were already tense when we left the NYI's apartment. Lucid had been out of contact for days and wasn't present, but it was decided that the bait patrol would go on without him. Zero and I took off on our boards with Tsaf a block behind us, strolling slowly, then Zimmer. Shortly into the patrol, Zero and I took a sharp turn and I stopped for a moment. The board had just felt too stiff to make the turn on the narrow Brooklyn street. Zero saw that I had stopped and skated over.

"What's wrong?" he asked, irritated.

"I—the board took that turn too stiffly," I said.

Zero grabbed the truck of the wheels on the front of the board. "These are too tight," he said, frowning. He got on his phone.

"Zimmer, I need you. This fuckin' guy here, his trucks are too tight on his board. I need you to go back to the apartment and get me a pair of pliers." Tsaf caught up with us. There was awkward silence.

A few minutes later Zimmer showed up. He was angry and everyone seemed tense. "You need to be sure your equipment is in working order before you go on patrol," he told me. Zero cranked on the truck and handed me back the board.

"Ride ahead and try it," he said. I jumped on the board and rode down the block and back.

"Yeah, OK," I said. I was feeling pretty stressed out.

We started moving again, but then there was technical trouble with the phones—Zero and Tsaf couldn't hear each other.

Zero let out a frustrated sigh. "Fuck this. That's it, I'm calling it."

He waited until Tsaf and Zimmer caught up. "I'm calling it," he told them. "We're having too many issues." Tsaf nodded and headed back to the apartment, a couple blocks away. Zimmer and Zero stood on the corner, quietly contemplating things.

"We should . . . let's go up to Broadway and patrol," Zimmer suggested.

"No. That wasn't the plan. We're not prepared for that."

"Well, I'm going to go. I want to patrol tonight." Zero watched him walk off and shook his head. He looked at me.

"Sorry about that, man. I wish it wouldn't have happened like that. I really wanted to show you what we do. I mean, how do you write that up?"

I told him that I actually appreciated him calling off the bait patrol if he felt things weren't in order.

"OK," he said. "You hungry? I can cook up some burgers."

We headed up to the NYI kitchen. Zero grabbed a frying pan and Tsaf walked into the room.

"Where's Zimmer?" she asked.

"He got all pissed off and headed down the street."

"He shouldn't patrol by himself."

"I can't tell him what to do."

Hanging Out in Williamsburg

The next day Zero seemed in a much better mood and we spent most of the day longboarding around Brooklyn, running errands. Zero was one of the most complicated individuals I met in my journeys. He is hard to describe in definitive terms. Sometimes he came across as an alpha male who barked orders and slammed people who disagreed with him. Other times he seemed like a highly meditative philosopher who envisioned a revolution of people taking care of each other.

And when we got on an empty subway car and he crooned a few bars of "Dreamer" by Supertramp, he seemed like a normal, carefree guy.

"That song's been stuck in my head all day," he told me as the subway rolled into Williamsburg.

We stopped at his eye doctor so he could get new lenses, ate at a hot dog stand, and visited the skate shop, where he shopped for longboard upgrades. I took a board he recommended out for a test drive. We also stopped by his day job. I was surprised to find that he didn't work as a tattoo artist or a motorcycle mechanic but as a clerk at a trendy clothing store. He said hi to his coworkers.

The day was late so we headed to the NYI's unofficial hangout spot—a bar in Williamsburg (they asked me not to name it) where Lucid worked security. Lucid has a strong build and a lot of tattoos but a very peaceful personality. He sat at the door of the bar, one eye on a book he was reading, *Born to Run* by Christopher McDougall, in which the author learns secrets of long-distance running from the Tarahumara Indians.

Zero and I caught a band and played pool, then he asked if I wanted to go out for a ride on the boards. We skated around back streets and through a park. Suddenly we spotted a young woman, alone, stumbling along clumsily in her high-heeled shoes. Zero watched her for a second.

"Let's do an impromptu bait patrol. I'll skate way ahead and you hang back behind her. When you see me turn, hold up your hand and give a thumbs-up so I know everything is OK." He took off, and I cruised lazily. We kept track of the woman for several blocks before we saw her get safely onto a bus.

Meeting in Washington Square Park

My last day in town I was invited to a Sunday afternoon meeting with Dark Guardian during the day at his long-time battleground, Washington Square Park. It was also a sort of peace offering—he had extended the invitation to the NYI as well. He would soon put his differences and past drama aside and join up with the team.

Zimmer showed up shortly after I did and shook hands with Dark Guardian underneath Washington Square Arch. Also joining us was a friend of DG who had yet to pick out a cool code name or flashy gear, and a new RLSH from New Jersey who had named himself the Conundrum. The Conundrum was sporting jeans and a Bad Religion T-shirt for the meeting, but his RLSH costume consisted of a gray hooded sweatshirt that was modified to zip over his entire head, with two bulbous goggles installed over the eyes, giving him the appearance of a five-foot-five man-frog.

The Conundrum, or "Conor Drums"* as he sometimes called himself, was a med student and was drawn to the unique activist

---

* Such aliases are common among RLSH, especially on places like Facebook, where hero names like Miss Fit and Rock N Roll are interpreted as "Missy Fitzgerald" and "Roxanne Roel."

aspect of the RLSH. "I believe we can turn our publicity stunts into downright global action," he optimistically stated on his MySpace profile.

Dark Guardian led the informal meeting, talking about patrol techniques and ideas for charity and humanitarian efforts. He talked about his history with the park.

After people began to split, Dark Guardian invited Zimmer, the Conundrum, and me out to lunch at a diner near the park. I was scheduled to depart NYC the next morning. We sat and talked about various RLSH and the Conundrum broke down the nutritional value of pizza for us.

At this point, Dark Guardian had an optimistic energy about RLSH working together to try to make a difference. Soon, however, a new Seattle superhero would become a divisive figure in the movement and become the target of sharp criticisms from Dark Guardian.

12

MR. JONES AND ME

Phoenix Jones watches a suspect as I watch Phoenix Jones in the background.
LUCIEN KNUTESON

After my visit with Thanatos in Vancouver, I had hopped on a Greyhound with the Irishman to take a trip to Seattle and see if there was any good material down there. We walked and drove around the area by the Pike Place Market for an hour or two. It was completely uneventful, and tired from our long week in Vancouver, we soon decided to retire to one of the Irishman's secret hideouts—an Irish pub, of course—to enjoy a pint of Guinness.

There were other Seattle RLSH at that point—Black Knight, White Baron, and Mr. Ravenblade. I tried to contact them but they were retired, on hiatus, or otherwise unavailable. While I was in town I e-mailed Seattle Police Department spokesman Detective Mark Jamieson. There were a couple of incidents I wanted to ask him about.

In a blog entry, Black Knight wrote about how he had intervened in a fight between a couple guys fighting outside a bar (a common Seattle pastime, I was to find out) when the fighters teamed up and attacked him, ripping off his helmet and kicking him. Black Knight had mentioned that a witness had called 9-1-1.

In another entry, written by Mr. Ravenblade, it was mentioned that police had encountered Black Knight, White Baron, and Mr. Ravenblade while on patrol and told them to remove their masks. I asked Detective Jamieson if he had any record of these events and what his take on them was.

He responded that he had no record of the RLSH. "I cannot locate any contact between Seattle police and [the RLSH]," Detective Jamieson stated. "I think the advice the group was given by the police, if it is in fact true, is good advice and should be heeded. One doesn't need to wear a costume or a mask to do the right thing. In fact, walking around in a mask will probably generate a lot of calls to 9-1-1. It is best to leave the crime fighting to the police."

Detective Jamieson was going to hear a lot more about masked men and calls to 9-1-1 soon enough. In November 2010, a costumed crime fighter named Phoenix Jones and his crew, the Rain City Superhero Movement (RCSM) appeared, seemingly out of nowhere.

In a report for a Seattle website, Phoenix Jones, a young African American man, announced that he was leader of the RCSM, which he claimed was nine members strong. They had names like Buster Doe and Red Dragon. Jones's costume at that point was very low budget—a ski mask with a fedora, gray tights, and a cape.

Despite his simple costume, there was something about him that captivated the media. Jones is very charismatic, sometimes funny, sometimes cocky. There is a certain quality to his cockiness that reminds me of Muhammad Ali, who would make bold claims and hurl insults, but always with a wink.

Jones was in top physical shape, and he was later revealed to be an experienced mixed martial arts fighter and a comic book fan. He cited Nightwing as his favorite comic book hero, but Jones's reveling in media soon drew comparisons to another DC comic superhero by disgruntled RLSH: Booster Gold. That character was invented in 1986 and his back story is that he comes from the twenty-fifth century, where he steals artifacts from a superhero museum and travels back to the twentieth century to make himself into a corporate, attention-hungry superhero who cashes in on his knowledge of history.

Like the time-traveling superhero, Phoenix Jones seemed to appear out of thin air and quickly became a perpetual source of stories, both in the media and in the Internet whisperings of various RLSH forums and social networking sites. Some of these stories were wild and exciting. Some were truly oddball.

New reports appeared every other week. Seattle news reported that Phoenix Jones got his nose broken in a fight. Video showed Phoenix Jones stopping a car break-in and placing the perp under citizen's arrest. Phoenix Jones claims that he was stabbed and even shot. Fellow Seattle RLSH Sky Man shared a story of how Phoenix Jones invited him to his headquarters (his house) but blindfolded him on the way there. Once they arrived, the duo enjoyed a snack of pudding.*

Jones claimed to have a successful run confiscating crack pipes and busting someone at a club with drugs. He taped a public service announcement for the Game Show Network. And after the film *Super* was released, Phoenix Jones met comedian Rainn Wilson, star of the film, for coffee. Afterward, in the parking lot, Jones handed Wilson his Taser and told him to zap him with it to show off his ability to "take a tase."

---

* "With sprinkles!" Sky Man reported enthusiastically.

The stories wouldn't stop.

Reception from the already established RLSH community was very divided. Long debates on his merits raged on Internet forums. Some said he was a liar, fabricating and exaggerating his street adventures. Others complained about his messages typed out in ALL CAPS. This anti-Phoenix camp argued that Phoenix Jones and his antics were bad for the RLSH in general. The pro-Phoenix constituency said this squawking was sour grapes and professional jealousy.

Phoenix himself battled back, claiming he was the only actual crime fighter out there and that his critics were merely "REAL LIFE SANDWICH HANDLERS." He refused to call himself an RLSH, rejecting that label and replacing it with his own RCSM tag. He refers to other RLSH he is fond of as "supers."

He was hated by some, inspiring to others, and viewed with a neutral caution by many.

Mr. Ravenblade, another Seattle RLSH who dressed in the typical ninja-in-a-trench-coat motif, began a weird and obsessive battle trying to bring ruin to Phoenix Jones. He claimed Jones was dangerous, "with a criminal record." His "record" turned out to be traffic violations and suspended license charges. Becoming more incensed, Ravenblade drafted "An Open Letter to Phoenix Jones, Hero in Training," on his blog, hoping to rally more RLSH to his anti-platform with a thousand-word screed.

"A lot of the top respected members of the RLSH community that has existed for years without you—both in Seattle and internationally around the world—are not happy at some of your actions and the claims of affiliation you have made that have in turn damaged our collective reputations. We have worked hard to earn our reputations, so it is understandable we are protective of them as it allows us to do greater good in our communities."

Other RLSH dismissed Mr. Ravenblade's claims. "You don't speak for the community, you speak for yourself," Nyx shot back in response to Ravenblade's open letter.

The word-count war between Mr. Ravenblade and Phoenix Jones moved to a new level. Ravenblade claimed Jones called him "multiple times through an unknown number and made threats about my physical safety at 1 AM." Ravenblade further claimed that Jones later drove by his house and made a threatening pointing gesture at him. Jones denied it. This led to a rather ridiculous superhero story line—Ravenblade got a lawyer and went through the process of having a restraining order placed, forcing the two costume-clad Seattleites to stay five hundred feet away from each other.

"What the hell is going on in Seattle?" I wondered, my eyes blurry from reading pages and pages of angry online rants and forum debates. I decided it was time to call Phoenix Jones and see if I could figure out who he was.

Shortly after his explosive appearance I did a phone interview with him, which I transcribed for my *Heroes in the Night* blog. In the interview he seemed taken aback by the negative RLSH reaction. During the interview he revealed his "origin story" to me. One thing he has been criticized for is changing the details of this story in different interviews.

"I was at a water park in my hometown, and someone broke into my car—there was glass all over the ground," Phoenix explained in the version he told me. "My son fell into it and cut his knee. I was telling everyone to call 9-1-1, but everyone just stood there and stared. One guy even started recording it for YouTube or something. And I was like—what is this? Why does the world suck?"

Enraged by this incident, and another in which Jones claimed a friend of his was badly beaten up outside a club the following week, he became inspired to become a ski mask–clad vigilante.

After my interview, I would occasionally blog on news out of Seattle, but I knew if I wanted to get the real scoop, I'd have to take a trip to Seattle and hit the streets with Phoenix in person. I began planning a trip, coordinating with someone who had stepped in as Jones's volunteer media booking agent/publicist: Peter Tangen.

Tangen wasn't sure of what to make of Jones at first and was cautiously skeptical. He began to change his mind as he spoke with him more and saw him as a force who could grab attention and share the message of the RLSH. Tangen began a hectic schedule of handling media requests and spinning them in a positive direction, talking to media around the world while stuck in Los Angeles traffic jams and in between shuttling around Hollywood for photo shoots.

Although he continued to promote other RLSH with the same passion he had brought to his Real Life Super Hero Project, some RLSH, the very people he had tirelessly supported, turned their cape-clad backs on him. They had begun to despise Phoenix Jones and his rising star so much that any of his allies were considered bad company.

As my departure to the Pacific Northwest approached, I arranged a talk with Jones on the phone.

"I think you're going to be here just in time, brother!" he told me excitedly. "We've got some intel on a place that we think is a meth lab. We're going to get a camera crew and bust into it live on camera if it checks out, and place them under citizen's arrest. I hope you're here when we go through with that!"

I hung up the phone, dazed. What had I gotten myself into now?

Arrival in Rain City

On Friday, October 7, 2011, my train was pulling into Seattle from Portland, where I had spent a few days. My phone started ringing with a "Restricted ID." I knew it was none other than Phoenix Jones. But when I answered the phone, there was a child's voice on the line.

"Hi . . . Tea . . . hi," the voice said. I heard talking in the background and then Jones was on the line. "Hey, that was my son! I wanted him to say hi to you!"

We talked briefly about meeting up for a patrol in the evening and decided to touch base again after I checked in with my friend in West Seattle where I was crashing. According to Phoenix, it had already been an action-packed week for him. The previous night he had been on patrol, keeping an eye on the Occupy Seattle protestors. He had heard police would be intervening and pepper-spraying the protestors so he had prepared a pepper spray "antidote" he could give them. Along the way, he claims he ran into what might have been anarchist Black Bloc members smashing a storefront window, so he chased them off. He told me his meth lab–crashing idea had fallen through.

I looked out the train window and thought about Phoenix Jones. And his son.

I found my friend's house and was picked up later that night by Phoenix Jones and his teammate, Mist. Jones was wearing a baseball cap and sweatshirt over his supersuit, a somewhat comical disguise on top of a disguise so he couldn't be identified while driving.

Jones had quickly traded in his gray tights, ski mask, and fedora for a more elaborate black and gold rubber suit, made by a company called Xtreme Design FX. This is the same company that made the Watchman's signature red rubber cowl and leather gloves. It fit him well except the neck was stiff and limited his ability to turn his head. He wore a bulletproof vest underneath the rubber and added a utility belt and running shoes. His eyes peered back and forth from the triangular eyeholes, and a goatee jutted out the bottom of the mask. Jones says the costume and additional gear cost him about $7,000.

While I was planning to come to Seattle, Phoenix had asked me to measure from my armpit to the bottom of my torso so he could secure a bulletproof vest for me. He handed it to me in the car and I found it fit surprisingly well, even comfortably.

We headed over to the University District, where his teammates Ghost and Pitch Black joined us. Jones leads a very ethnically diverse team. Mist is a tall, thin African American man with a mask split in half, the left side white, the right side blue. Pitch Black is a shorter African American man in a common RLSH outfit—a black mask, fedora, and trench coat, the "Rorschach look." Ghost is a heavy Hispanic man with the lower part of a ski mask, hooded sweatshirt, and leather jacket. Other team members—white, African American, and Hispanic—were not available for tonight's patrol.

Phoenix lamented the lack of more of his team; many of them were out due to illness, he said. Phoenix blamed this plague on long hours patrolling and the wet Seattle weather. "We've been pushing too hard," he admitted.

Not in superhero gear, but also along for the patrol, were Seattle writer A. J. Roberts and videographer Ryan McNamee.

The patrol was a long night of walking around, and somewhat uneventful, but it gave me a chance to see Phoenix in a positive light. In these bright moments, I could see the appeal of the superhero—Phoenix can be very charismatic, friendly, and funny. People are genuinely excited to see him. He is polite to women and he calls guys "brother." He shakes hands, poses for pictures, and laughs off insults. He has a good rapport with people he talks to on the street and with his teammates—they clearly have established a superhero brotherhood. And he is popular. Too popular to effectively move down the street in some spots.

In the crowded U-District he was mobbed for pictures everywhere he went, with constant high fives and fist bumps and people telling him to keep up the good work. He was so mobbed with picture requests that the patrol often was put on hold for long minutes while Jones posed for pictures with everyone and their mothers.

From the U-District we headed to a neighborhood named Belltown, where Phoenix has claimed some success in breaking up fights and stopping crime, including one of his most recent capers—stopping a man from stealing a party bus.

We did encounter a hot dog vendor who was glad to see the superheroes. He told me that Jones and company had scared off a couple of would-be muggers who targeted him. He told them he was so grateful that the next time he saw them, he was issuing the whole team VIP cards that would grant them free access to hot dogs at any of the stands he owned.

"Free hot dogs all the time for you!" he shouted after us as we continued the patrol.

The team stopped to stare down some people they thought were suspicious and selling drugs. They said they encountered some people in the same area whom they were sure had been hiding drugs in their mouths when they confronted them.

"Well, were they masticating?" Mist asked them.

"What!" Phoenix Jones replied.

"It means to chew. Were they chewing?" Mist said in a muffled voice through his mask.

"No," Jones said.

"Doesn't the moisture ruin it?" Pitch Black asked.

"Not if they . . ." Mist began.

"Coated in wax! They got it coated in wax," Jones exclaimed, interrupting.

"Or shrink wrap," Mist guessed.

"They seemed to be talking normally for having crack in their mouths, but I guess you can be an expert on anything," Jones declared, then turned his attention back to the man they thought was suspicious across the street.

"Hey! What's going on over there!" The man stared at them, dismissed them, and kept walking.

There was a heavy police presence in Belltown. Police crawled through the streets in an organized grid of squad cars when the bars closed, leaving no area unwatched. "We've been down here before and there's been no cops, but they're everywhere tonight," Jones observed.

Like other crime-patrolling superheroes, Jones received mixed reactions from police. Some officers have posed for pictures with him or given him the thumbs-up. Others, Jones told me, have gone out of their way to make life more difficult for him. As the media whirlwind rushed in, Detective Mark Jamieson was now deluged with dozens of interview requests to talk about Seattle's superheroes. He often appeared, exasperated, in news clips warning Jones and his followers to leave crime fighting to the Seattle Police Department.

Jones decided to call it a night and we began the long walk back to the U-District around 3 AM. It had been a quiet night—the biggest accomplishment was helping a man who was so inebriated he could hardly stand up get into a taxi. Jones stopped at a convenience store to buy a package of Skittles to share with us.

"I swear his diet consists entirely of Skittles, energy drinks, and teriyaki," A. J. Roberts laughed.

"And sometimes steak!" Jones added.

As we walked, the RCSM talk drifted to random subjects.

"I was watching *The Walking Dead*—you guys ever see that show?" Jones asked, turning around and walking a few paces backward while he addressed us. "There is a deleted scene where a woman is being chased by zombies and she pepper-sprays one of them and the zombie just eats her hand!" Jones laughed heartily and turned around. "I laugh so hard every time I see that—pepper spray is no good in a zombie attack!" The whole team laughed.

Saturday Night

The next night I met up with Jones around 8 PM. We were waiting for Lucien Knuteson, a local photographer, to meet up with us. I took the opportunity to walk around the grounds of the Space Needle with Jones and record an interview. We talked about the future of his team and difficulties he had faced with the media.

I asked how he reacted to people telling him he would certainly be seriously injured or killed. He answered, "When people got scared and said 'Oh my God, he's going to die,' what they really said is, 'He's stepping up, putting himself between danger and safety' and that is what I would expect everyone to do. And could I get stabbed? Yes, happened. Could I get shot? Yes, it's happened. Could I get hit with a baseball bat? Yes, it's happened. Can I get my nose broken? Yes, it's happened. But ideas are bulletproof. If they get me, they got to get the idea."

After Lucien arrived, we headed to Phoenix's car. Phoenix opened the trunk where he had a spare bulletproof vest. "Here you go, brother!" he shouted as he threw it over to Lucien. Lucien looked surprised and concerned.

The three of us cruised to a coffee shop named Chocolati Café to have a meeting with Phoenix's wife-turned-teammate, Purple Reign. Purple is an attractive, purple-haired ninja who is very kind and obviously very supportive of Phoenix and his mission. She decided to dress up in a costume of her own and help her husband and the team by researching crime stats. She would also use her persona to lead a charitable campaign to raise awareness and funds for charities working to help victims of domestic abuse. Purple Reign was in an abusive relationship herself before she met Jones, she says.

The couple can count charity fundraising as one of their superhero successes. Between the two of them, they've raised thousands of dollars. When Phoenix has been offered money for media appearances, he's instructed them to donate to a variety of charities instead.

I asked Phoenix if he'd like anything to drink. "Anything with lots of caramel!" he declared. The baristas were watching the costumed hero with a mix of amusement and concern.

"Ah," I told one of them, "a coffee and . . . anything with a lot of caramel."

Purple gave us a crime report based on crime stats she found online, trying to pinpoint criminal hot spots. Jones also showed me some bulletproof shields and a duffel bag full of weaponry he had. He had a couple collapsible batons, which he unfurled with a loud *snik*. It raised a few eyebrows in the café. In the duffel bag he also had a flash grenade, the type used by police to disperse rioters, and a roll of duct tape, which Phoenix said was for binding criminals' hands after placing them under citizen's arrest.

He also handed me his bottle of pepper spray to examine. I handled it carefully, afraid it might accidentally discharge. Phoenix's spray comes in a one-pound, pistol grip–style canister that looks like a mini fire extinguisher, made by a company that caters to law enforcement.

"Check this out," Phoenix said, pointing to the side of the canister. There was a number followed by the letters SHU. "I'm not sure what the SHU stands for," Phoenix admitted.

SHU stands for Scoville heat units, based on the Scoville scale, which is used to measure the spice heat of peppers. Your average jalapeño pepper weighs in at about 2,500 to 8,000 Scoville heat units. A cayenne will really get the blood flowing at 30,000 to 50,000 SHU, and raw habanero pepper can max out at 350,000 on the SHU scale. And Phoenix's pepper spray—a whopping 2 million SHU.

We said good-bye to Purple and headed out to patrol around Pioneer Square, an area I gathered was known to have problems with brawling outside of bars.

We encountered our first incident of the night pretty quickly. Lucien was shooting pictures of Phoenix in one of his natural elements, an alleyway. Meanwhile, my friend Groschopf (visiting from Portland, where he had recently moved) and I were giving them plenty of room to work when we saw a commotion in front of the bar next door.

I yelled to Jones that there was a fight, and he immediately ran and barreled into the crowd toward two men fighting. I lost him for a few moments, so it wasn't clear to me what happened, but apparently club bouncers and Phoenix sprayed the fighting men with pepper spray. I pushed my way through the crowd and found Phoenix. He was leading one of the men, who had been sprayed in the face, to a nearby food stand. He bought a bottle of water and poured it on the man's eyes, instructing him to blink.

The other man had removed his pepper-sprayed shirt and was extremely irate at Jones. He was walking back and forth across the street yelling, "You ain't no real nigga—you will never be a real nigga! You ain't no nigga! You ain't no superhero and you ain't no real nigga!" He walked into the street and yelled at Phoenix, then back to the sidewalk to yell some more.

After yelling that message several times, he switched his mantra to incorporate Image Comics superhero Spawn. "Get out of here you wannabe Spawn-ass motherfucker!" Phoenix Jones stood across the street, arms folded, studying the man carefully but not saying anything. "You wannabe Spawn! You ain't Spawn, motherfucker!"

Then a new observation occurred to the man. "Stan Lee never drew your black ass, you fake-ass superhero! Stan Lee never drew you! Stan Lee did not draw your black ass, motherfucker!"

Phoenix Jones, arms still crossed, glanced sideways at me. "Stan Lee didn't even draw comics, he wrote them," he told me.

Police arrived and were clearly familiar with Jones. They looked nonplussed—it was another night in Pioneer Square and here was Phoenix Jones again. They detained the shirtless man for questioning.

"I hate these superheroes! He is not a superhero! I fucking hate these superheroes!" the man shouted toward Phoenix as the officers ordered him to put his hands on the back of their squad car while they frisked him.

Phoenix proudly declared this as arrest number thirty-five for him. Minutes later, however, we saw the man, shirtless and swearing angrily, walking down the street to his car. Phoenix peeked from around a corner, watching the man. He got in his car and drove off. Phoenix spotted the responding officers and ran across the street to ask them what the deal was. He alleges that the officers told him that they didn't arrest him but that the man was in violation of his parole, which would be reported.

At this point we parted ways with Lucien and Groschopf and were joined by Ryan MacNamee and, later, Ghost.

We walked around for a while and later, outside the same club where we had witnessed the first fight, Phoenix spent some time observing an aggressive-looking group of men, shouting and gesturing. As he expected, they began fighting each other. Phoenix ran into the group and pepper-sprayed the men who were fighting—one had blood running down his face.

There were some moments of chaos and the police, who were nearby, showed up quickly. As I ran across the street, I suddenly felt a hot mist that burned my nose and eyes, making me flinch. I realized I had run through some of the spray that was drifting through the air.

One of the men who had been sprayed angrily confronted Phoenix, and when he saw Ryan filming, he began to push him around. The police, who were just around the corner, separated us from the group of men, spoke to both parties, and told everyone to go.

Phoenix was obviously using pepper spray a lot more frequently than usual, although it has long been part of his modus operandi. There is video of him using it on another individual starting a fight outside a club. Phoenix pepper-sprayed him and chased him down the street until police caught up and arrested the man. He used the spray again on the man trying to steal the party bus. And now he had already used it twice within a couple of hours.

We walked around without incident until around 1:30 or 2 AM. Phoenix spotted a group of suspicious, gangster-looking males. He decided to hang around to see what they were up to. One of them glared at him and repeatedly spat on the sidewalk. Another started telling Phoenix something about him being a "fake-ass Batman" and then said "You think I give a fuck about your pepper spray? Look what I got." He lifted his shirt to show us a gun tucked into his waistband. Jones decided to get us out of there quick. He called me and Ryan over, and then called to Ghost, who was having a tense talk with someone else in the group.

"Ghost!" Phoenix shouted. Ghost didn't hear him. "Ghost! Ghost! Ghost!" I could see a level of panic rising in Phoenix. "Ghost! Ghost! Ghost!" Ghost heard him and we quickly left. Phoenix ran across the street to tell the police, and they followed the man with the gun and his friend to their car, where they detained the suspect.

Phoenix was riled about the situation. "If I yell like that, it means you got to listen to me and we got to go," Phoenix said to Ghost.

"I didn't hear you!" Ghost replied.

"You didn't hear me? I yelled your name like eight times!"

They began to calm down. "OK, if you didn't hear me, I'm not mad," Phoenix told Ghost, slapping his shoulder.

The night had yielded three crazy encounters already, two of them involving pepper spray. But the most terrifying moment, the one that would be reported by media around the world and joked about on *Saturday Night Live*, was still ahead of us.

PEOPLE FIGHTING AND SUPERHEROES AND PEPPER SPRAY AND ... I DON'T KNOW

Phoenix Jones runs into the "pepper spray incident." RYAN MCNAMEE

Around 2:30 AM we were walking on First Avenue when Phoenix ran into a fan who had questions and wanted a picture. While he was talking, Ryan looked down a hill that led to parking lots near the waterfront and saw a fight in progress.

"Phoenix. Huge fight!" Ryan said, interrupting the fan.

Phoenix came over to take a look and then took off running as fast as he could down the hill. Ryan, Ghost, and I took off after him. As we ran down the hill, Phoenix shouted, "Get me 9-1-1!"

Running into the middle of the fight, Phoenix yelled "Back up!" a couple of times, then pepper-sprayed two of the people fighting. Pepper spray, however, is not an exact science. Others nearby felt the spray and it made them very angry. One woman, famously caught on video, began to pummel Phoenix repeatedly on the head with her high-heeled shoe. Phoenix took the abuse and tried to avoid her. She backed off for a moment.

Suddenly a car did a sharp U-turn and hit one of the men who had been fighting, then sped off. The man—hit in the side, mostly on his arm—stumbled off into the parking lot.

Phoenix shouted, "Tea! Call 9-1-1!" then ran after the car, shouting out its license plate number. I ran after him down the block while trying to get 9-1-1 on the line. The call went through, and I tried to catch my breath and explain to them what was going on and where we were. It was a frustrating conversation because I was unfamiliar with the Seattle streets and had no idea where I was, really, and my eyes searched frantically for street signs and address numbers.

We began to regroup. Phoenix and Ghost walked down the street to keep an eye on the group. The group amassed across the street, watching us and yelling in Russian. They were very pissed off. I had just told the situation to 9-1-1 on my phone, and while I was on the line, Phoenix had also hit the 9-1-1 panic button on his phone.

The woman ran across the street, her high-heeled shoe again in hand, to launch another attack. The men had gathered in a group and were obviously preparing to execute an attack of their own. One man was staring at us, speaking angrily in Russian and reaching into a coat another man was holding in front of him.

"What . . . are they going for a gun?" I asked, getting ready to hit the ground.

"This is Phoenix Jones, the Guardian of Seattle! We need police now!" Phoenix shouted to 9-1-1. He handed his phone over to me to take over the conversation. Suddenly, the group made an attack in concert, all of them running across the street at the same time, punching Ghost and pushing him into a giant potted plant, slamming Ryan into a wall so hard his camera turned off, and running at Phoenix.

Phoenix yelled that they needed to stay away, and when they charged him he doused a few of the men with a steady stream of pepper spray. I was telling 9-1-1 that we were under attack when I got punched on the right side of my face. I looked at my attacker—his face was red, irritated with the pepper spray. He looked at me in wild confusion. "You are with them—why!" he shouted. I held up my hands and told him to back up. He ran and joined his friends, who were retreating from Phoenix's pepper spray.

It was very chaotic, and a lot of the details I can only remember in flashes—I was trying to talk to 9-1-1 as well as keep track of the two groups of warring people. With some distance between the groups, I got off the phone with 9-1-1 and wiped my face to see if I was bleeding. Phoenix was across the street, calling for Ryan and me to join him.

Phoenix and I made it to a concrete median, then noticed the Russians revving up their Escalade to try and run us down.

"Take cover! Protect yourselves!" Phoenix shouted. He ran back across the street to Ryan and Ghost and they dove under a fence and ran into the ferry terminal. I crossed back to the other side and hid myself in the shadows of a concrete pillar. I had a clear view as the Escalade came roaring up to the ferry terminal entrance. A man got out of the passenger side and began picking up rocks and throwing them at Phoenix, all the while shouting in Russian.

At this point I remember thinking, "Oh, Lord, I hope everyone gets out of this alive." After a minute of rock throwing, the man got back in the Escalade and it screeched back to the parking lot on the other side of the street. Then, at last, came a sound I was glad to hear—approaching police sirens.

The police, however, were not pleased to see Phoenix Jones standing on the sidewalk waving them down. Phoenix alleges that one of the responding officers, Officer Camilo DePina, a stocky bulldog of a cop, has had issues with him in the past. Officer DePina and his partner immediately instructed Phoenix to put his pepper spray on the ground, remove his mask, and put his hands on the hood of the car.

Jones carefully peeled his rubber mask off, and to my surprise I saw that he had a giant hi-top fade–style haircut. It was similar to the one sported by Kid of the hip-hop duo Kid 'n Play. After somehow being jammed in underneath his rubber cowl, Jones's hi-top was now soaked in sweat and lying limp across his head.

Officer DePina barked out to the rest of us, "Anyone else want to join this party? Because I think we're going to arrest the whole bunch of you and clean things up. I'm tired of this game."

Officer DePina's partner told us, "Go away. Go away." Ghost took the officer's recommendation and left. Ryan and I walked about fifteen feet away, so we could give the officers room but still see what was going on.

After a few moments Officer DePina called for Ryan and me to come back over. He had checked with the party across the street and their ludicrous statement was that they were "having a good time, dancing in the street" when Phoenix crept up and pepper-sprayed them.

Their word was apparently good enough for the police—Phoenix was to be arrested on four counts of assault.

Officer DePina looked at the three of us—Phoenix maskless with his hands on the hood of the car, Ryan and me wide-eyed in the light of the squad car's headlights. He said, "This goes for all three of you, understand?" and read us our rights.

"Well," I thought, "here I go to jail."

But then Officer DePina called for our IDs and asked our business since we weren't "dressed like superheroes." We told him in simple terms that I was a writer and Ryan was shooting video.

Officer DePina watched a couple seconds of the video through Ryan's viewfinder but wasn't impressed. "I see chaos, but not fighting," he commented. He glanced at my ID. "So you came all the way from Wisconsin to write about this guy? Cool." He shrugged.

As they ran our IDs, Phoenix asked if he could put his mask back on, as he had been identified. Officer DePina nodded.

"Give me back my face!" Phoenix growled, and put the mask back on. This was a line from *Watchmen*, uttered by Rorschach when he is cornered and caught by police and unmasked.

"I felt naked without it," Phoenix said as he adjusted it. The police returned our IDs, handcuffed Phoenix, and put him in the back of the squad car.

A lot of people have asked me if I was scared during this incident. The fear didn't really set in until this moment. During the chaos I was so busy focusing on what was going on and who was where that I didn't have time. But after the squad car pulled away with Phoenix in the back, I began to realize that my hands were shaking.

Ryan and I had one more challenge ahead of us: getting back to his car. We were concerned because police had apparently let most of the party across the street go free, and we had a long way to walk and did not want to run into them again. There were only the two of us and . . .

"What happened?" Ghost suddenly appeared from behind some rocks. He was clearly in a lot of pain. He was holding his hand and wincing. "I broke my thumb!" he said in a gasp.

We started walking. We were uncertain what to do. Ryan called Peter Tangen and told him what had happened, out of breath with his voice quaking. Tangen told us to try to wake up Purple and tell her the situation while he spoke to a lawyer. Despite our offer to give him a ride, Ghost decided to drive to the emergency room, where he told them he had a late-night accident falling off a ladder.

Phoenix had entrusted me with his car keys, and after some aimless driving I was able to recall where he had parked his car. Ryan dropped me at my friend's house, where I lay in bed staring at the ceiling, my adrenaline still pumping. I thought about the events of the evening until I fell asleep briefly in the early morning.

Aftermath

Phoenix spent the night in a holding cell. He claims he was put in there with two people he had encountered earlier in the night who were booked because of him and that they tried to attack him. Like a lot of Phoenix's stories, this is hard to substantiate.

Police confiscated his supersuit and put it into the evidence locker, where it would remain for several months.

On Sunday, I tried to take it easy. I went to a gadgeteer meet-up in the suburbs with Victim, White Baron, Sky Man, and Sir Bob. It was a nice change of pace. I talked to Peter Tangen a couple times on the phone. Peter had been working around the clock, talking to Phoenix's lawyer and sorting out media. He informed me that the story had broken and had already hit the airwaves in Seattle and beyond.

A media storm was rolling in. By late morning, the *Smoking Gun* had outed Phoenix's secret identity. By the end of the week, the story would become a joke on *Saturday Night Live*'s "Weekend Update" segment: "Phoenix Jones, a self-proclaimed costumed vigilante, was arrested in Seattle after he allegedly used pepper spray on a group of people leaving a nightclub," Seth Meyers deadpanned. "Jones apparently became a superhero after he was bitten by a radioactive idiot."

Phoenix called me when he was released on bail the afternoon following his arrest. He sounded oddly cheerful and optimistic. "Are you sure you're OK? You sound like you're kind of shook up," he said. I guess I probably was. I told him I was OK, though.

On Monday, as I was packing up and preparing to leave town, I was invited to appear on a local radio talk program, *The John Curley Show*. They wanted Ryan and me to come in and talk about the "pepper spray incident," as it began to be called. Ryan picked me up and on the way over he told me Phoenix would probably be making a surprise visit to the studio.

I also got a call from Dark Guardian. I hadn't spoken to him since I saw him in Manhattan, but he had heard about the pepper spray incident. Dark Guardian had long been a loud critic of Phoenix Jones, angrily chastising him for his methods. This incident just added more depth to the rivalry between them.

"He rushed into a situation and reacted with very poor judgment," Dark Guardian later wrote in a statement. "He maced a group of people who were not attacking him. He was not reacting in self defense and the police have rightfully charged him with assault. This is an example of what not to do as a community crime fighter."

At the radio station, the show producers looked through the video Ryan had shot during the incident. "Ryan, let's play one of our favorite clips from this," John Curley said, laughing, as we listened through our headphones. It was Ryan talking to 9-1-1 on the phone, trying to describe the violent scene unfolding in front of him.

"There's people fighting and superheroes and pepper spray and . . . I don't know," he was reporting in exasperation.

After our interview, we found Phoenix, wearing a spare supersuit and a motorcycle helmet, and Purple Reign waiting on the newsroom floor. I gave Phoenix a hug. (What can I say? I was glad to see him alive.) After he talked with John Curley, we all got into Ryan's car. I had a plane to catch, so they dropped me off at the light rail station.

Phoenix got a phone call from his mother. I could tell she was extremely upset and that he was trying to calm her down. I asked him what she had said, but he quickly changed the subject. I asked him what he planned to do next, looking in the backseat where he and Purple were sitting. He looked at me through the visor of his motorcycle helmet.

"I'm just going to take it one day at a time," he said. He paused, then added defiantly, "And tonight, I'm going to go out on patrol like I usually do."

They dropped me off at the station, where I wandered toward an airport-bound train, shocked, amazed.

Phoenix Jones in Court

A few days after the pepper spray incident, Phoenix Jones had a court date. He showed up with a lawyer, and although his supersuit had been confiscated as evidence, he had a spare one. He wore a slightly different version of his infamous black and gold cowl and rubber torso to court with a nice dress shirt and slacks awkwardly juxtaposed over it.

A court officer told Phoenix to remove the mask, which he did, shielding his face from the courtroom with his hand. The prosecution did not file charges, but retained the right to file them later. After the hearing, Phoenix put his mask back on, but again dramatically removed it outside the courtroom, revealing to reporters that his secret identity was Benjamin Fodor, a father whose day job was working with autistic children in a day care setting. He also revealed his mixed martial arts fighting name, "the Flattop," after his distinctive hairstyle, with a record of 11 wins, 0 losses, 0 draws.*

Blowback from the incident wasn't over. Phoenix alleges he was pulled over by an officer who was hoping to issue him a ticket for a suspended license, a problem Phoenix had already temporarily amended. And then he lost his job. The Department of Social and Health Services sent a letter informing him that he was not allowed to work with his autistic children due to the pending status of the pepper spray incident.

Although some of his Seattle constituency continued to support him with encouraging words, others' opinions had turned. Media had originally reported that Jones had sprayed down a group of people who were merely reveling in the streets, and now people spit at and threatened him.

A little over a month later, the charges against him were dropped, but not before Seattle city attorney Peter Holmes made it clear he was not a Phoenix Jones fan and reprimanded him harshly in a statement.

"Mr. Fodor is no hero, just a deeply misguided individual," he told the Seattle press. "He has been warned that his actions put him in danger, and this latest episode demonstrates that innocent bystanders can also be harmed."

Absolutely none of this deterred Phoenix Jones. If anything, it made him more defiant. He had suffered multiple injuries. He had

---

* According to mixedmartialarts.com.

been shunned by his superhero peers and ripped into by the local media. He had been arrested, threatened, and lost his job. There were many reasons for him to hang up the rubber suit and call it a day. But when I would periodically check his Facebook page for updates, his status more often than not read something like "I'm out on patrol."

More RLSH Arrests

Phoenix Jones was not the first and would not be the last RLSH to end up on the wrong side of the law. The movement was finding that there was a fine line between safety patrols and what is considered illegal vigilante behavior. One person who has become an expert on the legal woes of superheroes is Zack Levine, who maintains a blog called *Superhero Law*.

"The idea started when I was in my first year of law school," Levine told me. "I used comic book characters and situations to remember the analysis for intentional torts and criminal law." Levine pointed out several legal issues RLSH face, starting with sometimes vague self-defense laws.

"The line between legal behavior and vigilante behavior is definitely unclear and not only different in every state, but it is constantly changing." He adds there are a lot of factors RLSH might not have even considered.

"The determination of what is 'reasonable' in the self-defense context takes into consideration things like relative size, the level of aggression used, and even statements made by the attacker."

Levine has uncovered another legal issue for RLSH in at least seven states: anti-mask laws. "Most (of these laws) are rooted in efforts to thwart organizations like the Ku Klux Klan from holding public meetings. The theory was that if these groups were unable to hide their identity in public, their activities and membership would be curbed. More modern anti-mask laws are focused on public safety. For example, many states have laws forbidding people from driving or entering a bank with a mask on."

In 2010, an RLSH named Viper, clad head to foot in a green spandex costume, was confronted by police when they found he had brought ninja throwing stars and a baton with him while patrolling the streets of Columbia, Tennessee. He also had a screwdriver, wrenches, and a cell phone in his utility belt. Police let him go with a warning.

Less than a month after Phoenix Jones's arrest, a young member of the Pacific Protectorate, the Ray, was beaten by police and arrested while he was trying to do "security" at an Occupy Oakland protest. He was wearing the lower half of a face mask and carrying Motor-Mouth's riot control shield, designed to look like the one carried by Captain America. When police closed in on protestors, they viewed the Ray as a threat and beat him unconscious. He woke up with two black eyes, handcuffed to a hospital bed. He was charged with "assault" and "failure to disburse." A reporter looking into the story didn't offer much sympathy—the Ray made a few racist comments during his interview and he was subsequently dumped from the Pacific Protectorate.

The most disturbing arrest of an RLSH was an incident in April 2012. It involved Bee Sting, a member of the Michigan Protectors who lived outside Flint, Michigan. The owner of the Twin Meadows Mobile Home Park in the Flint suburb of Burton had allegedly encouraged the Michigan Protectors to patrol his mobile home park to curb some of its crime issues. Bee Sting headed out to patrol the park with his teammate, Justicar, dressed in a bulletproof vest, leather jacket with a bee logo, knee and shin guards, leather gloves, and a utility belt. He also had a shotgun.

His last Facebook update before going on patrol read, "Time to roll. Everybody Bee safe." A recently posted picture showed off an arm gauntlet he had designed to hold shotgun shells.

"I love the smell of new gear in the morning," the caption quipped, parodying a famous quote from *Apocalypse Now*. "There's a zipper compartment as well—buck shot on the outside, all purpose on the inside."

Just after midnight Bee Sting confronted a man riding into the park, telling him his motorcycle was too loud. An argument between the two escalated and Bee Sting grabbed his shotgun. The two began to wrestle and the shotgun discharged in the skirmish, blasting a nearby trailer that happened to be empty. The frightening incident showed how dangerously close the RLSH concept could come to a fatality.

Bee Sting's teammate and witness, Justicar, was horrified and the incident left him having "thoughts of shredding my mask."

"I saw the aftermath of the victim's kids crying and I know they'll be haunted a long time after this, as I will, all over a bad decision about a noise complaint," Justicar told me. "Bee Sting made a critical error by bringing a shotgun to a shouting match."

Bee Sting's story brought comparisons to the story of George Zimmerman, a self-proclaimed neighborhood watchdog who shot an unarmed African American teenager, Trayvon Martin. That story started a firestorm of controversy about people taking the law into their own firearm-bearing hands.

RLSH RUN-INS WITH THE LAW
Illustrations by David Beyer Jr.

Phantom Patriot
Date: January 20, 2002
Location: Bohemian Grove (outside Monte Rio, CA)
Charges: Five felonies—two counts arson, one burglary, one possesion of a billy club, one exhibiting a firearm in the presence of a police officer.
Verdict: The Phantom Patriot, also known as Richard McCaslin, spent six years in prison and was paroled in 2008.

Viper

Date: June 30, 2010
Location: Columbia, TN
Charges: Carrying ninja
throwing stars and plastic batons.
Verdict: Let off with a warning.

Phoenix Jones

Date: October 9, 2011
Location: Seattle, WA
Charges: Four counts of assault
for the "pepper spray incident."
Verdict: Charges dropped.

The Ray

Date: November 2, 2011
Location: Oakland, CA
Charges: Battery on a peace
officer and remaining at the
scene of a riot.
Verdict: The Ray was bailed out
with a donation from Occupy
Oakland. His case is still pending.

Bee Sting

Date: April 26, 2012
Location: Burton, MI
Charges: Assault with a dangerous weapon and wearing body armor during commission of a violent crime.
Verdict: Pleaded guilty, spent 100 days in jail before being placed on probation.

Beast

Date: July 31, 2012
Location: Mansfield Township, NJ
Charges: Being disorderly and unlawful possession of handcuffs.
Verdict: Handcuffs charge dropped, pleaded guilty to disorderly conduct, which carries a fine of $133 plus court costs.

Other unfortunate echoes arose from the fact that pepper spray had become a villain of the Occupy movement. Disturbing images of young women in New York and an elderly woman in Seattle suffering the effects of being pepper-sprayed by police outraged and galvanized the Occupy protests. The "casually pepper-spraying cop," a photo of an officer nonchalantly pepper-spraying handcuffed students at the University of California at Davis, became an Internet meme.

Phoenix Jones began to receive further connections to this chemical villain after one of his teammates, Midnight Jack, sprayed demonstrators at a May Day protest parade in Seattle on May 1, 2012. Jones says he, Midnight Jack, and team member El Caballero were defending the federal building from protestors throwing rocks and bricks. The spraying of the protestors caused him to be identified with "the man."

"All right, Jones, we see you're on their side, man," one angry protestor shouted at the scene, while other protestors yelled insults and helicopters buzzed overhead. After that he would occasionally receive shouts and confrontations about his handling of May Day from random people while out on patrol. In one of these conflicts, caught by Phoenix Jones's "Phoenix-cam," an angry, inebriated woman berated Jones and his team for a solid eight minutes.

"When I first heard about you, I was like, 'This is cool,' and then your ass popped up at May Day," the woman yelled, pointing at Jones's face. "You know how much support you had until May Day happened? Do you know how much people don't like what you did because you ain't a cop, and you pepper-sprayed people like you was a cop, motherfucker!"

Another horrific event, the Aurora, Colorado, shooting, also affected the RLSH directly. A couple weeks after the July 20, 2012, shooting, a New Jersey RLSH named Beast was hanging out in the parking lot of a Home Depot, asking shoppers if they needed his assistance with any superhero chores. He was wearing tactical gear and a domino mask. Customers and store employees began to fear they were witnessing a copycat of the shooting and called 9-1-1. Police arrested Beast, drove him to a nearby mental hospital, and charged him with disorderly conduct.

It was becoming a difficult time to be a Real Life Superhero.

14

AN AGE OF HEROES?

RLSH at work during the HOPE 2011 mission. GREGG SIMPSON

While researching this book, I occasionally saw something posted on the RLSH forums that would optimistically declare an upcoming year as the "Year of the RLSH" or even a "dawn of a new age of heroes."

Could this be true? I wondered, and what would an "age of heroes" consist of?

Portland, Oregon

Before my trip to Seattle I had spent a couple days in Portland. I met up with Knight Owl again. He took me to the dojo where he studied krav maga, which is a recommended martial art for RLSH, he told me. It's heavy on martial and light on art. Training sessions are intense, and after a solid hour of getting my ass kicked, I sat down exhausted.

Knight Owl said I did well—people have thrown up after their first class. We got hot wings and headed back into Portland to meet Anti-Man, a creepy-looking RLSH clad in black rags stitched together. The next night I patrolled briefly with two other Portland RLSH, Iconoclast and Dark Wolf. I also met up with Zetaman again. But he was no longer Zetaman. He was just Illya King.

It was the first day of the Occupy Portland protests, so we went to check out the mass of protestors milling about the Willamette River. We went to his favorite comic book shop, Cosmic Monkey, and then to Floyd's Coffee Shop to talk about his life post-Zetaman. He was reluctant—it had been a painful exit.

Illya's RLSH world started to deteriorate after he hosted SA4 in Portland. He and his wife, Apocalypse Meow, separated and eventually divorced. To make matters worse, he discovered that she had been having "erotic conversations" with another RLSH. Although it was difficult, he still believed in Zetaman and pushed forward.

In January 2011, Thanatos called for a Pacific Northwest team-up. He and others wanted to give Phoenix Jones a chance, feeling bad about his initial poor reception. Illya said that up until that point he found Jones to be "pompous" but hadn't formed much of an opinion beyond that. When he arrived in Seattle, Illya's encounter with Jones was bad from the get go, he said.

"I first met Phoenix Jones outside of my car. He asked if I had called the media and I said, 'No, me and [the girl I was dating] have been on the road since three.'

"He got agitated and was yelling about someone calling the media."

As they got into the patrol, Illya pointed out someone who was selling coke. "Instead of reporting the dealer, Jones demanded the dealer hand over the drugs and took them and dumped them down a sewer, then walked off. I chased after him, asking if we should report this. He didn't want to."

Next, Illya said, they witnessed a fight between "a few street people."

"Jones pushed both of them and said, 'If you want to fight someone, fight me.' . . . I didn't think it was a good way to break up a fight," Illya reflected.

After being summoned into a bar to pose for pictures for a bachelorette party, Jones led the assembled RLSH to a café. "He claimed they had a special back room for his team," Illya laughed. At the café Illya and Jones argued about techniques, methods of handling aggressive homeless people, and about the number of arrests Jones had claimed. Illya said that on a peaceful note they both apologized for things they had said about each other online. Illya left to give his girlfriend a ride, then returned to the gathering of RLSH at the café.

"The rest of the party was there—Knight Owl, Thanatos, Icarus, Sky Man, White Baron, Irishman, Victim, and Red Dragon." What followed next was dramatically dubbed "the Battle of Seattle."

"Phoenix Jones said to the whole group, 'You know, I don't think you're a good guy. You're a rotten guy. Why don't you go back to Portland and leave Seattle to me?'

"I swear the seconds seemed like minutes. I looked around the room. Victim and Irishman were laughing. Icarus, Thanatos, and Knight Owl just turned their heads. Sky Man said, 'C'mon, guys.'

"I looked around for a second or two and realized I was out and this guy was in. Phoenix Jones is what they wanted and not someone like me.

"I said, 'If that's the way you all feel, good day, gentlemen.' White Baron followed me and apologized for Jones's behavior. I stormed off."

I asked Phoenix Jones about this incident in a follow-up phone call. His story mostly followed Illya's account but he said the major issue was that Illya "spent most of the night lecturing me on how to be a good RLSH." Frustrated by the unsolicited advice on his home turf, he told Illya he wasn't welcome to join him on patrol. Phoenix Jones expressed regret at the drama between him and other RLSH, but he thinks he can lead a new Age of Heroes.

"I think Dark Guardian and Zetaman are great superheroes, but they're the old way of doing it and I'm the new," Jones told me.

Illya was deeply wounded by the incident. Down and out, he hit the streets of Seattle alone that night to hand out the supplies he had bought to the homeless. He helped one woman build a shelter out of cardboard and their roles were reversed.

"God bless her soul," Illya recalled. "When I told her about the night I had, she hugged me and told me I was welcome in Seattle any time."

After returning to Portland, Illya said the straw that broke Zetaman's back was a blog post by the RLSV Malvado. Malvado had posted gossip, "true, exaggerated, and lies," Illya said, about Illya's sexual relationship with his ex-wife, his current girlfriend, and even his mother's mental health history. Illya turned his back on the RLSH community.

"That blog post sealed my conviction that the RLSH community as a whole is nothing more than an Internet social circle that cares for who is popular and who isn't."

Illya retired his blue body armor and began to focus on school and a new girlfriend. He started taking classes at the same krav maga school as Knight Owl and got in shape. His weight loss and healthier appearance was noticeable to me after seeing him at SA3. He began to channel some of his criticism into a comic book series he drew, *Naked Man Comics*. Among the superhero satire lineup is Pepper Gold, who bears an uncanny resemblance to Phoenix Jones.

Illya's altruistic side found a channel, too. He began to volunteer at the Macdonald Center, a low-income and mental health facility in downtown Portland, leading a workshop titled "Find Your Inner Superhero." At first the program was designed to feature RLSH-type persona adoption, but Illya and the other program organizers dropped it when they felt it was a bit much for the Macdonald Center residents.

"Having someone in front of them in cape and cowl really screws around with the tenuous grip street people have on reality."

The program switched to using actual comics creation as the format, which Illya says is "designed to stimulate free thinking with writing and comic storytelling."

Illya does not plan to return to the RLSH world. "I miss what I thought was a good idea based on my love of comics. I do not want to return to the cesspool that is the RLSH community. If I did it would be a backslide and welcoming the abuse back again. I'd go back to feeling bad about myself and letting others make me feel bad."

Illya had wanted to be part of the new Age of Heroes, but the dream had died.

Later, Illya called me. "I'm sorry, I feel like I was really negative. I wish there was something positive I could give you. But there isn't."

San Diego, California

For others, the dream lived on as a positive inspiration. In 2011 I travelled to San Diego for the biggest nerd-out event in the universe, the San Diego Comic Con.

A group of RLSH had established a new annual tradition: HOPE (Homeless Outreach Program Effect). This year was their second annual HOPE event and the biggest RLSH meet-up ever, with thirty-some RLSH traveling to San Diego from all over the country. Some were also there to use the proximity to check out Comic Con, others were there simply to enjoy the camaraderie of their fellow RLSH and lend a helping hand to HOPE.

The event was Razorhawk's idea. He had done a fair share of the organizing with help from DC's Guardian and Mr. Xtreme, who led a San Diego team called the Xtreme Justice League.

I met Anonyman, a young RLSH from Saskatoon, at the airport and we took the bus to a beachfront condo several RLSH had rented for the weekend.

Urban Avenger, a member of the XJL, had let me borrow his Comic Con pass for a few hours so I could get in and take a look around. I stood there with major sensory overload, watching thousands of people walk around the con dressed as every character you can imagine (and some you couldn't) from comic books, sci fi, video games, and horror movies.

A caravan headed to the HOPE staging area the next morning in the parking lot of a high school. The RLSH had a trailer full of two hundred sleeping bags and two hundred backpacks filled with supplies, toiletries, and socks. A refrigerated food truck held over a thousand pounds of food: bottles of juice, fruit, sandwiches, granola bars. The parking lot was soon filled with RLSH. There were a lot of familiar faces—Knight Owl, Razorhawk, Geist, DC's Guardian, and Thanatos.

"I knew our paths would cross again, my friend," Thanatos said when he saw me. He had even more new tattoos.

There were people I had spoken to but not yet met—Mr. Xtreme, Superhero, Miss Fit,* and Vigilante Spider. And there were more, many more. Some I vaguely recognized, others I didn't.

We split into teams to cover a grid of an area that had a high number of homeless people. My team captain was Mr. Xtreme. My teammates included Thanatos, Anonyman, Prof. Midnight, and the Handler, a Los Angeles dog trainer accompanied by her German shepherd, Gio. We began to walk down Sixteenth Street in the hot San Diego sun. We soon found a row of homeless people who had built makeshift shelters along a fence out of shopping carts, tarps, milk crates, and random flotsam and jetsam. We began to reach into our supply and handed it out. Down the block, the truck with the backpacks and sleeping bags and the food truck had stopped—they had run into a large gathering of homeless people and decided to stay stationary and work from that point. I hopped in the back of the food truck to help a consultant-turned-superhero named Sage and a couple other volunteers bag up food.

---

* I thought the best way of seeing Miss Fit's biceps in action was to challenge her to an arm-wrestling contest. After a long struggle, we agreed to a draw. I think she was humoring me.

I won't forget the scene that followed. As word spread that there was free food and supplies, both trucks, parked across the street from each other, were swarmed by people in need. I looked out the back of the food truck. There was a large crowd of people, extending their hands toward us. Sage, the rest of the volunteers, and I put together bags of sandwiches, fruit, juice, and granola bars and handed them out as fast as we could. When we ran out of bags, we filled up empty boxes. When we ran low on boxes, we filled the last of them up with food and gave them to Good Samaritan and Knight Owl to pass out.

When the action died down for a moment, I stepped out of the truck to get some air and check out the scene. It was surreal, but moving. Thanatos had his hand on a homeless man's shoulder. The man had a bushy beard and was missing several teeth. The two of them were laughing and talking about the old Adam West *Batman* show. DC's Guardian was in the street. Such a large crowd had showed up that he worried it was a safety hazard, so he stood in the street expertly directing traffic. Across the street, Superhero was instructing people to form an orderly assembly while Mr. Xtreme, Vigilante Spider, and Miss Fit helped hand out the backpacks and sleeping bags.

These people could have done anything with their summer vacations. They could have spent their time less than a mile away, where Comic Con was in full swing. But they chose to come here, sweat profusely under their spandex costumes, and work as a team handing out supplies to San Diego's homeless population.

In less than an hour, all the supplies were gone. The trucks had been completely cleaned out. The RLSH were in high spirits, hugging each other and giving each other high fives. To them, the Age of Heroes was a reality. It had not been an epic comic book mission, but it was a successful mission.

"It's weird how much these guys mean to me," Razorhawk told me as we walked. "It's the one thing I feel like I got right in my life, besides my family." He said he was definitely going to plan a HOPE 2012 and wanted to double the number of supplies.

Alexandria, Minnesota

Razorhawk and Geist had been part of another mission that I found very humbling. They had befriended a young man named Power Boy.

One day Geist got an e-mail from a woman, who said her family had read about the RLSH online. Her young son had become a fan of Geist's, a fellow Minnesotan. They lived not too far away, in Alexandria, Minnesota, and the idea of a superhero in his neck of the woods thrilled him.

"She said that her son, Ben, wanted to buy an action figure of me," Geist said. "I really did laugh out loud. I said, 'Sorry, but I'm not exactly on the market,' or something like that. Then she asked if I'd be willing to meet Ben when they're in Rochester visiting the Mayo Clinic next month. And I said—Mayo Clinic? Is everything OK?"

It was then that Geist learned that Ben, age nine, had a disease called adrenoleukodystrophy, ALD for short. It's a rare, inherited disorder that leads to progressive brain damage, failure of the adrenal glands, and eventually death. There is no known cure.

Geist told Ben's mother that he would be glad to meet him. He sent Ben a care package with a signed photo and an LED light. He even delivered a Geist action figure, custom made by a friend, a one-of-a-kind item.

His teammates on the Great Lakes Alliance pitched in to help. Razorhawk made costumes for Ben, or, as he now dubbed himself, Power Boy, and his three siblings—Little Tornado, Super Sergeant, and Pink Lantern—the Fearsome Four.

Power Boy found his superhero friend base growing—RLSH from around the country began sending him gifts and photos, or just dropping by online to say hi. Geist organized an RLSH coloring book, inspired by Power Boy, which featured black-and-white art of Power Boy's RLSH friends.

"Ben, now officially Power Boy, doesn't fear the tests so much anymore," his mother said. She noted that the family goes to the Mayo Clinic at least every six months to run a battery of tests. "We

Night Bug and Rock N Roll sending well wishes to Power Boy. COURTESY OF THE CAI

have slowly become friends with lots of RLSH and it has expanded our world so much. It helps us all in times of pain and agony."

"There's nothing about meeting with Ben that doesn't get tears streaming down my cheeks, man," Geist told me. "I'm very emotional about it and I'm also inspired by how the rest of the RLSH community and the just-plain-fans are stepping in to help Ben." Power Boy's mother says the Age of Heroes had touched their hearts and had given hope to the whole family.

"Becoming RLSH has helped all four of the kids," Power Boy's mother told me. "It has shown them that they have friends and that many people of all walks of life do care about others. We have found hope and family among the RLSH."

As for Power Boy's future, she said, "We are can only hope he will beat this and be one of the few who have."

An Expanding Initiative

Two big supporters of Power Boy are Rock N Roll and Night Bug, the couple who began their superhero journey together at the movie theater in San Francisco. I met them at the HOPE event, and later Rock talked to me about Power Boy over the phone. Like Geist, she felt very emotional about the story, starting with seeing a picture of Power Boy lying in a hospital bed.

"I have a son the same age as him, so I contacted them and said 'I can't imagine what you're going through,'" Rock told me. "'If you need anything at all, let me know.' And that was it—we just started talking and talking."

She became a part of Power Boy's rapidly growing group of superhero friends. She and Night Bug helped organize an online fundraiser to help pay for Power Boy's visits to the Mayo Clinic. The couple also formed the California Initiative (CAI)—a new branch that spun off from the NYI. Since my visit to the Initiative, they had become a rapidly expanding franchise.

Zero reflected back on the summer I visited the NYI as a dark period of the group's history. He cited a lack of resources and manpower. "(Since then) we've gained and lost a lot of members for various reasons," he told me in a follow-up interview. Dark Guardian had buried the hatchet with the group and had become a member of the NYI. Conflict between Zimmer and Zero continued to heat up, leading Zimmer to be ousted from the group. He headed back to Austin to work on his tech ideas for a company he started, Zimtelligence.

The NYI membership rose to over a dozen—men and women with names like Short Cut, Blitz, Tango, and Thre3. They continued to study martial arts and patrolling techniques, including bait patrols.

"On the second bait patrol we did with Tango, we collected a lot of license plate numbers of creepers who tried to get her into cars (one by force, the rest by trying to lure her) and we caught a dude who had been trying to break into women's houses all night. He was following them home; we cornered the guy and police were able to apprehend him without any problem."

The expanded NYI lineup found other projects to engage themselves in, too. After the bodies of several prostitutes were found in the woods of Long Island, it became clear that a serial killer was at large. The NYI decided to offer their services to protect prostitutes at risk and to announce this on a website the Long Island Killer (as he was being called) likely could have found victims, Craigslist.

"The Long Island Killer is out there," the announcement read. "He's a scary bastard and it's starting to seem like he is focusing on you pretty ladies because some people are slower to report you missing and also because apparently the law doesn't respect your personal choices and is slower to follow through when it comes to you."

The NYI urged a check-in system with friends and, if that wasn't available, suggested the prostitutes could use them as an emergency line. "We also want to offer our services as the NYI: Namely, practical martial arts training for free as well as improvised weapons training free of charge," the post continued. "We care about you. We want you alive in this world, just like everyone else."

The group also offered their security services at the Occupy Wall Street encampment. They spent long shifts watching over protestors to make sure they were all right, at one point catching a man who was molesting protestors in their sleep and turning him over to police.

New Branches

Soon two new branches of the Initiative formed. The Virginia Initiative was founded by crime fighters Death's Head Moth and a man named Ira Ui'Raghallaigh, who continued to track drug dealers and gang members. Rock N Roll, Night Bug, and half a dozen others like Eon and Olde School formed the California Initiative. They focused on things like patrols, charity events, and teaching free self-defense classes.

Disagreements on methodology led them to operate their group separately from Motor-Mouth's group, the Pacific Protectorate. For the first time, two separate groups were in operation in the same general area.

I met up with the CAI while I was visiting San Francisco. Rock N Roll, Night Bug, and Olde School invited me to join them on a needle pick-up in the Mission District.

Olde School—dressed in a fedora, tie, and bright yellow tennis shoes—does needle pick-ups for a couple hours most Saturday mornings. The CAI have nicknames for the different alleys. Lovers Lane is known for all the used condoms and Poop Cake Alley for—you guessed it—human feces. Olde School's original goal was to pick up one hundred used needles for the year, but twenty days into January he had already collected twenty-seven. He snaps on a pair of latex gloves, carefully picks the needle up, and places it into a portable biohazard container. On my expedition with the group we scanned the alleys and an area near the train tracks and found ten used needles.

I asked Olde School why he would spend hours on a Saturday morning doing such a thankless, unsavory task. "The world is a fucked-up place," he told me matter-of-factly, "so I like to spend a couple hours making it better."

More Initiative branches opened. Lucid moved to Los Angeles, where he founded a CAI:LA branch. Fear, also known as Stitch, started an Arizona Initiative, and more formed in Washington state, Louisiana, and Colorado.

They were spreading like chapters of a motorcycle gang of do-gooders, working toward the goal of a Fifty State Initiative.

Zero says that the Initiative isn't about trying to usher in an Age of Heroes, just groups of concerned allies. "The world lacks decency," he told me. "We aren't trying to be badass dudes, just decent human beings. I see dark times coming. But I also see something maybe others don't—this is all going to turn around. And I'm no optimist; I just have a gut feeling about it."

A Mixed Legacy

I was amused by the juxtaposition of two comments I saw on an online article about the Watchman.

The first one glowed: "Good for him, Milwaukee needs more of this! If the government fails, it is up to the individual to take responsibility. Yes, he's at risk, but at least he stands up for something."

The second one said, simply, "This is the dumbest story I've ever read."

The legacy of the RLSH will no doubt be a mixed one. They will sometimes viewed as good-natured, everyday people with an unusual hobby, like Knight Owl or Civitron. Other times they'll be viewed as delusional and dangerous, like Bee Sting. Charitable events like HOPE will cross paths with the madness of the pepper spray incident.

Opinion of the movement as a whole will depend greatly on individual perspective. To people like Peter Tangen and other RLSH advocates, they represent a symbol of individuals making the world a better place, a group that gives us hope that superheroes secretly walk among us and inspire us to be better people. They say the Age of Heroes is on the horizon.

To critics like the RLSV, the movement is a failure, bogged down by too much human error and ego. They say the Age of Heroes is over.

Remembering Rouroni

In May 2012, there was an RLSH fatality. He was a young man from San Diego who called himself Rouroni, an alternate spelling of a popular manga and anime series about a samurai. He was a member of the Xtreme Justice League and dressed in a ninja costume with an Asian-style rice paddy hat. I met him briefly at HOPE 2011 alongside the rest of his team members during the hustle and bustle of the homeless handout. He introduced himself to me with his real name, Alex. He died not in a showdown with criminals but in a car accident after he lost control of his vehicle on a slippery road.

"He'd been with the team almost two years now and patrolled as often as he could with us. He was an important factor of our team," Rouroni's XJL teammate Urban Avenger told me. "He never wanted to be in the spotlight or take credit for anything. He was really the epitome of what an RLSH should be. We all learned a lot from him."

His family decided they would embrace his RLSH identity. They invited his teammates to attend his funeral, wearing their superhero costumes, and act as pallbearers. His gravestone dually noted his real name and his RLSH identity.

Rouroni's mom is named Jeanette, but her friends call her "Jett" for short. She told me about Alex and about Rouroni. Alex was a kind person who volunteered with his church's youth ministry, making a special point to try to befriend outsiders. "He had a heart for those who didn't quite fit in," Jeanette recalled. When Alex told her that he was also going on patrols with the XJL, Jeanette felt concerns for his safety but didn't try to deter him.

"I had normal motherly concerns he might get hurt," she told me. "But it should be noted that despite the potential danger, I at no point felt the need to discourage his participation. One of the things I loved most about my son was his willingness to stand up for what he thought was right and not sit by apathetically while bad things happened. I raised him to get involved. So how could I fault him for doing what I encouraged him to do?"

After Rouroni's death, Jeanette decided that she wanted to carry on his legacy, so she became a superhero herself. She got a green wolf mask, a tunic-style spandex shirt, rubber pants, and a green velvet cape. She was now the Emerald Fáel (*fáel* is Gaelic for "wolf," she explained), another everyday person who has chosen the title of Real Life Superhero.

"I guess you could say that I've been adopted by the RLSH community. Many of the RLSH reached out to me after Rouroni's accident to support me. Some were shocked I would accept them, as their own families rejected and belittled their RLSH participation."

Emerald Fáel began to volunteer. "Working at the food bank, volunteering at Stand Up for Kids, participating in homeless outreach, running in the Warrior Dash for St. Jude's Children's Research Hospital,* and den mother to the XJL," she laughed. "Shhh, maybe I shouldn't have said that!" She also attended HOPE 2012, which was dedicated to Rouroni and bigger than Razorhawk had anticipated.

Sometimes she would stop by the graveyard after the events to report on them to Rouroni. "This may not be the life I would have chosen," Emerald Fáel told me. "I certainly would not have wanted to walk this path without my child. But let me assure you, when I see my son again in heaven, he is going to be very proud to call me mom."

I thought about what being a superhero meant, and ultimately I decided that the Age of Heroes, like beauty, was all in the eye of the beholder. For some people, it is already here.

---

* Emerald Fáel was on a team of RLSH for the Warrior Run. The team leader was Miss Fit and included members of the NYI, CAI, and XJL. It was the most successful RLSH fundraiser to date. A little over $15,000 was raised by the team.

Epilogue

MASKING UP

Argo (center) with the Watchman and Blackbird. COURTESY OF THE CHALLENGERS

One warm afternoon, I sat in my backyard as I talked to the Watchman on the phone. We had been talking on a regular basis for a couple of years and he was filling me in on the Challenger's latest patrols.

Then he said, "I got a question for you."

"Sure, OK," I said.

"Have you ever thought about doing this?" he asked.

There was a long pause. It was a question I had been asked before, one I always laughed off by saying, "No, I don't look good in spandex." But when the Watchman asked me, it somehow caught me off guard.

I had thought about it, I told him. I saw the appeal in all of it, the secret adventure, the comic book theatrics. The RLSH were very receptive to me and more than one had declared, "You're one of us."

The thought of becoming a costumed crusader and writing about it had crossed my mind early on, but I had quickly rejected it. It was too gimmicky and self-serving. The idea was a hollow piece of stunt journalism—after all, if I were writing a book about the lives of professional chefs, I wouldn't hang out with them dressed as a chef, would I? I wanted to write a book documenting RLSH, not pretend that I was one.

The Watchman thought this point over, then told me, "But the only way you'll truly get to experience what it's like to walk on a patrol as RLSH is to dress as one and try it." I got off the phone and sat in my backyard, deep in thought. Was this the point of no return?

A couple weeks later, I experienced my first RLSH adrenaline rush. A package had arrived in the mail. I took it inside my house, made sure my roommate wasn't home, and tore it open. A floppy piece of blue spandex slid into my hands. It was a mask created by Razorhawk through Atomic HeroWear, designed to my specifications. I went into the bathroom, adjusted it over my face, and—I couldn't help myself—practiced a few kung fu moves.

"That's right," I told the reflection in the mirror, nodding defiantly. "I am Argo. You cannot defeat me, criminal!" More kung fu moves.

The name for my RLSH persona was originally the Argyle Gargoyle, but this was so ridiculous even I couldn't pronounce it, so I shortened it to the more user-friendly Argo.

When thinking of the persona, I kept in mind two of my favorite comic book artists from the Silver Age of comics, Steve Ditko and Jack Kirby. Ditko created the look of Marvel characters like Spider-Man and Doctor Strange as well as other offbeat characters like the noir-style detective named the Question and the weirdo antihero the Creeper. Jack Kirby cocreated the X-Men, Captain America, Fantastic Four, and the Silver Surfer, among countless others.

I was imagining an eccentric Ditko-style superhero persona that combined Spider-Man's mask, a shirt and tie, and my longboard as part of the persona much like the Silver Surfer utilizes a surfboard. After a couple sketches in a notebook, I began assembling the various pieces of the Argo costume. I bought skateboard knee and elbow pads online; an argyle sweater vest, shirt, and tie at a thrift store; some ninja tabi boots from a martial art supply store. I got some black army pants from another popular shopping spot for RLSH—the army surplus store.

With my gear collected, I was ready to hit the street . . . or was I?

When I spoke to Zero in the NYI headquarters, he had told me that putting on his gear felt like a religious experience. But when I was putting on my gear, I experienced something else: extreme nervousness. What would my poor mom think? What would my friends say? Something about it just didn't feel right.

When I spoke to Bob Burden, creator of the Mystery Men comic, he had told me an irony about himself—that he couldn't bring himself to wear a costume at all, despite all the costumed characters he had created.

"The idea gives me the heebie-jeebies," he told me. "I don't know what it is. When I was young I had a cowboy hat and spurs and six shooters and I just looked in the mirror one day and thought, You ain't no cowboy."

When I looked in the mirror now, I felt a steady, rising level of alarm.

You ain't no superhero, I thought.

It was early September 2012 and I was set to meet the Challengers on the streets of Riverwest for a patrol of my neighborhood in less than an hour, and sweat was already building under my spandex mask and argyle sweater vest. Would we be arrested? Beaten up by pepper spray–soaked Russians? Shot? I inhaled deeply, the mouth of the spandex mask popping inward.

Around 10:30 PM I got a call from the Watchman to let me know that the Challengers were outside my house, waiting for me in Blackbird's jeep. I sneaked quickly out of my house and jumped in, joining Crimson Crusader in the backseat. The Watchman sat in the passenger seat, and the three RLSH, like me, were wearing their costumes sans masks.

"What's up, pimp?" Blackbird greeted me, as he pulled out into traffic. He told us we would drive to a quiet, dead-end street nearby so we could put on our masks and head out on patrol from there. He reached for the stereo volume and pumped up the electropop dance hit "Acceptable in the 80s" by Calvin Harris. Blackbird sometimes performs as a DJ and spins a wide range of music, but while he patrols in his jeep he likes to pump up with electronica or rap by Wu Tang Clan or Notorious B.I.G.

I was audio-recording the patrol. For the next several minutes after we parked, there is no talking on the recording, only the bumping track by Calvin Harris and the odd but unmistakable sound of rubber and leather stretching against car upholstery. There are sounds of crinkling leather, Velcro, and squirming and shifting as the four of us wrestled to put on masks, gloves, and other gear in the confines of the car.

We were all masked up and ready to hit the street when a car pulled into the dead end, shining its headlights on us, then did a U-turn and parked nearby. A second car rolled up and parked on the other side of the street and two carloads of friends got out and began walking in the middle of the street toward us. Some of them stared curiously through the windshield.

"Great," said Blackbird, trying to ignore them despite his luminescent bird eyes and sharp profiled beak. The Watchman looked casually out the window in his red rubber mask.

"So much for a private entrance," Crimson Crusader laughed.

"Yeah—whose idea was this?" the Watchman mocked Blackbird.

"Maybe we should park somewhere else," I suggested.

"Right," Blackbird said. He pulled the jeep up a block and, hitting a green light, headed through the intersection. He and the Watchman both looked left into traffic and directly at a squad car sitting at the traffic lights. The squad car turned and followed us.

"Oh shit," Blackbird said. He quickly ripped off his mask with one hand and drove with the other. The rest of us took our masks off, too.

"Damn!" Blackbird said, looking in his rearview mirror at the squad car quietly rolling behind, gliding after us like a shark. "Hooooooo. Worst night ever. Only time I've driven an inch with my mask on, and it had to be right then."

My throat felt dry. We had made it a total of one block before we started getting tracked by the police. I started thinking about who I could call for bail.

Crimson Crusader was laughing heartily and looked out the back window. "They stopped tailing us," he reported.

"Jeeesus," Blackbird said. "They were probably like, 'Did we just see that? Naaah . . .'" We laughed. Blackbird parked the jeep near one of our familiar meet-up points—the basketball courts on Center Street.

"I wonder if he ran my license and it said something about us getting stopped in Walker's Point," Blackbird said, reflecting on the run-in we had had with police the first night he met me and the Watchman.

"What? I missed that," Crimson Crusader said.

"That was before your time, boy," the Watchman said, imitating an army drill sergeant.

"Be glad you did," Blackbird said, shaking his head and switching the jeep off. "It was a shit show."

We walked around Center Street. I occasionally would jump on the board and skate ahead a couple blocks and skate back. The streets were quiet except for the occasional typical reaction. We passed a man smoking a cigarette who said a bewildered, "Uh, hi."

A hippie girl unlocking her bicycle for a late-night bike ride said a friendly, "Good evening, gentlemen."

Blackbird had a destination in mind—Reservoir Park. "A lady got her throat slashed in a mugging here last week," he told us. The forty-five-year-old woman, a mother and grandmother, had been murdered in the park the prior weekend. A mentally ill man stabbed her in the throat with a box cutter, strangled her, and then ran off with her purse.

We walked to the top of the hill in Reservoir Park and looked out at the lit-up, crisp skyline of downtown. I had walked by the murder scene on patrol with the Challengers dozens of times, but none of us had been out the night of the stabbing. Now all that we could do was stare at the skyline and wish that we had been there, that we could have appeared in the night like comic book heroes to stop the killer.

We continued to walk around the neighborhood. I had one last nerve-wracking moment on the final leg of our patrol. We saw a van parking half a block in front of us and as we approached, I saw my friends Beth and Bubba climb out the cargo doors.

I tensed up, wondering if I should run or hide in some nearby bushes. I looked at them silently, nodded, then looked straight ahead and quickly stepped past them, putting the other RLSH as a buffer between us.

"Hey, superheroes!" Beth said. "Were you guys out on patrol? These are the guys Tea is writing about in his book!" Beth said to Bubba.

"Hi, guys," Bubba said, smiling sarcastically.

We kept walking. When we were down the block, I turned to the Watchman. "Of all the people to run into," I said.

"I don't think they recognized you," the Watchman replied.

After we rolled around the mostly abandoned streets of the east side in Blackbird's jeep, the Challengers dropped me off at home. I was tired from the adrenaline rush and the thrill of the costumed patrol. I shook their hands and thanked them for taking me out on patrol.

I crept quietly back into my room and threw my Argo mask into my sock drawer—a curious memento from my strange journey with the RLSH.

I felt a mix of dismay and relief. On one hand, imagine if we had been able to run comic book–style after a purse snatcher or popped into a dark alley to thwart one of the muggings that plague the neighborhood on a regular basis. It would have been a fireball of a story. On the other hand, I was just glad I had made it through my last RLSH patrol without bodily harm.

The Challengers had embraced me as one of their own, but after trying it out I determined the costumed lifestyle wasn't really my thing. I like hanging out with the Challengers; I think they are nice guys who are trying to do a good thing, albeit in a strange way. They have fun, they have adventure, they perform small-scale heroics.

I didn't find any comfort in the mask, like so many RLSH do. I didn't feel like a beacon of hope in the dark—I felt like a big, tall walking target. I guess I'm more of a jeans and T-shirt type of guy.

For that one night, though, I was an RLSH, a member of the Challengers. I was Argo.

I was one of the heroes in the night.

ACKNOWLEDGMENTS

I'm really very humbled at the number of people I have to thank. Number one on the list is Jan Christensen, a real life Wonder Woman. She helped me revise early drafts of this book. It wouldn't have been possible without her guidance and wisdom.

A huge thanks also goes out to the RLSH community. They welcomed me into their world, showed genuine hospitality, and gave me an unprecedented look into their secret lives. I interviewed over 150 RLSH, and although I couldn't possibly write about every one, each interview helped inform me of the bigger picture. These people in particular helped me over and over: the Watchman, Blackbird, and the rest of my hometown defenders, the Challengers, Razorhawk, Geist, the NYI (especially Zero and Zimmer), Thanatos, Knight Owl, Illya King, the CAI, Richard McCaslin, Urban Avenger, Motor-Mouth, Civitron, Phoenix Jones and Purple Reign, and Phantom Zero. Agent Beryllium and Lord Malignance were helpful villains.

People who joined me for part of the adventure—the Robins to my Batman—or offered help shaping this book include: J. Jason Groschopf, Paul Kjelland, David Beyer Jr., Peter Tangen, Beth Bakkum, Gregg Simpson, Matt Miller, Sarah GM, Matt Pniewski, Matt Harrison, Pierre-Elie de Pibrac, Jessica Baumann, Kurt Hartwig, and everyone who helped out for the Superhero Dance Party and Motionary Comics events.

I'd like to thank Jerome Pohlen and all the mystery men and women at Chicago Review Press for their outstanding work. The

J. Jonah Jamesons at the following publications gave me a venue to explore and write about the topic: *Milwaukee* magazine, *Boston Phoenix*, *New York Press*, *Riverwest Currents*, *Forces of Geek*, and *Delayed Gratification*.

During the course of writing the book, I found out about a great charity in my own neighborhood: Meta House (www.metahouse. org), an internationally recognized drug and alcohol abuse family treatment center for women and their children. In keeping with the charitable nature of the RLSH, I will be donating a percentage of royalties from this book to them, and I thank them for their outstanding work.

Last, I'd like to thank my parents, Marty and Joy, and my sisters Megan, Margot, and Rita. If I've overlooked anyone, please know that you are nothing short of an epic superhero to me.

ONLINE RESOURCES

***Heroes in the Night* blog:** http://heroesinthenight.blogspot.com
RLSH site and forum: www.reallifesuperheroes.org
STAND: www.standsuperhero.com
Atomic HeroWear: http://atomicherowear.weebly.com
Superheroes Anonymous: www.superheroesanonymous.com
Real Life Super Hero Project: www.reallifesuperheroes.com
The Oracle Project: http://theoracleproject.wikispaces.com
Superhero Academy: http://blogtalkradio.com/superhero_academy
Superhero Law: http://superherolaw.com
ROACH: www.joinroach.com

NOTES

I interviewed over 150 RLSH by e-mail, by telephone, in person, and sometimes via multiple methods. I spoke to some very briefly and others repeatedly over a course of years. My first interview was with the Watchman, March 1, 2009, and my last was a follow-up with Phoenix Jones on November 11, 2012. In the following chapter-by-chapter list, "AI" indicates my author interviews.

1. American Superheroes

AI: The Watchman, Miss Fit, Catman, Citizen Prime, Captain Black, Treesong, Crossfire the Crusader, Bob Burden, Geist, Thanatos, Silver Sentinel.

Tea Krulos, "Everyday Heroes," *Milwaukee* magazine, September 2009.

Captain Black, "The RLSH Party Is NOT About Politics," Real Life Superheroes.org, April 7, 2010, http://captainblack.reallifesuperheroes.org (post removed).

Bob Burden, *Flaming Carrot* #16 (Dark Horse Comics, June 1987).

Alan Moore and Dave Gibbons, *Watchmen* (DC Comics, 1986–87).

"How Much Does It Cost to Be Batman?," *Centives* blog, July 17, 2012, www.centives.net/S/2012/how-much-does-it-cost-to-be-batman/.

A. M. Rosenthal, *Thirty-Eight Witnesses* (New York: McGraw-Hill, 1964).

Jim Rasenberger, "Kitty, 40 Years Later," *New York Times*, February 8, 2004.

2. Boy Scouts and Batmen

AI: DC's Guardian, Dragonheart, Agent Mixsae, Death's Head Moth, Nightwatch, Zero, Tothian, Red Voltage, Zetaman.

Stan Lee and George Mair, *Excelsior! The Amazing Life of Stan Lee* (New York: Fireside, 2002).

"Vigilante" definition: *The Merriam-Webster Dictionary*, new edition (New York: Merriam-Webster, 2004).

Creature Feature Internet radio show, September 12, 2009, www.blogtalkradio.com/rlsv/2009/09/13/creature-feature.

Elmo Ingenthron and Mary Hartman, *Bald Knobbers: Vigilantes on the Ozarks Frontier* (Gretna, LA: Pelican Publishing, 1988).

3. Early Prototypes

AI: Terrifica, Captain Ozone, Captain Jackson, the Eye, Superhero, Knight Owl, Zimmer, Wolf, Richard McCaslin.

Ray Fox, *Raising Kane: The Fox Chronicles* (Montgomery, IL: Kindred Spirits Press, 1999).

Douglas Martin, "Obituary: James Phillips, 70, Environmentalist Who Was Called the Fox," *New York Times*, October 22, 2001.

John Etheredge, "Friends, 'Kindred Spirits,' Recall the Fox," *Oswego Ledger-Sentinel*, April 27, 2006.

United Press International, "Captain Sticky Combats Crime," *Boca Raton News*, August 7, 1974.

Jack Williams, "Obituary: Richard Pesta; Captain Sticky Championed Consumer Causes," *San Diego Union-Tribune*, February 18, 2004.

Stan Findelle, "Captain Sticky," *New Musical Express*, July 19, 1975.

Ky "the Rocketman" Michaelson, "Human Fly," Rocketman Enterprises official website, 2005, www.the-rocketman.com/human-fly.html.

Bill Mantlo and Lee Elias, *The Human Fly* #1 (Marvel Comics, 1977).

Bill Mantlo and Frank Robbins, *The Human Fly* #5 (Marvel Comics, 1977).

Jefferey R. Werner, "What Can a Passenger Do If the Flight Is Booked Solid? The Human Fly Has One Solution," *People* magazine, July 19, 1976.

Super Amigos, directed by Arturo Perez Torres, 2007.

Chris Kline, "Defender of Justice Superbarrio Roams Mexico City," CNN.com, July 19, 1997, www.cnn.com/WORLD/9707/19/mexico.superhero/.

Bryan Robinson, "Meet the Anti-Sex in the City Superhero," ABCNews.com, November 5, 2002, http://abcnews.go.com/US/Valentine/story?id=91072.

Grant Stoddard, "The Anti-Cupid: Able to Stop an Ill-Advised Hookup in a Single Bound," *New York* magazine, November 8, 2004.

Captain Ozone documentary video, Captain Ozone official website, 2006, available at http://web.archive.org/web/20060215061638/http://www.captainozone.com/1/1home.HTML.

Zoltan Scrivener, "At Last—a Real Superhero!" *Car and Driver*, November 2004.

BBC News, "'Superhero' Takes on Clampers," BBC.com, September 16, 2003, http://news.bbc.co.uk/2/hi/uk_news/england/3112670.stm.

"Angle Grinder Man," WWMT News 3, November 12, 2003, available at www
.youtube.com/watch?v=TBz4NtXRh48.

Lou Anders, "The Batman of Birmingham," *Bowing to the Future* blog, February 18,
2006, http://louanders.blogspot.com/2006/02/batman-of-birmingham.html.

"Holy Update: Birmingham Batman's Rescue Mobile Has Been Saved!"
Southernist.com, April 20, 2009, www.southernist.com/2009/04/20/holy
-update-birmingham-batmans-rescue-mobile-has-been-saved/.

Captain Jackson official website, www.captainjackson.org.

John Bebow, "Unmasked, Hero Is Human," *Detroit Free Press*, December 22, 2005.

"A Really Super Hero," *Web Drifter* Internet radio show #17, January 8, 2008,
www.revision3.com/webdrifter/theeye.

Night Rider, *How to Be a Super-Hero* (Morgantown, WV: GEM Enterprises,
1980).

Richard McCaslin, *Prison Penned Comics* (self-published, 2008).

Dark Secrets: Inside Bohemian Grove, directed by Alex Jones, 2000.

Peter Martin Phillips, "A Relative Advantage: Sociology of the San Francisco
Bohemian Club" (doctoral dissertation, University of California, Davis,
1994).

Peter Firmrite, "Masked Man Enters, Attacks Bohemian Grove: 'Phantom'
Expected Armed Resistance," *San Francisco Chronicle*, January 24, 2002.

Kelly St. John, "Bohemian Grove Commando Found Guilty," *San Francisco
Chronicle*, April 17, 2002.

4. Great Lakes Alliance

AI: The Watchman, Razorhawk, Celtic Viking, Doc Spectral, Geist.

Chao Xiong, "St. Thomas Student Missing After Abruptly Leaving Cell Phone
Conversation," *Minneapolis Star-Tribune*, April 6, 2009.

Emily Kaiser, "Body of Missing St. Thomas Student Found in Mississippi River,"
Minneapolis City Pages, May 4, 2009.

Jessica McBride, "The Smiley Faces," *Milwaukee* magazine, October 2008.

Lora Pabst, Patrice Relerford, and Matt McKinney, "Dangerous Fire Clears Out St.
Charles," *Minneapolis Star-Tribune*, April 18, 2009.

Geist, "Disaster in St. Charles," MySpace blog post, April 17, 2009, available at
http://rlshgeist.blogspot.com/2010/05/classic-tale-disaster-in-st-charles
.html.

Geist, "Geist's Great Misadventure: A Learning Experience," MySpace blog post,
November 2, 2009, available at http://rlshgeist.blogspot.com/2010/05/classic
-tale-geists-great-misadventure.html.

Ward Rubrecht, "Superheroes in Real Life," *Minneapolis City Pages*, January 16,
2008.

5. The Secret City

AI: Civitron, Joseph Rebelo, Life, Ben Goldman, Dark Guardian, Knight Owl, Phantom Zero, Nyx, Zetaman, Basilisk, Recluse, Amazonia, Aurélia Perreau, Scavenger.

Tea Krulos, "Super Friends," *Boston Phoenix*, December 11, 2009.

America's Most Wanted, FOX, February 11, 2006.

Josh Brogadir, "Guardian Angels Met with Resistance in New Bedford," NECN .com, July 10, 2009, www.necn.com/Boston/New-England/2009/07/10 /Guardian-Angels-met-with/1247274869.html.

Alysha Palumbo, "Citizen Group Marches in New Bedford," WPRI.com, August 2, 2009, www.wpri.com/dpp/news/local_news/local_wpri_guardian_angels _march_in_parade_in_new_bedford_20090802_jle.

6. Coming Out of the Phone Booth

AI: Zetaman, Apocalypse Meow, the Watchman, MoonDragon, Rock N Roll, Phantom Zero, Silver Sentinel, Citizen Smoke, Andrea Kuszewski, Urban Avenger, Civitron.

Andrea Kuszewski, "Addicted to Being Good? The Psychopathology of Heroism," *Rogue Neuron*, September 28, 2009, www.science20.com/rogue_neuron /addicted_being_good_psychopathology_heroism-60137.

Mark Concannon, "The Watchman," FOX 6 News Milwaukee, November 18, 2009.

Mike De Sisti, "Riverwest Has a Real-Life Avenger," *Milwaukee Journal Sentinel*, October 3, 2010.

7. A Tapestry of Evil

AI: Executrix, the Potentate, Calamity, Agent Beryllium, the Overlord, Lord Malignance, Malvado, Poop Knife, Tiny Terror, Master Legend, Geist, Treesong.

"Cincinnati Superhero Patrols Streets Fighting Crime," WLWT News, April 27, 2009.

"Shadow Hare Wins Over Queen City: Hundreds Support Cincinnati's Masked Marvel," WLWT News, April 29, 2009.

Dark Horizon, "Re: Attention: Real-Life Superheroes," YouTube video, December 26, 2008, www.youtube.com/watch?v=9N8PsTXs7V8.

High Noon Tortoise, "Calling Out Shadow Hare," YouTube video, May 4, 2009, www.youtube.com/watch?v=R0rM6WECi8c.

Calamity, "Meanwhile . . ." *Calamity* blog, May 7, 2010, http://grandmastercalamity.blogspot.com/2010/05/meanwhile.html.

Agent Beryllium, "About," *Codename: Beryllium* blog, accessed September 23, 2009, http://codenameberyllium.blogspot.com (page removed).

The Potentate, "DC's Guardian," *Cahiers Du Villainy* blog, July 16, 2009, http://joinroach.blogspot.com/2009/07/dcs-guardian.html.

Lavender Leopard, "Nyx: Guardian of Hot Topic," *Panthera Lavandula* blog, May 4, 2010, http://lavenderleopard.blogspot.com/2010/05/nyx-guardian-of-hot -topic.html.

Master Legend, "RLSHSF—Meet at Pride Festival," nonpublic forum posting on Real Life Superheroes—the Forum, March 4, 2010, http://therlsh.net/t2553 -rlshsf-california-meet-at-pride-festival.

Brown, Jennifer, "12 Shot Dead, 58 Wounded in Aurora Movie Theater During *Batman* Premier [*sic*]," *Denver Post*, July 21, 2012.

The Potentate, "ROACH, I Am Dissapoint [*sic*]," *Cahiers Du Villainy* blog, June 1, 2010, http://joinroach.blogspot.com/2010/06/roach-i-am-dissapoint.html.

8. The Man in the Green Skull Mask

AI: Thanatos, Knight Owl, Motor-Mouth, Victim, Lady Catacomb, the Irishman.

"About," *Olympic Tent Village* blog, http://olympictentvillage.wordpress.com/about/.

Thanatos, "I'll Share a Dream I Have with You Just This Once," MySpace blog post, March 13, 2010, www.myspace.com/thanatos2008ms/blog/530892364.

Linda Solomon, "Black Bloc Riot at the 2010 Olympic Games Damages Hudson Bay Company Store in Vancouver's City Centre," *Vancouver Observer*, February 13, 2010.

Thanatos, "More of the People That I Meet," MySpace blog post, November 8, 2009, www.myspace.com/thanatos2008ms/blog/517725665.

Thanatos, "The Rose of Pender Street," MySpace blog post, May 31, 2009, www.myspace.com/thanatos2008ms/blog/492124933.

9. International Justice Injection

AI: Anonyman, Polar Man, Vampireto, Alma Fuerte, NN, O Gaviao, the Statesman, Entomo, Laserskater, Gost Face, Iron Lamb, Captain Australia, Thylacine, Flying Fox, Peter Tangen.

Chip Kidd and Jiro Kuwata, *Bat-Manga!: The Secret History of Batman in Japan* (New York: Pantheon Books, 2008).

NN, "Despertando–Waking Up," MySpace blog post, March 27, 2009, www.myspace.com/nnandarondando/blog/479547609.

NN, "Dengue," MySpace blog post, April 16, 2009, www.myspace.com /nnandarondando/blog/483589714.

"Everyday Heroes Collective Makes Performances on the Streets to Show the Importance of Small Acts," *O Globo*, March 23, 2010.

The Statesman: The account of the London meet-up was written in a private section of the Heroes Network forum, which the Statesman copied and e-mailed to the author in November 2009.

The Statesman, "The Statesman Gives Firsthand Account of Riot," *Heroes in the Night* blog, August 10, 2011, http://heroesinthenight.blogspot.com/2011/08 /statesman-gives-firsthand-account-of.html.

Entomo, "Report of Paranormal Faculties" (dossier-style report, 2009), e-mailed to the author by Entomo.

Laserskater, "New Year's Special: Table of Final Results," nonpublic MySpace blog post, January 1, 2012, www.myspace.com/laserskater/blog/545091244.

Red Arrow, "Red Arrow," YouTube video, October 11, 2006, www.youtube.com/watch?v=RyMWCJ9AUbU.

Red Arrow, "Red Arrow 2—A Christmas Mission," YouTube video, February 22, 2007, www.youtube.com/watch?v=wFW2XL8XlfM.

Lin Meilian, "Who Was That Masked Woman!" *Global Times*, July 29, 2011.

"Under the Hood," Fauna Fighters official website, 2011, www.faunafighters.com .au/Under-The-Hood.html.

"Lion Heart," Real Life Super Hero Project, March 25, 2011, www.reallifesuperheroes.com/index_bak.php/2011/03/25/lion-heart/.

10. Challengers, Assemble!

AI: The Watchman, Blackbird, Metadata, Charade, Crimson Crusader, Electron, Nightvision.

Tea Krulos, "Operation: Sidewalk Chalk," *Riverwest Currents*, December 2009.

11. Brooklyn's Ex-superheroes

AI: Dark Guardian, Zero, Zimmer, Tsaf, Lucid, Z, the Conundrum.

Tea Krulos, "Brooklyn's Own Superheroes," *New York Press*, July 13, 2010.

Ben Goldman/Superheroes Anonymous, "Dark Guardian Confronts a Drug Dealer in Washington Square Park," Vimeo video, March 8, 2009, www.vimeo.com/3529737.

Squeegeeman, "Squeegee-Vote Squeegeeman," YouTube video, October 18, 2008, www.youtube.com/watch?v=owGBJnPhMIQ.

"The Sexes: The Lavender Panthers," *Time*, October 8, 1973.

"About," NYC Resistor official website, www.nycresistor.com/about/.

Graham Rayman, "The NYPD Tapes: Inside Bed-Stuy's 81st precinct," *Village Voice*, May 4, 2010.

12. Mr. Jones and Me

AI: Detective Mark Jamieson, Phoenix Jones, Mr. Ravenblade, Sky Man, Peter Tangen, Ghost, Mist, Pitch Black, Purple Reign.

Jenny Kuglin, "Phoenix Jones: Real-Life Superhero," KOMOnews.com, November 19, 2010, http://capitolhill.komonews.com/content/phoenix-jones-real-life -superhero.

Tea Krulos, "The Phoenix Jones Interview," *Heroes in the Night* blog, November 24, 2010, http://heroesinthenight.blogspot.com/2010/11/part-2-phoenix -jones-interview.html.

Interview with Rainn Wilson, *Jimmy Kimmel Live*, March 22, 2011.

Keegan Hamilton, "The (Alleged) Adventures of Phoenix Jones," *Seattle Weekly*, June 1, 2011.

Mr. Ravenblade, "An Open Letter to Phoenix Jones, Hero in Training," forum posting on Real Life Superheroes—the Forum, November 20, 2010, available at http://slog.thestranger.com/slog/archives/2010/11/22/seattle-super-hero -fight.

Scoville Heat Units for Peppers (SHU), www.scovillescaleforpeppers.com.

13. People Fighting and Pepper Spray and Superheroes and . . . I Don't Know

AI: Phoenix Jones, Peter Tangen, Dark Guardian, Zack Levine, Motor-Mouth, Justicar.

Saturday Night Live, NBC, October 15, 2011.

The John Curley Show, 97.3 KIRO FM, October 10, 2011.

Jonah Spangenthal-Lee, "Phoenix Jones Loses Job, Barred from Working with Children," *Seattle Met*, November 2, 2011, www.seattlemet.com/news-and -profiles/publicola/articles/phoenix-jones-loses-job-barred-from-working -with-children.

Casey McNerthney and Seattlepi.com staff, "'Superhero' Phoenix Jones Won't Be Charged with Assault," Seattlepi.com, November 23, 2011, www.seattlepi .com/local/article/Superhero-Phoenix-Jones-charged-with-assault-2284701 .php.

Lauren Smiley, "Enter: A Superhero; The Ray Faced Down Cops to Help Occupy, but His True Mission Is Darker," *SF Weekly*, December 14, 2011.

Roberto Acosta, "Burton Police Arrest Michigan Protectors Member Bee Sting for Felonious Assault at Twin Meadows," MLive, April 26, 2012, www.mlive .com/news/flint/index.ssf/2012/04/burton_police_arrest_michigan.html.

Kelly St. John, "Bohemian Grove Commando Found Guilty," *San Francisco Chronicle*, April 17, 2002.

"Man Dons Costume to Fight Crime," *Columbia Daily Herald*, July 4, 2010.

Lauren Smiley, "Superhero in Exile: The Ray Goes It Alone," *SF Weekly*, January 18, 2012.

Melissa Anders, "Fellow Superhero Bee Sting Says Petoskey Batman Was Just Trying to Help," MLive, October 5, 2012, www.mlive.com/news/index .ssf/2012/10/fellow_superhero_bee_sting_say.html.

Philip Molnar, "Warren County Superhero 'Beast' Pleads Guilty to Disorderly Conduct," *Express-Times*, September 18, 2012, www.lehighvalleylive.com /warren-county/express-times/index.ssf/2012/09/warren_county _superhero_beast.html.

Ryan McNamee, "Phoenix Jones: Pepper Sprays No Protestors," YouTube video, May 2, 2012, www.youtube.com/watch?v=0kR3dmRXGJg.

"THEPHOENIXJONES Recorded Live," Ustream, October 20, 2012, www.ustream.tv/recorded/26299902.

Express-Times staff, "Batman Look-Alike Wanted to 'Inspire Hope' Before Arrest Outside of Home Depot," Lehighvalleylive.com, August 1, 2012, www.lehighvalleylive.com/warren-county/express-times/index.ssf/2012/08 /batman-like_mask-clad_man_says.html.

14. An Age of Heroes?

AI: Illya King, Phoenix Jones, Razorhawk, Thanatos, Mr. Xtreme, Miss Fit, Geist, Brandy Roseth, Rock N Roll, Zero, Night Bug, Olde School, Urban Avenger, Emerald Fáel.

"About," Power Boy ALD Awareness Facebook page, www.facebook.com/pages /Power-Boy-ALD-Awareness/250983988272890?sk=info.

"MN Family's Real Super Hero Powers Battle Genetic Disease," CBS 4 Minneapolis, October 25, 2012, http://minnesota.cbslocal.com/video /7885045-mn-familys-real-super-hero-powers-battle-genetic-disease/.

Richard Esposito and Jessica Hopper, "New York Serial Killer: Three More Bodies Found on Beach," ABCNews.com, April 4, 2011, http://abcnews.go.com/US /long-island-serial-killer-discovery-bodies-beach-raises/story?id=13294531.

NYI, "To All Ladies: Free Protection and Safety System (Long Island Killer)," Craigslist posting, April 16, 2011, available at http://web.archive.org /web/20110503015500/http://newyork.craigslist.org/mnh/cas/2329212396 .html.

Epilogue: Masking Up

AI: The Watchman, Blackbird, Crimson Crusader, Zero, Bob Burden.
Mike Johnson and Jesse Garza, "Suspect Charged in Kilbourn Park Slaying,"
Milwaukee Journal Sentinel, September 6, 2012.

INDEX